Reconciliation
in Global Context

Contents

Acknowledgments

The outlines of this book were first discussed at a four-day research colloquium on reconciliation in June 2015. As director of the Martin-Springer Institute at Northern Arizona University (NAU), I had been able to assemble a team of international scholars and scholar-practitioners with assistance of a grant from NAU's Center of International Education. The Martin-Springer Institute and the Jena Center for Reconciliation Studies (under the directorship of Prof. Martin Leiner) organized the research colloquium at the Friedrich-Schiller University in Jena, Germany. At the end of the extensive discussions during those four days, we decided to move forward with the idea of a publication. In subsequent months, we were able to recruit additional international scholars to submit chapter contributions.

We would like to thank NAU's Center of International Education, the Jena Center for Reconciliation Studies, and the Martin-Springer Institute: Global Engagement through Holocaust Awareness for their support of this project.

Björn Krondorfer
Flagstaff, Arizona
October 2017

Cover image: "Mostar Old Bridge, Bosnia and Herzegovina," by Naomi Morrison

Published by State University of New York Press, Albany

For information, contact State University of New York Press, Albany, NY
www.sunypress.edu

Library of Congress Cataloging-in-Publication Data

Names: Krondorfer, Björn, editor.
Title: Reconciliation in global context : why it is needed and how it works /
   edited by Björn Krondorfer.
Description: Albany : State University of New York Press, [2018] | Includes
   bibliographical references and index.
Identifiers: LCCN 2017058363 | ISBN 9781438471815 (hardcover : alk. paper) |
   ISBN 9781438471822 (ebook)
Subjects: LCSH: Peace-building—Case studies. | Conflict management—Case
   studies. | Reconciliation—Case studies.
Classification: LCC JZ5597 .R45 2018 | DDC 303.6/6—dc23
LC record available at https://lccn.loc.gov/2017058363

10 9 8 7 6 5 4 3 2 1

Reconciliation
in Global Context

Why It Is Needed and How It Works

Edited by

Björn Krondorfer

Introduction

Social and Political Reconciliation

BJÖRN KRONDORFER

We open the newspaper, watch and listen to the news, or follow social media, and we are inundated with reports on old and fresh conflict zones around the world. And yet, less apparent in political rhetoric and public awareness are the many attempts at bringing together conflicting and warring parties through various large- and small-scale reconciliatory efforts.

The question of how to redress wrongdoings and work toward reconciliation between former adversaries is as enduring as the observation that human history has been marred by violent conflicts that have left scores of individuals and communities harmed and traumatized. Reconciliation is both an idea and a practice that seeks individual and collective healing in situations where seemingly irreparable harm has left people in broken relationships characterized by fear, mistrust, and anger. While proponents of forms of reconciliation differ in their understanding of the term, the questions in post-conflict situations remain the same: Can enmity be replaced by amity? Can the seemingly "unforgivable" be transformed into peaceful coexistence? Is reconciliation desirable? Is it possible? What intellectual resources and practical experiences do different communities provide to stitch together a ripped and stained social fabric?

In the broad terms of social repair, the concept of reconciliation shifts the focus away from asking either about how to prevent atrocities from occurring or whether to intervene militarily and politically in conflict zones. Rather than being primarily a means of *prevention* or *intervention,* reconciliation can be seen as an issue of "postvention." It refers to efforts of bringing together communities and societies ripped apart by violent conflict, of establishing conditions for coexistence, of social healing, and of overcoming fear and mistrust on collective and individual levels. Insofar as postvention efforts can contribute to preventing recurring cycles of violence, the lines between pre-conflict and post-conflict cannot be clearly drawn.

Reconciliation is of seminal importance in today's world, since we need to find pathways of living together in communities and societies in the aftermath of violence. Recent studies in memory and trauma point to the long-lasting effects of unhealed wounds from the past. If left unattended, they fester and become a source of renewed outbreaks of violent conflicts.

This volume on *Reconciliation in Global Context: Why It Is Needed and How It Works* argues for the merit of reconciliation and for the need for global conversations around this topic. The various contributors describe and analyze examples of "reconciliatory practices" in different national and political environments.

As a team of scholars and scholar-practitioners from the United States, South Africa, Ireland, Israel, Zimbabwe, Germany, Palestine, Belgium, Bosnia and Herzegovina, Serbia, Switzerland, and The Netherlands, we bring expertise from different academic disciplines to this topic. All of us are keenly aware of the long-term effects of diverse forms of political violence, whether it concerns the Holocaust as a paradigmatic example of genocidal violence or the repercussions of European colonialism in Africa; the racism of Apartheid systems or the breakdown of the authority of nation-states; interreligious and interethnic conflicts or political conditions of ideological entrenchment. Each of the countries represented in this volume addresses a different set of past and present conflicts; what connects them are examples of where and when reconciliation "happens."

Reconciliation as a Concept

The term *reconciliation* itself has strong religious connotations, but it is employed today also in international debates about transitional and restorative justice. It did not enter into the philosophical vocabulary until late in the twentieth century, though the Western philosophical and political traditions have certainly discussed concepts related to reconciliation (such as right conduct, virtue ethics, forgiveness, tolerance, and rapprochement). Arguments have been put forth that query the assumption that reconciliation is a moral good in and of itself. For example, one trajectory of the Aristotelian tradition—among whom one can count Adam Smith (1854/2000), Margaret Walker (2006), and Thomas Brudholm (2008)—is to value anger as an appropriate response to injury and injustice. In this view, (legal) retribution and (emotional) resentment—rather than reconciliation and forgiveness—are seen as ethically appropriate and politically effective ways to ensure moral and social repair.

In the aftermath of the Holocaust, the international community and civic initiatives have called for greater accountability toward crimes and awareness of the legacy of traumatic memories. Although retributive justice based on the idea of punishment is still a strong international mechanism to seek legal redress, reconciliation is a different way of thinking about the needs of communities in which people have experienced acts of mass violence. The concept of reconciliation can be approached politically, as an issue of coexistence and interdependence; psychologically, as an issue of social affect within interpersonal relations and intersubjectivity; judicially, as an issue of restorative justice and rehabilitation; philosophically, as an issue of resentment and forgivability; and religiously, as an issue of healing, mercy, and atonement. In this volume, the contributors pay attention to these levels of inquiry, asking whether reconciliation is necessary, under what conditions it might thrive, how it works, and where its limits are.

In the last decades, the political dimension of reconciliation has become more prominent because of the work of various national truth commissions. Given that reconciliation has entered the vocabulary in international and interstate relations, we can ask whether reconciliation should become a tool in the power of the state, or, to the contrary, whether it should be put into the hands of individual agents. Likewise, we can ask whether deeds of radical evil are unforgivable (as argued by German-Jewish political philosopher Hannah Arendt [1989]) or whether we need to advance a transformative vision of personal and political reconciliation, as South African archbishop Desmond Tutu has suggested (Tutu 1999; also Minow 1998).

Among the key terms in the study of reconciliation are trust, forgiveness, truth, justice, trauma, empathy, societal healing, rehabilitation, conflict management, and transformation. Advocates of reconciliation emphasize that reconciliation is not a static concept but an active dynamic that propels former adversaries into newly defined relationships. We therefore suggest speaking of "reconciliatory practices" or "reconciliatory processes" to indicate the open-endedness of the work that needs to be done. Rather than being prescriptive of a particular goal, reconciliation is a commitment to a specific posture of thinking and acting. In this sense, reconciliation might be best understood as a core phenomenon of human interaction that is future-oriented, constructive, and empathetic and that transcends the limitation of self-interested action by moving toward an other-directed care.

A Polysemic Phenomenon

The contributions to this volume are embedded in the enduring question of how to make life viable in communities and societies in the aftermath of political mass violence and atrocities. Reconciliation—as an ethical concept, a moral good, and a social and political practice—is one promising possibility to counteract the damaging long-term effects left in the wake of such violence. Reconciliation might be difficult to implement, and yet it is needed in communities that have been literally and symbolically disfigured by widespread injustices and violence-induced harm.

As a concept and phenomenon, reconciliation is polysemic: it cannot be contained in or reduced to a single meaning. This becomes apparent when we look, for example, at the multiple ways through which we can organize our understanding of reconciliation: Do we approach it as a phenomenon that is personal or political? Social or intrapsychic? Institutional or attitudinal? Relational or structural? Interpersonal or communal? Do we pursue a bottom-up or top-down approach when implementing reconciliation? Do we focus on individual transformation or social change? Do we invest in national efforts, legal paths of transformative justice, philosophical inquiry, or quasi-therapeutic settings?

Valerie Rosoux, in an entry on reconciliation as part of peace-building processes, distinguishes between three approaches: "structural, social-psychological and spiritual" (2008, 544). Whereas the first (structural) focuses on fixing political, economic, cultural, and security problems in order to establish cooperation and coexistence between the affected parties, the latter two prioritize the improvement of relationships between parties. According to Rosoux, the social-psychological approach emphasizes "cognitive and emotional aspects" in order to affect attitudinal and motivational changes, whereas the spiritual approach emphasizes "collective healing and forgiveness." The social-psychological approach aims at "forging a *new* relationship," the spiritual approach at "*restoring* a broken relationship" (ibid., 545; emphasis in original).

Rosoux's suggestion to differentiate between "restoring" relationships and "forging new" relationships may not be fully persuasive, but her point of distinguishing between structural and relational approaches is important. Whereas a structural approach tries to change societal structures (legal, economic, institutional, etc.), the relational approach to reconciliation occurs when, according to Al Ramiah and Hewstone, "members of previously hostile groups come to mutual acceptance" and "experience a changed orientation toward one another" (2013, 535).

In the background of our contributors' inquiry is an understanding of the polysemic nature of the phenomenon of reconciliation. Though the chosen focus of this volume is on psychosocial and relational aspects of reconciliation, those aspects cannot be grasped without alertness to politics and policy issues. Hence, the contributors address both the *interpersonal* dimension (religious, ethical, psychological) and the *political* dimension (institutional, judicial, policy-based) of reconciliation.

Political and Social Reconciliation

When conceptualizing reconciliatory practices, it is helpful to distinguish between *political* reconciliation and *social* reconciliation, a difference that somewhat parallels Rosoux's (2008) distinction between the structural and social-psychological approaches as outlined above.

Political reconciliation has the purpose of "moving beyond collective forms of enmity" (Pope 2014, 179; also De Gruchy 2002, 26). It prioritizes issues of structural interdependence (economic, sociopolitical, security) over interpersonal relationships, and is usually negotiated by officially authorized bodies, such as truth commissions. *Social reconciliation,* on the other hand, seeks to overcome "alienation between and within communities" (Pope 2014, 179; also De Gruchy 2002, 27). It prioritizes human relationships (psychological, emotional, cognitive, reparative) over structural concerns, and is usually practiced on grassroots and communal levels, such as intergroup dialogues and encounters. These two kinds of reconciliation differ in their emphasis and prioritization of two basic elements that are operative in the practice of reconciliation: knowledge and acknowledgment. Discussing briefly this difference below, we will further introduce the elements of truth telling, storytelling, and emotional memory work.

Let us begin with *knowledge*. Knowledge is necessary in order to establish a factual basis regarding the acts of wrongdoing that precede the need for affected parties to reconcile. Establishing a knowledge base is necessary for political reconciliation. Although facts in the aftermath of violent conflicts will always remain contested within a politicized context, at least an attempt must be made by domestic or international bodies to arrive at some legal and moral judgment on past wrongdoings. By collecting testimonies and scouring archives, various truth commissions over the last three decades have been seeking to establish some "truth," even if such commissions may decide to abstain from recommending particular options, such as retribution, restoration, reparations, or amnesty (Cobban 2007; Hayner 2002; Rotberg and Thompson 2000).

In social reconciliation, however, the verification of factual knowledge is less urgent. In these settings, knowledge is transmitted through a different mode of communication, often through storytelling, in which the truth of personal memory is more vital than forensic evidence.

In both political and social reconciliation, a form and forum of credible and genuine communication are needed in order to create a trusted base in which "knowledge" becomes verified and accepted. Otherwise, the knowledge that is gained will fail to motivate political transitions or social change. The difference between political and social reconciliation is that the former gives credibility to truth telling (ruled by legal or quasi-legal frameworks), while the latter puts its trust into storytelling (ruled by what is perceived as personal sincerity and integrity). In political reconciliation, truth telling is seen as a valuable tool to heal some of the rifts between social macro-units, often in the service of advancing national unity.[1] Social reconciliation, on the other hand, relies on storytelling to build up trust between people in order to forge human and communal bonds on the microlevel.

Truth telling and storytelling operate on different principles. They follow what we might call different reconciliation "moods." In the case of truth telling in national truth commissions, the prevailing mood could be described as social verification and public drama. Truth telling in these cases can be backed up with archival and forensic evidence, be incentivized with legal promises of amnesty, and may lead to public apologies (Tavuchis 1991; Govier and Verwoerd 2002b). The resulting proceedings and reports are debated, assessed, and criticized by numerous national and international players (media, politicians, judges, interest groups, journalists, scholars, clergy, etc.). It is no exaggeration to state that every official truth commission has received its share of public criticism.

In distinction to truth telling in political reconciliation, the prevailing mood of storytelling in social reconciliation can be described as personal honesty and interpersonal reliability (Bar-On 2000). Storytelling in settings such as intergroup dialogues is backed up by the integrity of the personal narrative (Chaitin 2011, 55–75). Many of these groups opt for some degree of confidentiality about what transpires in their meetings. The incentive for participants is emotional release, being listened to, and human connectedness.

Besides knowledge, it is *acknowledgment* that really matters to the injured parties, as scholars and practitioners of restorative justice and reconciliation have repeatedly pointed out.[2] Acknowledgment confers recognition of suffering to individual victims and victimized communities. Whereas knowledge alone is limited to gathering evidence and factual information, acknowledgment is a moral activity. It is partisan insofar as it gives voice and agency back to people who have been harmed and victimized. In this sense, acknowledgment is a crucial step toward moral repair. "Moral repair," philosopher Margaret Walker argues, "is the process of moving from the situation of loss and damage to a situation where some degree of stability in moral relations is restored" (2006, 6).

Emotional (Memory) Work

A vital part of the task of acknowledging the harms inflicted and endured is to engage in emotional memory work. Since reconciliation is not needed unless wrongdoing has occurred in the past, memory and remembering play a critical role in the processes of social healing. Because the inflicted and received injuries may have been suppressed, or otherwise have remained publicly unacknowledged, the act of remembering is as important as it is burdened by unresolved emotions (Gobodo-Madikizela 2012). Depending on the degree and extent of the harm inflicted, we can speak of traumatic memories (in case of intolerable harms) or injurious memories (in case of harms that do not lead to psychic disintegration and fragmentation). In either case, the activating of memories—whether in public settings, such as truth commissions, or in interpersonal settings, like intergroup dialogues—is emotionally painful.

Memory work—as opposed to memory in and of itself—refers to an active process of working through the past. Simply put, we all have memories, but not all of us are willing to engage them critically. Memory work remains cognizant of the interplay between the traumatic content of injury, the narrative form it takes to get communicated, and the socio-political context within which it gets a hearing. Memory work, hence, is a form of both critical and empathetic inquiry. "Memory work," Annette Kuhn writes, "makes possible to explore connections between 'public' historical events, structures of feeling, family dramas, relations of class, national identity and gender, and 'personal' memory" (1995, 4).

When it comes to emotional memory work in *political reconciliation,* the record is checkered at best. Some national truth commissions, for example, restrict themselves to legal frameworks and proceed perfunctorily. They do not offer psychological support services or do not regard people's emotions accompanying injurious and traumatic memories as important for the reconciliatory mechanisms they employ. This can lead to a loss of credibility in the eyes of victims.[3] In other cases, however, such as the South African Truth and Reconciliation Commission, mental health assistance is provided (Hamber 2009).[4] And yet, as Priscilla Hayner reminds us, "truth commissions . . . do not offer long-term therapy; they offer survivors a one-time opportunity to tell their story" (2002, 135).

In the case of *social reconciliation,* emotional work (including emotional memory work) is a core element in addressing fractured and injured interpersonal relations. Space is provided to express anguish. Emotional memory work opens doors to those unforgiven zones of human agony where people have experienced manifestations of human cruelty and grave immorality. Confronted with moral injury and physical trauma, an instinctive reaction might be to recoil from facing it, or to leave such labor to the professional intervention of psychiatrists and psychotherapist. Within intergroup settings, however, the task of emotional memory work is not therapeutic healing of individuals but is, instead, geared toward the integration of human agony in the presence of the Other.

Mechanisms of *political reconciliation* might be criticized for neglecting the value of emotions; practices of *social reconciliation,* on the other hand, might be cautioned against giving emotions too much weight. In the latter case, such caution is prudent in order to avoid giving emotive responses a priori credibility. It is important to remind ourselves that the power of anguished personal testimony lies in its immediacy, which renders it instinctively persuasive. It has a direct impact on the listener. A personal narrative in intergroup settings might be compelling precisely because it articulates strong emotions. Participants, however, may not be sufficiently alert to how personal stories are shaped by, and actively shape, affective identifications with large-group identities. Thus, such stories may reproduce rather than repair the injurious memory of a group's social identity. In other words, to face memories productively we need critical distancing devices that allow us to engage our emotions also cognitively. This kind of reconciliatory process I have described elsewhere as a form of "cultural therapy" (Krondorfer 1995, 91). As cultural therapy, reconciliation in intergroup settings reaches beyond political and legal frameworks (even when pursuing alternative forms of justice),[5] but also beyond the confines of personal therapy (even when injured and traumatized individuals might benefit from therapeutic interventions). The practice of interpersonal reconciliation in group settings is one in which the psychosocial, psychopolitical, and emotional dimensions are addressed that underlie and feed specific conflicts (Hamber and Gallagher 2014; Volkan 2013).

Becoming aware of the affective dimension that undergirds much of the discourse and practice of reconciliation allows us to pay attention to aspects of reconciliation that get easily sidelined if the focus remains predominantly on structural reform and policy-driven debates. Questions of the weight of trauma, the stumbling block of large-group identification, the usefulness of apologies, or the merit of empathy now move to the foreground.

In sum: This volume largely subscribes to a conceptual framework that understands reconciliation in relational and psychosocial terms, while deemphasizing its structural and policy aspects. Reconciliation here is understood as a restoring of "right relations" (Llewellyn and Philpott 2014b, 23) and as a way of "coming together again, in restored relationship, after a rift from actual or perceived wrongdoing" (Govier 2002, 141). In the same vein, others have spoken about reconciliation as an overcoming of "distrust and animosity" (Krondorfer 1995, 71) or a "building or rebuilding of trust . . . in the wake of tension and alienation" in relationships (Govier and Verwoerd 2002a, 185). All contributors to this volume nevertheless remain keenly aware of the political dimension of reconciliation in each national context. While some authors accentuate the question of *Why Reconciliation Is Needed* (by contrasting, for example, failed official policies with reconciliation efforts on the ground), others focus on the question of *How Reconciliation Works* (by describing, for example, detailed interpersonal encounters with groups in conflict). What brings us—this team of scholars—together are shared assumptions about reconciliation as a deep commitment to the flourishing of "the conditions of human relationship" within a conception of justice after trust in human relationships has been gravely violated or destroyed (Llewellyn and Philpott 2014b, 22).

Structure of This Book

The scholars we have pulled together as a team for this volume are embedded in national contexts and also represent multiple nationalities. Hence, our experiences with and comprehension of conflict are deeply rooted in acknowledging the power of social identities within national borders while also recognizing the practical need for reconciliation across cultural, ethnic, religious, and national boundaries. All of us have had direct experiences with reconciliation efforts, from facilitating psychosocial intergroup workshops to critically evaluating official policies vis-à-vis actual needs in communities. For this reason, we have asked all contributors to integrate into their analysis some reflections on personal motivation. These two features—multiple national identities, and the inclusion of select biographical notes on our motives and journeys—make *Reconciliation in Global Context: Why It Is Needed and How It Works* unique.

This volume does not aim at being comprehensive with respect to analyzing reconciliation processes, either in terms of geographical scope or disciplinary breadth. Rather, we use our experiences to exemplify how reconciliatory efforts work in different (national) settings and why they are needed. The exemplary nature of our endeavors in specific zones of conflict are aimed to inspire other scholars and scholar-practitioners to reflect on the value, necessity, and limits of reconciliation in their own settings, blending academic concerns with practical engagement.

The chapters are arranged along an arc that spans from cases describing and interpreting actual processes with groups in conflict to cases in which the conceptual merits and constraints of reconciliation are brought to the fore. The volume begins with Björn Krondorfer's reflections on how the framework of interpersonal and psychosocial reconciliation makes possible deep encounters between people who have been historically in conflict or are currently in conflict. He illustrates select key features of this kind of work with examples from his facilitation of Israeli-Palestinian and German-Jewish groups. Having grown up in postwar Germany and now residing in the Unites States for the last three decades, Krondorfer is keenly aware of the binding and, at times, blinding potency of large-group identifications.

Wilhelm Verwoerd and Alistair Little report and reflect on their reconciliation work with individuals who are ex-combatants and veterans. Motivated by their own experiences with social identities rooted in political-national aspirations, Verwoerd and Little have reached out to ex-combatants especially from South Africa and Northern Ireland. Alistair, as a teenager, had participated in political violence as a loyalist in Northern Ireland (he was later imprisoned); Wilhelm comes from a white, Afrikaner family background in South Africa, with a grandfather who is considered the architect of Apartheid. Together, Alistair and Wilhelm present a cogent argument of why apologizing for wrongdoing—an act that seems so desirable in reconciliatory processes—can turn into stumbling blocks when working with people who once belonged to opposing militant and military organizations.

Joram Tarusarira, born to the Shona people in Zimbabwe and today pursuing his academic career in The Netherlands, analyzes the ongoing civil strife in Zimbabwe through the analytical lens of instrumentalist nationalism. This provides him a platform to trace and list the negative psychological repertoire that inflicts people in violent political situations; to counteract such negative effects on the social fabric of communities, he suggests creating forums of psychosocial reconciliation. Tarusarira ends his chapter with sharing his experiences with applying the "Training for Transformation" method to the Zimbabwean conflict.

Zilka Spahić Šiljak and Julianne Funk are the co-authors of the chapter on Bosnian Muslim peacemakers in postwar former Yugoslavia. Zilka is a Bosnian Muslim and feminist scholar and activist; Julianne is an American-born scholar and Christian peace activist who divides her time between her academic study in Switzerland and NGO work in Bosnia. Together, Spahić Šiljak and Funk reflect on the need to include religious peace agents into the reconciliation efforts in Bosnia and Herzegovina. Although faith-based activists have been largely shunned by secular NGOs working in Bosnia—because these NGOs regard "religion" as a major culprit in the 1990s ethno-religious wars in former Yugoslavia—Spahić Šiljak and Funk make a compelling case that the inclusion of religiously motivated activists benefits the still-divided communities.

What Spahić Šiljak and Funk describe as "vocation" regarding the commitment to peace activism by individual Muslims corresponds on a communal level with the Arabic idea of *wasat* (middle). In a footnote, they mention *wasat* as a form of moderate Islam, an Islamic middle way that promotes interfaith and interethnic dialogue. Zeina Barakat, a Palestinian woman who completed her PhD at a German university, makes *wasat* an important tenet of her chapter on reconciliation options for Palestinians. Though *wasat* is more implicitly assumed than explicitly stated in much of Barakat's chapter, she argues for following a middle path of moderation during times of conflict so that justice, tolerance, and reconciliation can flourish. Having joined at some point the Wasatia movement of Mohammad Dajani Daoudi, she also refers to Hölderlin's maxim, "Reconciliation happens in the middle of strife." By including the eighteenth-century German poet into her *wasat* path, she creatively blends insights from different cultures. Based on her experience of growing up in an unending conflict, Barakat strongly advocates for reconciliation to happen in the midst of conflict—rather than waiting for an end of conflict before setting up reconciliatory mechanisms.

Avner Dinur is an Israeli scholar and peace activist who has facilitated heterogeneous groups and has participated in trilateral encounters between Israelis, Palestinians, and Germans. Like Zeina Barakat, he is deeply troubled by the entrenchment of both the Palestinian and Israeli communities that prevents any meaningful solution to the conflict. He argues for a conceptualization of reconciliation that takes seriously the need of each community to be recognized by the other the way it is, and not the way one wishes the other to be. Recognition of each other's social identity and collective narrative must be part of any reconciliatory practice. At the same time, Dinur argues, each side has to be willing to make room for the other and identify those issues that are valued by both. Land, trauma, and violence, Dinur suggests, are three central components that are important to each community; hence, addressing them together would open possibilities for a shared ethos in the future.

In the last chapter, we return to the post-conflict setting in former Yugoslavia. Heleen Touquet, a researcher from Belgium who specializes in post-conflict peacebuilding in the Balkans, and Ana Milošević, born into the Socialist Federation of Yugoslavia, of Serb nationality, and now studying in Belgium and The Netherlands, lead us into a discussion of the political failure of reconciliation. They show how and why there is little patience for any talk about reconciliation in the now-divided enclaves of Muslim Bosniaks, Orthodox Serbs, and Catholic Croats. They trace some of these knee-jerk hostile reactions to the imposition of a particular model of reconciliation by international third parties, and in particular by the European Union. In addition, local, regional, and national leaders have politically manipulated and misused reconciliation to either exculpate themselves or to further their nationalist agendas. These factors, Touquet and Milošević argue, have inhibited the transformative potential of reconciliation to flourish, at the expense of recognizing in meaningful ways the suffering of victims and especially of survivors of sexual violence.

In her Epilogue, Valerie Rosoux, an expert in international relations, comments on this volume's chapters in analytical and creative ways, asking hard questions but also appreciating the relational approach to reconciliatory practices we have chosen to take in this book. She concludes with a cautionary and challenging remark: Do the reconciliatory practices we are engaged in actually help the communities in whose name we promote reconciliation? For if they do not, we may have lapsed into valuing an abstract principle more than the relational and open-ended spirit of reconciliation and may have reverted to a self-interested action rather than a commitment to an other-directed care.

Notes

1. On political reconciliation and nation-building, see Teitel (2003) and Wüstenberg (2003; 2009). Generally speaking, around the time of the collapse of the Soviet Union in the 1980s, which was "a period of accelerated democratization and political fragmentation," transitional justice shifted from international trials of retributive justice to forums of political reconciliation and restorative justice "associated with nation-building" (Teitel 2003, 71). Theologian Ralf Wüstenberg, who echoes this perspective in his comparative analysis of post-Apartheid South Africa and post-1989 Germany, writes: "To overcome the division of the past, political decision making prioritized nation-building" (2003, 139). For a positive ethical assessment of political reconciliation, see also Philpott (2012).

2. Philpott (2008, 128–31). For distinction of knowledge and acknowledgment, see Hayner (2002, 24–27).

3. Hayner's study of various truth commissions list significant differences. Among those with little credibility are, for example, Zimbabwe's Commission of Inquiry that was never made available to the public or the nonrelease of the Burundi investigations. The *Nunca Mas* report of the National Commission in Argentina, to name another example, was politically contested but effective; but it explicitly shunned "reconciliation" because, in Argentina's context, it was perceived as a code word for doing nothing (Hayner 2002).

4. Brandon Hamber, born in South Africa and director of a conflict research institute in Belfast, is a clinical psychologist, who has been involved with the South African Truth and Reconciliation Commission and has written about the process of reconciliation and the psychological implications of political violence.

5. Alternative forms of justice can be transitional, traditional, or restorative justice. See Roht-Arriaza and Mariezcurrena (2006); Kritz (1995); Llewellyn and Philpott (2014a); Braithwaite (2014).

Works Cited

Arendt. Hannah. 1989. *The Human Condition.* Chicago: University of Chicago Press.

Bar-On, Dan, ed. 2000. *Bridging the Gap: Storytelling as a Way to Work through Political and Collective Hostilities.* Hamburg: Körber-Stiftung.

Braithwaite, John. 2014. "Traditional Justice." In *Restorative Justice, Reconciliation, and Peacebuilding,* edited by Jennifer Llewellyn and Daniel Philpott, 214–39. New York: Oxford University Press.

Brudholm, Thomas. 2008. *Resentment's Virtue: Jean Amery and the Refusal to Forgive.* Philadelphia: Temple University Press.

Chaitin, Julia. 2011. *Peace-Building in Israel and Palestine: Social Psychology and Grassroots Initiatives.* New York: Palgrave Macmillan.

Cobban, Helena. 2007. *Amnesty after Atrocity? Healing Nations after Genocide and War Crimes.* Boulder, CO: Paradigm.

De Gruchy, John. 2002. *Reconciliation: Restoring Justice.* Minneapolis: Fortress.

Gobodo-Madikizela, Pumla. 2012. "Remembering the Past: Nostalgia, Traumatic Memory, and the Legacy of Apartheid." *Peace and Conflict: Journal of Peace Psychology* 18(3): 252–67.

Govier, Trudy. 2002. *Forgiveness and Revenge.* New York: Routledge.

———, and Wilhelm Verwoerd. 2002a. "Trust and the Problem of National Reconciliation." *Philosophy of the Social Sciences* 32(2) (June): 178–205.

———. 2002b. "The Promise and Pitfalls of Apology." *Journal of Social Philosophy* 33 (Spring): 67–82.

Hamber, Brandon. 2009. *Transforming Societies after Political Violence; Truth, Reconciliation, and Mental Health.* Cham/Heidelberg/New York: Springer.

———, and Elizabeth Gallagher, eds. 2014. *Psychosocial Perspectives on Peacebuilding.* Cham/Heidelberg/New York: Springer.

Hayner, Priscilla. 2002. *Unspeakable Truths: Facing the Challenge of Truth Commissions.* New York: Routledge.

Kritz, Neil, ed. 1995. *Transitional Justice: How Emerging Democracies Reckon with Former Regimes.* Washington, DC: United States Institute for Peace Press.

Krondorfer, Björn. 1995. *Remembrance and Reconciliation: Encounters between Young Jews and Germans.* New Haven: Yale University Press.

Kuhn, Annette. 1995. *Family Secrets: Acts of Memory and Imagination.* London, New York: Verso.

Llewellyn, Jennifer, and Daniel Philpott, eds. 2014a. *Restorative Justice, Reconciliation, and Peacebuilding.* New York: Oxford University Press.

———. 2014b. "Restorative Justice and Reconciliation: Twin Frameworks for Peacebuilding." In *Restorative Justice, Reconciliation, and Peacebuilding,* edited by Llewellyn and Philpott, 14–36. New York: Oxford University Press.

Minow, Martha. 1998. *Between Vengeance and Forgiveness: Facing History After Genocide and Mass Violence.* Boston: Beacon Press.

Philpott, Daniel. 2008. "Reconciliation: An Ethic for Responding to Evil in Global Politics." In *Confronting Evil in International Relations: Ethical Responses to Problems of Moral Agency*, edited by Renee Jeffrey, 115–49. New York: Palgrave Macmillan.

———. 2012. *Just and Unjust Peace: An Ethic of Political Reconciliation.* New York: Oxford University Press.

Pope, Stephen. 2014. "The Role of Forgiveness in Reconciliation and Restorative Justice: A Christian Perspective." In *Restorative Justice, Reconciliation, and Peacebuilding*, edited by Llewellyn and Philpott, 174–96. New York: Oxford University Press.

Roht-Arriaza, Naomi, and Javier Mariezcurrena, eds. 2006. *Transitional Justice in the Twenty-First Century: Beyond Truth versus Justice.* Cambridge: Cambridge University Press.

Rotberg, Robert, and Dennis Thompson, eds. 2000. *Truth v. Justice: The Morality of Truth Commissions.* Princeton: Princeton University Press.

Rosoux, Valerie. 2008. "Reconciliation as a Peace-Building Process: Scope and Limits." In *The Sage Handbook of Conflict Resolution*, edited by Jacob Bercovitch, Victor Kremenyuk, and William Zartman, 543–63. Los Angeles: Sage.

Smith, Adam. 1854/2000. *The Theory of Moral Sentiments.* New York: Prometheus Books.

Tavuchis, Nicholas. 1991. *Mea Culpa: A Sociology of Apology and Reconciliation.* Stanford: Stanford University Press.

Teitel, Ruti. 2003. "Transitional Justice Genealogy." *Harvard Human Rights Journal* 16: 69–94.

Tutu, Desmond. 1999. *No Future without Forgiveness.* New York: Doubleday.

Volkan, Vamik. 2013. *Enemies on the Couch: A Psychopolitical Journey through War and Peace.* Durham: Pitchstone.

Walker, Margaret. 2006. *Moral Repair: Reconstructing Moral Relations after Wrongdoing.* Cambridge: Cambridge University Press.

Wüstenberg, Ralf. 2003. *Die Politische Dimension der Versöhnung: Eine theologische Studie zum Umgang mit Schuld nach den Systemumbrüchen in Südafrika und Deutschland.* Gütersloh: Chr. Kaiser.

———. 2009. *The Political Dimension of Reconciliation: A Theological Analysis of Ways of Dealing with Guilt during the Transition to Democracy in South Africa and (East) Germany*, trans. Randi Lundell. Grand Rapids: Eerdmans.

1

Interpersonal Reconciliation with Groups in Conflict

Israelis and Palestinians, Germans and Jews

Björn Krondorfer

In the summer of 2014, when the Israel Defense Forces (IDF) and Hamas in Gaza fought a lethal fifty-one-day war, I met with Israelis, Palestinians, and Germans in a location in the West Bank, close enough to the border to be within relatively safe reach for Jewish Israeli citizens. We met to engage in difficult conversations among people in conflict, with people who have been hurt, injured, traumatized, fearful, and distrustful—in the belief that it is continuous human contact that prepares us for better times, even when everything around us seems to fall apart. Besides the actual dead and injured, this war had pushed Palestinians and Israelis even farther apart, demanding and enforcing group loyalty. Internally, each community ostracized and punished individuals who dared to stay in touch with people from the other side. And yet, a group of Israelis, Palestinians, and Germans met for four days, revealing to each other their fears and opening their hearts.

On the last day of the seminar, the Palestinian Authority unexpectedly called our retreat center, claiming that we had no permission to meet and that we had to leave. As it turned out, this was not true, since it was a German NGO that had organized the meeting; hence, there was no requirement to inform the Palestinian Authority, which, in turn, would have informed the Israeli security.[1] However, this call led to turmoil and

confusion among the participants. A young Israeli psychologist and grandchild of Holocaust survivors no longer felt safe and accused the leadership
of failing to provide security. He got so frightened that his whole body
began to shake. He asked why the Palestinian Authority even knew that
we were meeting here. His fear spread like wildfire through the group.
Fear is contagious. It took us a long time to contain it, with the eventual
result that the young man decided to stay with us for the remainder of
the seminar (Krondorfer 2015a).

A year later, in 2015, we met again at the same location with a group
of about twenty Palestinians, Israelis, and Germans ranging in age from the
late twenties to mid-seventies. The memory of the previous year's violent
confrontation was still alive but it had receded enough for people to join
together in an interpersonal setting to explore the effects and meaning
of "borders" in our lives. For Palestinians, the pressure to abide by the
"anti-normalization" campaign was strong. This political campaign refuses
to accept the status quo of the occupation by discouraging and disallow-
ing any Palestinian-Israeli cooperation. Palestinians are not supposed to
meet with Israelis unless such meetings lead to political-structural changes
regarding the occupation. Given the "anti-normalization" campaign, the
willingness of Palestinians to join our mixed seminar required courage:
their attendance went against their community's consensus. For the Israeli
participants, the high personal risk that marked their attendance of the
summer seminar during the 2014 war had been lessened in 2015, but
the continued siege mentality of Israeli society left them with a persistent
unease about meeting with Palestinians in Palestinian territory.

Had the seminar followed a conventional dialogue format, where
people congratulate themselves simply for conversing with each other, the
Palestinians could have judged it as part of the "normalization" campaign,
and hence unacceptable. I suggested to the group that starting an "anti-fear"
campaign might be more helpful than subscribing to an anti-normalization
code if the goal is to move both sides out of the current quagmire. I
also wanted a commitment from each member in the group to make our
four-day meeting "real" and to commit to the hard work of reconciliation.
This set into motion a more honest but also more demanding process.
As a result, the issue of trust and mistrust forcefully emerged on the last
day. I will return to this later.

In this chapter, I reflect on the dynamics of interpersonal encounters
between groups who have been historically in conflict or find themselves
in an ongoing conflict. Those dynamics include the role of personal and

collective memories and large-group identities, chosen traumas and unsettling empathy, trust and fear. Specifically, I am illustrating these dynamics with examples from my work with Israelis and Palestinians (case 1) and Germans and Jews (case 2). Reconciliation in this context is understood as a relational practice.

By emphasizing the relational quality of reconciliation over policies geared toward structural changes, I am following a framework of social reconciliation as outlined in the Introduction to this volume. I am not, however, arguing in favor of an individualized personal approach that disregards the political settings within which interpersonal encounters take place. When I facilitate groups in conflict it is very clear that the specific contours of interpersonal encounters manifest themselves in political history and that the dynamics unfolding in such processes are embedded in the deep structures of social identity.

Biographical Interlude

How did I get involved in working with groups in conflict? Some background about my personal path toward facilitating interpersonal encounters will help to contextualize my thoughts on reconciliatory processes.

I was born in Germany fourteen years after the end of World War II and after the end of Nazi Germany's murderous ethnic cleansing operations and genocidal campaign against European Jews. I belong to West Germany's postwar generations. Although there is no direct causal link between my generational belonging and my engagement in reconciliation (after all, most of my peers have little interest in such matters), my postwar German identity remains a strong motivational source. Growing up in the comforts of a fairly stable democracy, I also grew up with stories and images of suffering that Germans endured during the last years of the war and the early postwar years. In this sense, I belong to the "second generation," surrounded by and participating in the postwar master narrative of German suffering.[2] My parents received most of their education during the Nazi regime and experienced the end of the Third Reich as young adults. In 1945, they were, respectively, seventeen and eighteen years old. Both lost their childhood homes and also family members in the war.

My father was born in 1927 in the *Sudetenland*, the part of the Czech Republic that had a strong German population. When he returned to his home in Moravia in 1946, after spending one year as a POW in a Czech prison, he found his mother alone in the apartment. His father was still in captivity in the Soviet Union. No stories exist in my family about my grandfather's POW experience. My father's younger brother, age sixteen, had killed himself accidentally when mishandling antiaircraft weaponry in a military training unit. In the summer of 1946, my father and his mother were expelled by the postwar Czech government and, after a long train ride in cattle cars, found themselves in a small town in Hesse, a region under the control of the American Allied forces. In Hesse, he eventually met my mother.

My mother grew up in Königsberg in East Prussia, today Kaliningrad in Russia. In January 1945, at age seventeen, she fled from the advancing Soviet army. She was sent by her mother to find her way across war-torn Europe by herself. She reunited with her family in West Germany, also in a small town in Hesse. Her father, a German army officer, had died of cancer in 1941. Her mother now had the arduous task of building up, out of nothing, a new existence in West Germany for her four children (for whom she had earlier received the bronze *Mutterkreuz,* the Nazi medal awarded to highly procreant German mothers).

My social identification with Germany as a nation was weak until I came to the United States as a graduate student in 1983. It was weak insofar as I took my German identity as a given, in no need of further reflection. The stories passed on in my family about the Hitler regime, which almost exclusively focused on moments of personal affliction during the war years, were similarly taken for granted. Those seemingly dependable narratives, as well as my uncontested sense of belonging, were unsettled when I encountered the Jewish community in Philadelphia and befriended both rabbinical students of my age and Holocaust survivors of my parents' age. I no longer was simply "Björn." I was now primarily "German," a representative of my age group who had to account for the lives, deeds, and choices my parents and grandparents had made during the Nazi regime and, by implication, during the years of the Holocaust.

I plunged into the study of the Holocaust. The more I studied, the more German I became. It was both confusing and exhilarating, eliciting feelings of guilt and, at times, shame. It was gratifying to explore the complexity of history while interacting with my Jewish peers. Occasionally, it also gave me—and I admit this with some embarrassment—a sense of smugness: I was the "good German" willing to face the past.

Over time, the family narrative of German war affliction got shaken up when stories emerged that put my family in proximity to the Holocaust.

Sometimes, these were passing moments, when, for example, my mother pointed herself out in a black-and-white photo as a young teenager at a birthday party in Königsberg, and then pointed to a girl right next to her, stating that she was Jewish. When I asked to tell me more about her, she abruptly ended the conversation (Krondorfer 2001). A graver moment occurred later, albeit only accidentally. After I had already spent ten years in the United States, I learned from my father that he had been stationed as a seventeen-year-old soldier-in-training near Blechhammer (Blachovnia), a Jewish slave labor camp in Upper Silesia, Poland. For one year, from 1943 to 1944, his task was to "protect" a German industrial site from Allied bombing raids (Krondorfer 2000; 2002).

During those years of growing awareness of the legacy of war and genocide in German history in general, and in my family history in particular, I worked with people in a number of interactive environments to explore our differences vis-à-vis the long-lasting effects of the past. These included working with ethnically and nationally diverse student groups, religious leaders, community organizations, and visual and performance artists. I have also facilitated workshops on the intergenerational transmission of traumatic memories and led trilateral, intergenerational encounters for Israelis, Palestinians, and Germans in the West Bank, Jerusalem, Greece, and Germany.[3]

Developing sensitivity toward the dynamics of power asymmetries and becoming aware of the perception gaps between marginalized and dominant communities (see Baumeister 1997, 18–19) are now an indispensable part of my work with groups in conflict. Grounded in my own history, I became sensitized to facing the effects and aftereffects of my large-group identity. Questions of German accountability and acknowledgment of wrongdoing—and the accompanying moral emotions, such as guilt and shame—could not be avoided. Rather, they needed to be juxtaposed to and integrated with the perspectives of victimized communities. I learned that interpersonal encounters remain incomplete unless one addresses the perspectives of both the victimized communities and perpetrator mentalities. In the face of a Jewish presence, for example, the master narratives of postwar German suffering got exposed as one-sided, distorted, and misleading. Previously unquestioned "truths" conveyed in family memories became unsettled. Concomitantly, collective loyalties upheld and enforced in such narratives were also shaken up.

The fact that these dynamics involved vicarious identification with the guilt and complicity of perpetrator society did not diminish the impact of those experiences (Vetlesen 2005; Brunner and von Seltmann 2006.). In the case of Germany, the perpetrators themselves, with few exceptions, did not engage with the people they had victimized, and so it fell onto the new postwar generations to pick up this unfinished task. Such vicarious identifications raised awareness for how family memories are transmitted intergenerationally and are passed on to new generations below the surface of conscious cognition and reflection.

Over time, I understood that reconciliation is not just a mental state or a moral intention—and certainly nothing that one can do by oneself—but a commitment to engage with the other. When interacting with people within demanding, yet protected environments, it is important to disrupt patterns in which the "othering" of the other fuels subterranean tensions, misconceptions, prejudice, and toxic projections and counterprojections. The goal of interpersonal reconciliation is not to make the other into someone whom one wishes to be according to one's own ideals. Nor can the other become someone who resembles oneself or mirrors one's own values. Rather, it is the respect for and integration of differences. It is trying to see others in their own right and granting them their own experiences, frailties, and imperfections. When I speak of the relational nature of reconciliation, otherness is not dissolved into sameness. Trust is earned and (re)established when engaging the other as "other," while simultaneously engaging (self-) critically with people from one's own community and family.

Trauma and Trust: Israeli–Palestinian Conflict

It is now time to return to the trilateral meeting in the West Bank in the summer of 2015 with which I began this chapter. I mentioned above that the issue of trust was put on the table on the last day of this workshop/seminar. To clarify: this meeting, like similar trilateral gatherings for Israelis, Palestinians, and Germans that I have been part of for several years, was not called a reconciliation seminar. As a matter of fact, the term *reconciliation* was neither mentioned in any of the brochures and invitations nor in the seminar itself. The absence of this term, however, does not matter here, since the point is not to argue philosophically for the validity of an abstract notion but to utilize "reconciliation" as a way to analyze dynamics as they emerge and express themselves in guided, interpersonal group processes. The framework of social and relational reconciliation, as described and defined in the Introduction of this volume, is one lens through which we can understand such processes. Another framework, for example, would be to read such meetings through the lens of trauma (Krondorfer 2015b). This would not fundamentally change our understanding of the nature of these interpersonal encounters, but simply bring diverse elements of analysis to the fore.

To provide a little more context, we need to go back to an early moment during the 2015 seminar on borders.[4] On the third day, the group of Israelis, Palestinians, and Germans reached a consensus to explore, under the guidance of my facilitation team, the issue of "collective trauma." We separated each national group and asked them to write on a card what they perceive as their own collective trauma. We also asked them to write on two separate cards what they perceive are the traumas of the other two groups. The German group, for example, named their own trauma "Collective Guilt"; for the Israeli trauma, the Germans identified "anti-semitism," and for the Palestinians, the "Nakba"—the 1948 expulsion of Palestinians from their homes and villages (Meir 2009). The Palestinians named their own trauma also the "Nakba"; for the Germans, they said "Holocaust & Guilt," and for the Israelis, "Holocaust & Victimization." The Israelis, finally, named their own trauma "Holocaust & Hostile Environ-ment"; for the Germans, they identified "Third Generation Conflict," and for Palestinians, "Nakba & Life under Occupation." Looking at this list, it is apparent that there was a lot of overlap in the perceptions of each other's traumata, but they also contained a number of nuances.[5]

The point of these cards was not to debate academically the historical accuracy of the collective traumata as identified by the participants. Not that accuracy is unimportant, but those debates need to happen elsewhere, such as in scholarly settings. What counts in interpersonal reconciliatory settings is the *perception* of historical wrongs and the *identification* with such wrongs. Put differently, what needs to happen is to become aware of the degree with which we identify with our own large group and how we perceive others. Both components—collective self-identification and the perception of the respective other—are intimately linked in encounters between groups in conflict. Part of the task of reconciliatory processes is to address and dis-entangle them, and to bring to consciousness those elements of large-group identity that are either destructive or valuable. To enter into such processes, we might say, simultaneously summons and threatens large-group identities.

The fact that the Israelis, Germans, and Palestinians in the 2015 meeting agreed to look together at their collective traumas already sig-

naled a high degree of maturity and self-awareness among them. Most
groups, especially in the initial stages of their encounter, are not ready
to jointly and deliberately explore collective traumas. Rather, it is more
common for groups to unselfconsciously act out collective traumas
through the clash of competing narratives of suffering. Such competitive
narratives are often marred by mutual accusations, suspicions, and denials,
and elicit projections or other compensatory mental maneuvers. Yet, as
we will see soon, even this more mature group that we had assembled
in the 2015 seminar had difficulties when handling the variously named
collective traumas on their cards. We will return to this situation shortly.
But first we might ask: Why do we summon large-group identities and
collective traumas in reconciliatory settings? Is not the invocation of
the past antithetical to reconciliation efforts in the present? Would it
not be best to leave the past aside and focus on the immediate need
for social change and the task of finding political solutions? To answer:
it is, indeed, important to return to difficult histories and legacies in
reconciliatory settings. As already stated in this volume's Introduction,
emotional memory work is a core component of social reconciliation.
Anguish over past wrongdoings is not resolved if injurious or traumatic
memories are ignored. To the contrary, ignoring them deepens social
anxieties and heightens collective distrust.

Chosen Traumas

According to Vamik Volkan, a large-group identity can be described as a
"persistent sense of sameness," shared "subjective experiences," and a sense
of "we-ness" that fosters social cohesion within a group of people (2013,
77).[6] Large-group identities are powerful because they provide a sense
of security and belonging. As a psychologist and psychiatrist, Volkan had
worked for many years internationally with groups in conflict. He came
to realize that historical events are one of the most important amplifiers
that constitute a large-group identity (other amplifiers include language,
shared physical characteristics, food, etc.). The power of historical events,
Volkan states, does not depend on whether they are perceived in "realistic
or mythologized" terms (ibid., 78). Whether they are imagined or real,
factual or misperceived, they always constitute a strong motivational force.
As such, historical events are remembered and retold by groups as "chosen
glories" or "chosen traumas."

Chosen traumas, according to Volkan, are psychologically more complex than chosen glories, because the latter increase "collective self-esteem," while the former represent a "much stronger" identity marker (2013, 158f). This might explain why, for example, it did not even occur to the Palestinian, German, Israeli participants of the 2015 seminar on borders to look at national "glories." Instead, without being prompted from anyone externally, they chose as their subject "collective traumas."[7]

A chosen trauma refers to those historical events that a group collectively remembers as a time of having "suffered catastrophic loss, humiliation, and helplessness at the hands of its enemies" (Volkan 2013, 158). To avoid any misunderstanding, Volkan clarifies that no group "chooses" to be victimized. Yet, groups of people come to agree upon a tragic, harmful, or traumatic event in their past, which they grant a foundational status. As a foundational event, it secures group cohesion and is dwelled upon in the spheres of politics, culture, and family. Once isolated and identified, this becomes the "chosen trauma" of a given group—a culturally adopted and accepted reference point for understanding oneself within a collective history.

The driving force behind a chosen trauma is not factual accuracy. "It is not necessary for the historical or popular accounts of these past events to be accurate, consistent, logical, or indisputable," Bruce Edwards observes. "What is important for the group is that the mental doubles of these traumas . . . are shared by all members of the group . . . and support the group in times of collective stress" (Edwards 1998, 1). When we separated the Israeli, German, and Palestinian participants into national groups, they quickly identified the Holocaust and the Nakba as collective traumas. Whether or not this naming is based on an accurate analysis is, however, another question. For example, in the 2015 seminar the Holocaust was mentioned as a collective trauma for both the Jewish Israelis and the Germans. In other words, the Holocaust had to do double duty, serving as chosen trauma for the victimized community as well as the perpetrator society. Granted, the participants chose the Holocaust as collective trauma under a different system of valuation for each group. Regarding Israelis, it was paired with "hostile environment"; regarding Germans, it was paired with "guilt." From a point of view of critical trauma studies, one may ask, however, whether "guilt" is a valid category for trauma, for it does not easily match standard medical, psychological, or ethical trauma definitions. Similarly, we can ask whether the 1948 Nakba was, on military and political grounds, the most disruptive force for Palestinians in the Israeli-Palestinian conflict.[8] Yet, it is the Nakba that today is the reference point in the master narrative of Palestinian suffering (Bashir and Goldberg 2014; Meir 2009).

Such critical interventions are important. They do, however, miss the point about the emotional validity of traumas identified by groups within the dynamics of reconciliatory settings. In terms of social persuasiveness, it is less significant that accounts of the past are consistent and accurate, as Edwards points out. Rather, what counts is the ability to generate group cohesiveness through a trauma's mental double. Put differently: had we asked the Palestinian, Israeli, and German participants to enter into a political and academic discussion about the historical correctness of the collective traumata that each group had identified on their notecards, we would have missed an opportunity to lead the participants to potentially transformative insights. Had we simply opened the floor for a cerebral discussion, the result, in all likelihood, would have been a highly politicized debate dominated by polemics and by more or less informed opinions. Such a discussion would have operated under the rules of engagement of normative political narratives rather than a reconciliatory mode of empathic rapprochement.

Plenty of intellectual and political efforts have been invested in justifying chosen traumas. The reconciliatory processes I am facilitating, however, aim at touching levels of affective identification. Processes that foreground the social and relational dimension of reconciliation need to attend to working with emotions. To reach the affective levels, it is important to integrate nonverbal techniques and interactive, body-centered exercises that, at times, may resemble elements of group therapy (such as constellation, gestalt, psychodrama, theme-centered, interactional).[9]

In the case of the 2015 seminar in the West Bank, the facilitation team suggested to explore each national group's choices regarding "collective trauma." Using their notecards, we focused our attention on each national group separately, during which time the other two groups served as active witnesses.

To exemplify the way we work, I will limit my description only to the Israeli group. To recall: the Israeli group had identified their own collective trauma as "Holocaust & Hostile Environment," while naming the trauma for Germans "Third Generation Conflict" and for Palestinians "Nakba & Life under Occupation." In a first round, we placed the Israeli group in the center, while everyone else was sitting around them, listening into their conversation. This setup is called the "fishbowl" exercise. Since all the Israelis participants were skilled in verbal eloquence, the conversation was engaging, intelligent, politically correct, and polite.

In a second round, we arranged the space differently: on one end, we seated the German group in a half-circle, and on the other end, the Palestinians, also in a half-circle. The Germans and Palestinians became, so to speak, active witnesses of what was about to happen in the center, where we had placed the Israelis. In other words, we placed the Jewish Israeli group right in the middle of the German collective trauma on one side (Holocaust/Guilt/Third Generation Conflict) and the Palestinian collective trauma on the other side (Nakba/Life under Occupation).

We asked the Israeli participants to get up from their chairs, arrange themselves in the center in relation to the Palestinians and Germans, and add a simple physical gesture that might express something about how they feel or perceive themselves in that middle space. Torn between two "collective traumas"—one in the past, the other in the present—all of them turned their attention to the Palestinian group while turning their backs (or, in some case, their half backs) to the German group.

In a feedback session, we learned that turning their back to the German group was not meant—as one might surmise from the constellation visible in the room—to ignore the Germans and the legacy of the Holocaust. As a matter of fact, we learned for the first time that several of the Israeli participants traced their family roots to Europe and were directly related to the Holocaust as children and grandchildren of survivors. Turning their back to the Germans was not an expression of being disconnected to the European past, but a gesture of trust toward the German participants. Because the Germans were perceived as having faced the Holocaust themselves, the Israelis felt that they were given enough space to attend to the urgency of the Palestinian plight. With their backs supported by the German presence, the Israelis felt compelled to attend to the current situation with Palestinians rather than return to the European past.

The Palestinian group, however, responded with skepticism to the attention it got from the Israelis.[10] It was clear that the Palestinian participants—visible through their body postures and listless facial expressions—remained somewhat unmoved and reticent. This, in turn, left the Israelis unhappy. They felt frustrated by their inability to connect to Palestinians. They also sensed that, as Israelis, they might not have delved deeply enough into issues of their own social identification. They genuinely did not know what was missing. They felt that they had expressed themselves eloquently, with plenty of information and explanations, but realized that all their explaining did not bridge the emotional gap to the Palestinians.

"I was afraid you arrange for our kidnapping"

The dramatic scenario described above happened on the same day when religious Jewish extremists had firebombed a Palestinian home in Duba, West Bank, killing the toddler Ali Dawabsheh and severely burning his parents and brother (Ali's parents died a few weeks later from their burns). Tensions were high in Israel and the West Bank, and it affected also the dynamics within our protected space. Everyone was on alert, and the participants constantly checked their phones for news. The firebombing came on the heels of the fatal stabbing of Shira Banki by another Jewish religious extremist the day before. The Jewish Israeli Shira had marched in the gay pride parade in Jerusalem when the assault took place.

Our day ended with an open forum conversation. Later, in the same evening, some Jewish Israelis joined a Palestinian participant at his nearby home in the West Bank to walk his dog. A seemingly innocuous event! Yet, given the volatile and politically charged atmosphere of the day, it required courage, especially since Israelis had to be willing to cross at night into Area A of the West Bank. Entry into Area A is not permitted to Israelis, but this group went anyway. Walking around the forbidden zone, they met with friends of their Palestinian companion, and together they went to the wall that separates Israel from the Palestinian territories, seeing it for the first time from the Palestinian side.

The next morning—it was the last day of our seminar—we picked up where we had left the constellation work the previous day. We (the facilitators) invited the Israelis to return to their places in the middle of two traumas and proceeded by asking them some tough questions about motives and motivations regarding their political engagement. Why is it so important, we asked, to demonstrate to us that "you are good Israelis"?

At first, the Israeli participants were taking aback by the question and rejected the assumption that they were "trying to prove anything." They insisted that they simply showed who they truly are, and were not placating the Palestinian participants. After the initial puzzlement and protest, though, they were willing to engage the challenge we had put out for them.

A young Israeli man, who actually stood closest to the Germans seated in a half-circle (but with his body turned to the Palestinians and with both arms outstretched to them), revealed for the first time that his grandparents had survived Bergen-Belsen and Auschwitz. Almost in the same breath, he asserted how much he wanted to understand and connect to Palestinians. For him, our seminar was the first in-depth encounter with Palestinians. Then he started a long-winded speech to explain his personal and political motivations. I eventually had to interrupt him because I saw the eyes of Palestinians glaze over. "Instead of the wave of words and explanations," I said, "tell us what you feel." He stopped, and after a few moment of silence, he said in a low voice: "Fear . . . fear . . . fear."

One of the young Israeli women, still skeptical about the validity of our challenge of being a "good Israeli," turned to the Palestinians and asked them directly whether it is true that they were still distrusting them. Her question led to several remarkable exchanges. I will mention two.

First, the woman who asked the question had placed herself in such a way that she faced the Palestinian half-circle, with some distance between them. As soon as she asked the question, one student-age Palestinian man leaped to the occasion and affirmed her query. Yes, he confided, he continues to mistrust them. These two young people—in their mid-twenties— exchanged words with each other, but largely averted eye contact. "Is it true," the Israeli woman asked, "that you do not trust us? I am different from the majority Israeli society because I am committed to working for peace with the Palestinians." "Yes, it is true," the Palestinian man answered, "I still don't trust you because I still see in front of me an Israeli." When asked how she felt when hearing his response, she said: "I feel like shit."

A few moments later, the Palestinian clarified in so many words that he does not trust Israelis unless they agree to his political views and demands. Predictably, this led to a short exchange of harsh responses. The situation could have easily unraveled into a polemic debate about politics, had the facilitator team not intervened. We interrupted and asked the Palestinian to reconsider his position. "You can't have Israelis according to your wishes," we suggested. "You can't make Israelis into people the way you like them. They cannot become Palestinian like you. But here, in front of you, is a real person, a real Israeli, who is committed to change. You need to relate to and work with real people."

The second exchange I want to mention here is the contribution of another Israeli woman, who, the previous night, had joined the small group of Israelis venturing into the West Bank's forbidden Area A. In her professional life, she is a teacher in a Jewish school near Jerusalem for troubled teenagers, many of them exhibiting hard-line, ultranationalist, anti-Arab views. The previous day, she had talked about the challenges of educating those troubled teenagers. Now she turned to the Palestinian man who had taken them into Area A in the evening and addressed him directly. Looking into his eyes, she admitted that she had become really scared and frightened when, during their nightly walk, he had made several phone calls in Arabic. She told him candidly: "I was afraid you make calls to arrange for our kidnapping, or do some other harm to us." Surprisingly, the Palestinian man did not get upset. Instead, for the first time in our four-day seminar, he relaxed. He loosened his tightly crossed arms around his chest. He thanked her for the honesty. He said that he expected all along such fear and mistrust among Israelis. He was now able to relate to her differently. He could see her now as a human being, fearful in her own ways, and no longer simply a representative of Israel.

It is with this scene that I want to end my observations about the Palestinian-Israeli encounter. This Israeli teacher and Palestinian man had broken through fears, suspicion, and mistrust by admitting discomfiting emotions openly. It enabled them to trust each other a little more.

Skeptical readers may wonder whether my choice of ending with this scene is a rhetorical move in order to suggest a happy ending. It is not. The interaction really happened, and it is not a "happy end" that I am promoting. Govier and Verwoerd, in a philosophical argument about the central role of trust in national reconciliation, state insightfully that the rebuilding of trust in reconciliation does not aim at creating "a state of blissfully enduring unity." Rather, the building of trust, which is "essential to viable relationships," is an "ongoing process" that can never be reduced to a "singular event" (Govier and Verwoerd 2002, 185–86). The interaction we witnessed between the Israeli woman and Palestinian man opened levels to hitherto absent trust. On a microlevel, these two people exemplified the work that needs to be done individually. On a group level, we can further distinguish between a communal midlevel and a national macrolevel of engagement. On each of these levels, the ways we communicate and the ways we try to manage conflict need to follow their own rules of engagement in order to seek alternatives in an otherwise stale political discourse. What happened on the microlevel cannot be simply transposed, in terms of method and approach, to the midlevel and macrolevel. However, it is "inevitable and timely," Bashir and Goldberg write with reference to the Holocaust and the Nakba, that Israeli Jews and Palestinians will have to enter together into "productive engagement" with their two traumatic "memories, histories, and identities" (2014, 78). Efforts to rebuilding trust in reconciliation are an essential part of such productive engagement (see also Chaitin 2011).

Unsettling Empathy

People spending time together in reconciliatory settings build up meaningful relations and share moments of trust, creative freedom, laughter, and joy. Yet, there is nothing easy about such interpersonal processes for groups in conflict. The intense dynamics developing among and between people in conflict can be deeply unsettling. Such "unsettling," I argue, is productive. Combined with empathy, a sense of being unsettled in one's expectations and assumptions is necessary if we aspire to a modicum of personal transformation and societal change. In the many years of facilitating and observing interpersonal processes with groups in conflict, I have learned that unsettling empathy is a crucial component of reconciliation. As a matter of fact, it is in moments of unsettling empathy that people get drawn into transformative experiences.[11]

Unsettling empathy consists of two elements: a *willingness* to be challenged by the other, and the *ability* to turn this challenge into a positive force. It requires a *willingness* to be unsettled by the presence of the other regarding one's own attitudes and assumptions about the world, one's identification with large-group identities and, to some extent, regarding one's deeply held beliefs and values. Unsettling empathy also requires the *ability* to embrace such a challenge as productive in order to enter into fruitful engagement with the other, without having to give up who we are.

Unsettling empathy in reconciliatory settings resists harmonious unity and closure. Reconciliation does not prove its effectiveness when people hold hands and sing "Kumbaya."[12] The seemingly "happy end" of the 2015 seminar—when a Palestinian recognized the humanity of a Jewish-Israeli woman after she had confided her fears and mistrust—is not a singular event that marks it a success story. Rather, it was an unsettling empathetic experience between two people divided by a mistrust not completely their own—a mistrust larger than themselves since it has been etched deeply into their social identity as members of their respective communities.

Unsettling empathy also resists the blurring of boundaries, as it occurred in our seminar when a Palestinian demanded that Israelis need to agree with his own political position in order for him to trust them. Requesting from Israelis an empathetic agreement with his political views erased the "otherness" of his Israeli partners. Reconciliation, however, does not work in such unilateral ways. Amos Goldberg, a Jewish Israeli Holocaust scholar working in the field of trauma studies, writes in the context of the Nakba and the Holocaust:

> Empathy does not ask subjects to put themselves in the victim's shoes, to take the victim's place, but to identify specifically with the traumatic core of the victim's existence, thereby recognizing the *separateness,* lack and radical otherness that are inevitable components of relations with trauma victims and, in fact, of social relationships in general. (Goldberg 2015, 16–17; emphasis added)

Unsettling empathy, in other words, leads us to care for the other while respecting the differences between us. Social, interpersonal reconciliation demands our willingness to engage with the other as she or he is, not as we wish them to be. Hence, the unsettling empathy that does its work in reconciliatory processes is costly: it compels us to question our assumptions about the other and about ourselves. It is not a pleasant experience the moment it occurs, but it is a transformative one.

Memory and Fear: On German Family History

When our lives are not interrupted by war, premature death, or genocidal violence, we live in a "two-hundred-year present," a concept that sociologist and peace researcher Elise Boulding expounded on many occasions.[13] This is a presence measured by physical touch. This must surely be impossible, a skeptical reader might quickly object, since our individual life expectancy certainly cannot span two hundred years. The two-hundred-year present by physical touch, however, is a span that reaches from those who have touched us when we were born to those whom we may touch before we die. I have been touched by my grandparents, who were born around 1900. With some luck, I may be able to touch the yet-to-be-born children of my daughters, my future grandchildren, who, if they have auspicious lives, may reach into the decade of 2090s. From 1900s to 2090s, this is the two-hundred-year present of my life.

Once we become aware of the people we are connected to by physical touch, we may realize that we are not just autonomous, independent beings floating outside of history. History neither begins with us, nor does it end with us. Traumatic histories also do not begin with us or end with us. We live in a continuum of relationships, and we do so through our families and through the communities we inhabit and which we pass along to our children and children's children. Aware of how far we stretch backward and forward, we can recognize the responsibility that comes with a two-hundred-year present: we are called to account for the past as well as to imagine the future.

Those who have touched us may have done so with the love and caring they were bringing to their families. But the touch we have received from the generations before us can also be burdened by the wrongdoings of previous times. Their touch may have marked us with hurt or shame. At times, a touch can be poisonous, and we spend a lifetime in convalescence. In such cases we have no choice but to find ways to repair the damage done by those who have touched us, so that we do not pass on the poison to our children and grandchildren.

Every family, every community, every nation has skeletons in their closets. These hidden bones can be of minor or major social importance, but if left silenced and denied, they will impact future relations. On a smaller scale, a skeleton in the closet can be a child out of wedlock; it can be the homosexuality of an uncle in the 1950s or the bigotry of a grandmother at the turn of the century. On a larger scale, we can think of how national histories intersect with individual lives. In the United States, for example, awareness of living in a two-hundred-year present makes slavery not a remote event but reveals a presence to which Americans are very much connected. In Germany, it is the Holocaust that exudes a strong presence in families and communities.

On several occasions, I have been able to introduce the idea of a two-hundred-year present through embodied constellations, where workshop participants create a generational chain of their family histories in the context of interpersonal encounters. The mechanics of such an exercise is fairly simple: a participant volunteers to show his or her family history. As the protagonist, he or she would be asked to stand in the center of a line, representing him or herself at the current stage of life. The protagonist then invites four other people, each representing a parent and a grandparent standing on one side of the protagonist, and a child and grandchild standing on the other side. A generational chain thus becomes visible as a constellation in space. Whether the protagonist already has children or grandchildren does not really matter: they can be imagined, as we always have to imagine the future.

In mixed groups of Germans and Jews, the constellation of a two-hundred-year present can be very compelling, because it conveys tangibly the effects of traumatic histories in families belonging to victimized communities or a perpetrator society. In the example below, I focus on German family history. I will describe one German woman's display of her family's generational chain. As in most cases when Germans reconstruct their family histories, hers also revealed a gap in the intergenerational chain related to World War II and the Holocaust. The disrupted or broken link usually occurs in the transition from the generation that lived through the war and the Holocaust to those born after 1945. This gap is often marked by muddled emotions, turmoil, darkness, silence, and fear.

The particular constellation I will sketch below happened in a mixed German-Jewish workshop on memory, with a focus on intergenerational relations.[14] For this one-day workshop in Germany about twenty participants had signed up, including non-Jewish German university students, children of Holocaust survivors living in Germany, people born in the final years of the war and the 1950s, and a few people who had been adults during the 1940s, including a Holocaust survivor. Midway through the workshop, we approached the topic of German family history, a delicate issue in heterogeneous groups of Germans and Jews. It is not easy for Germans in the presence of Jews to open a window into their family story that might reveal a perpetrator perspective and mentality; it is also not easy for Jews to witness their German peers struggling with the ambiguities of loyalty and love in families touched by moral failure and criminal complicity (Berens 1996; Krondorfer 1995).

Frauengeschichte: A Woman's Family Constellation

After briefly introducing the idea of a two-hundred-year present, a German woman, who was born not long after World War II ended, volunteered to present her family's generational chain. What she showed us left her, by the end, deeply disturbed, so much so that afterward she said she almost regretted having stepped forward. Still later, in a letter I received a few weeks after the workshop, she took again ownership of her choice. She had been profoundly unsettled by the experience, she admitted in the letter, with the result that she suffered for days from symptoms of withdrawal, nightmares, unprovoked sobbing, and speechlessness. But she no longer felt any anger about these symptoms. Rather, she said, she now realized that something must have drawn her to sign up for this workshop in the first place, perhaps to cope with something still unresolved in her family. "The moment I had decided to attend the seminar," she wrote, "I had already made a choice without being fully conscious of it. This was even truer for my spontaneous decision to volunteer for creating a generational chain. I was clearly not forced to do it."

What happened? In a first step, the woman, whom I will call Annette, picked from among the participants a representative for each of the generations. With herself in the center of the generational link, she chose two people to represent her daughter and granddaughter (both standing to her right and representing future generations), then her mother (standing to her left and representing past generations). So far, these were only women. Only for her grandparents' generation did Annette pick a man, to represent her grandfather.

In a second step, we asked Annette to provide a little more information about each of the characters in her family chain, just enough to know who was who and what their relations to each other might be. Intriguingly, she only placed her grandfather into the context of German history. We learned that he had been raised at the end of the German "Kaiserreich" (Wilhelmine Empire) and remained "kaisertreu" (loyal to the monarchy). Described as unapproachable, stern, and cold, the grandfather remained nameless. It is not that Annette wanted to keep his name a secret, she just couldn't remember it.

In contrast to the nameless grandfather, the women in her family chain were all characterized in relational terms. We learned what kind of relations they had with each other and how close or distant their personal-emotional ties had been. An image emerged in the room that presented her German family as women's history. This impression was bolstered when each of the five people in the generational chain was asked to express physically how they related to the person next to them. All four women created a gesture that connected them by physical touch; only the grandfather stood isolated. It was a striking image of strength and solidarity among the women, with the man lost in his own space.

To show a constellation of one's family biography is, for the protagonist, something personal and unique: it reveals intimate details about
specific family dynamics. At the same time, such a constellation also gives
insight into the dynamics and representation of a large-group identity. The
individual and the collective levels merge and interact. What is deeply
personal for the protagonist in a constellation of a generational chain is,
at the same time, profoundly illuminating for the group participants at
the collective level. To maintain a balance between personal insight and
collective dynamics is what distinguishes such sessions from individual
therapy and what makes them beneficial for groups in conflict in reconciliatory settings.

In a third step, we invited the other group participants, who were
watching the constellation from outside, to offer some feedback on what
they were witnessing. A range of small observations was shared, expressing
some unease about a sculpture that so ostensibly portrayed women's solidarity. "It feels like a postwar reconstruction of German women's history,"
someone said. "I like it because it acknowledges the labor of the '*Trümmerfrauen*' [women who cleared the rubble after the war in the destroyed
German cities][15] and women's stride toward emancipation."

"Yes, I see this too," someone else added, "but the image also seems
to suggest women's innocence. I don't see the war or the horrors of the
Holocaust, and I do not see how these women were involved in this history."

Indeed, the constructed generational chain seemed to convey that only
men—in the person of the grandfather—were "historical" figures related
to Germany's national history. Women were characterized only by their
internal relationships and seemed to float outside of the realm of polity.
Isolated as the grandfather was from the four generations of women, with
no physical touch between him and them, the message seemed to be that
"*Tätergeschichte*" (history of perpetrators) is "*Männergeschichte*" (men's history).
It preserved the myth of the innocence of German women.[16] With the
disappearance of fathers in the Annette's generational two-hundred-year
present, the perpetrators seemed to have disappeared too.

"The fact that we created this chain of women," Annette later wrote,
"seemed natural to me, because I am a woman, and so are my daughter and granddaughter. It was also clear to me that my mother had to
be there. I did not even think about my father." During the workshop
itself, after being prompted by the group's feedback, Annette revealed a
few remembered details about the Nazi past. But her memories remained
vague and merely suggestive. She talked about brothers of her nameless

grandfather, who had apparently died during the war. As it turned out, though, she had initially misspoken, since the brothers she had mentioned were actually her father's brothers. In other words, these brothers were her uncles and young men during the Nazi regime. One of her uncles, we learned in passing, was a member of the feared SS. Shadows of the Nazi past entered into the constellation, but only in muddled ways—like a dark presence refusing to take on a clear shape or form.

"The whole time," Annette said, "I was in charge of keeping the generational chain together." When she shared this insight, it became clear how strenuous her position had been: much effort had been invested into keeping up an image of women's bonding and strength. In a fourth step, then, we invited Annette to remove herself from the generational chain. After a moment of hesitation, she vacated her place. As soon as she left, something unexpectedly happened. The four generations remaining in the generational chain spontaneously started to move, without being prompted to do so. They rearranged themselves anew in space. No longer lined-up in a generational chain, the three women surrounded the grandfather. He suddenly found himself in the center of the family constellation, encircled by the women representing Annette's mother, daughter, and granddaughter.

Annette watched this unexpected change with visibly growing anxiety. She was almost in a state of panic, pacing back and forth. She finally settled in a place far away from the newly formed sculpture, her body exuding mental and emotional turmoil. She looked frightened. The solidarity among women, which she had so carefully maintained and for which she had felt responsible, had collapsed right in front of her eyes. The isolated, stern grandfather had become the center of attention. "I was shocked to the depth of my soul," Annette would later say, recalling the new sculpture. "Under no circumstance would I have returned to this sculpture, even if my refusal to join would have cost me the loss of my daughter and granddaughter." Danger and calamity, Annette said, emanated from her grandfather, and a deep sense of darkness. She remembered that when she had been seven years old and her grandfather died, she stood at his open casket and thought, "It is good that he died."

In a fifth step, we asked the people representing Annette's family members how they felt standing in the spontaneously formed new sculpture, with the grandfather in the center. The daughter mentioned how uncomfortable it made her. She needed more distance to the grandfather. We invited her to move. The participants representing her daughter and the granddaughter together stepped away, leaving a large spatial gap between

themselves and the older generations (Annette's mother and grandfather).
We asked the woman representing Annette's daughter to acknowledge the
gap and to describe it to us. Lowering her eyes and looking down at
the floor, as if looking into an abyss rather than across to the preceding
generations, Annette's daughter was at a loss of words. "I do not see much,
I do not know what to say." It was an empty space for her. Though not
entirely. She also said that she had little interest in finding out about the
abyss, this Nazi past. She did not want to do her mother's work.

Annette was still watching, anxiety-filled, from a distance. Yet, the new
constellation also freed her from her paralysis. She rejoined the sculpture
and placed herself next to her granddaughter and daughter. But she did
not step into the gap in order to fill the empty space. She was no longer
trying to hold the intergenerational chain together. She no longer tried
to bridge the gap—an abyss of "darkness," as she would later write in a
letter. The chain was broken, separating the postwar generations from the
war generation of mother and grandfather.

"The truth almost drove me mad"

In the final round of conversation between protagonist, her family "representatives," and the group at large, we shared our observations but could
push our interpretations only so far. Annette was mentally exhausted and
needed time and space to digest all that had happened. Clearly, something
deep and unsettling had occurred, not only for Annette personally, but for
the group as a whole. The German participants identified with various
aspects of the two-hundred-year present in German families. The question was raised whether the unresolved task of acknowledging the gap or
abyss between the generations was delegated to Annette's daughter, and
whether it was fair to burden the new postwar generation with this task.
The participants of Jewish background, however, responded differently.
Though they were largely grateful for having been allowed to witness an
intimate moment in German family history, they were uneasy nevertheless. Because it is so rare that groups separated and yet united by a shared
antagonistic past reveal to each other guarded aspects of their own culture
and family, the Jewish participants reacted defensively.

What happened? Whatever the specific darkness was that remained
unnamed in Annette's family constellation, the session still humanized the
onerous struggle that marks so many German families after the Holocaust.

In other words, the Jewish participants were able to get a peek into the intimate struggles of German families regarding their social identity embedded in a perpetrator legacy. Revealing cultural secrets in the presence of the other can break down protective barriers by which we define ourselves over against the other. When those old identity boundaries get threatened, we call upon mental defenses to build up new walls. As a matter of fact, we can often observe that if one side opens the wall too much, the other side builds up its own wall. Psychologist Dan Bar-On called this the "double wall phenomenon" (1989, 328).[17]

In this particular workshop, an instance of strong defensive discomfort erupted during the last round of conversation shortly before we were about to part ways. It happened when the only attending, aging Holocaust survivor accused one of the young German participants of harboring pro-Nazi sentiments. The accusation was very much unwarranted. Feeling deeply insulted, the young man yelled back at the survivor and was ready to leave the room in anger. Only the intervention of other group participants prevented further escalation.

This interaction between the Holocaust survivor and the German man of the postwar generation was brief, but nevertheless loaded with suspicion and anger. It operated on several complex and interwoven levels that cannot be fully unpacked here. In the context of our discussion, it is sufficient to read it as a defensive reaction to having been unsettled by the breaking down of social identity boundaries, which, it seems, was triggered when witnessing Annette's struggle with her German family history. In the workshop, empathic understanding emerged between and among participants tied to each other by a traumatic past. The survivor's unprovoked accusation, rooted in his own fears, can thus be read as an attempt to quell anxieties over the loss of old boundaries. Those boundaries had neatly kept apart the narratives of victims and perpetrators after 1945, creating a publicly accepted moral equilibrium and keeping in check mistrust, recriminations, and suspicions. A loosening of those boundaries stirred an existential anxiety and moral panic in the survivor.

Coda: during this workshop itself, we never learned what the gap represented or what the abyss symbolized in the intergenerational German family chain that Annette had shown us. Presumably, it had to do with secrets kept about the Nazi past. Given that the gap in Annette's family constellation occurred precisely at the period that separated the postwar generations from the war generation seemed to suggest a silencing and veiling of the Nazi past. We can't be sure, however, since what was hidden might have been family secret altogether disconnected to Nazism. Or it could have been a mixture of both. From Annette's story we knew for certain that the grandfather had played an important role in the family. In a correspondence a few weeks after the workshop, Annette wrote to me that she had consulted with other family members to find out her grandfather's name. No one remembered! Her extended family, she wrote, recalled him as tall, hard, cold, penny-pinching, commanding, never giving gifts, and never touching anyone. Only a sister-in-law, who never met him personally, eventually remembered his name.

In our ensuing correspondence, I gently encouraged Annette to place herself in the gap that had been created in her generational chain and to imaginatively explore what she might find there. She wrote back, saying she could not do so. "I imagine sitting right at the edge of this gulf and looking down," she wrote. What she discovered at the edge, however, was anything but pleasant. It was an "enormous, dark, sharp-edged, dangerous abyss. You could neither place yourself in it, nor could you jump across it. It would only be possible to descend into it and ascend on the other side—that is, if you were able to make it across. You would have to go into the midst of hell. From the abyss emanated flames, smoke, stench. And dreadful screams, sobbing—the whole abyss nothing but a nameless horror."

For more than ten years in her life, Annette added, she had made efforts to descend into the abyss to find out the truth about her family. "I eventually found the truth in the abyss," she wrote, "and the truth almost drove me mad." Whatever she found, it remains her secret.

Outlook

To return to troubled times is not meant to reinscribe what is already known historically, but to change and transform contemporary relations. In this sense, it does not really matter that the exact nature of the truth that Annette found was not shared and that it remained her knowledge alone. Yet, her willingness to risk vulnerability in the presence of others, including those who might have been victimized as Jews by members of her German family, is what it takes to move into a posture unsettling empathy. Similarly, the Israeli woman had risked vulnerability in the presence of Palestinians, admitting her fear of being kidnapped by them. When these moments occur, it compels us to reconsider our assumptions and renders us vulnerable in the presence of the other. Revealing an internal tension in the social body of one's own community in the presence of those with whom one lives in conflict is part of the posture of unsettling empathy. This conflict can lie in the past, like the Holocaust. In this case, becoming aware of our two-hundred-year present makes those historical traumas far less removed than we sometimes assume. Or the conflict is ongoing in the present, as in Israel-Palestine. In this case, our two-hundred-year present calls us into responsibility toward the future. We have been touched by the generations before us, but what do we want pass on? What part of their touch needs to stop with our own generation because we do not want to pass on any contamination? What generational embraces can we accept, and which one do we need to reject? Unsettling empathy leaves people shaken up in their assumptions about themselves and others, and opens them up to future possibilities.

There are no magic bullets in this line of reconciliatory work. Evidence of transformative change does not lie in miracles. I have described two exceptionally intense scenarios from interpersonal reconciliation with groups in conflict: trauma and trust in the Palestinian-Israeli case, memory and fear in the case of German family history. I have suggested, prudently and cautiously, some interpretive possibilities without plumbing the full depth and complexity inherent in such processes. Importantly, the examples I chose to share and investigate reveal reconciliatory possibilities.

More often than not, it is in small gestures that we see the emergence of transformative changes. If success were measured by standards of grand political solutions alone, interpersonal encounters in reconciliatory settings would be disappointing. No peace agreement descended upon the troubled territory of Israel and Palestine after our seminars in 2014 and 2015; no sudden cultural healing of traumatic memories occurred in Germany after our workshop on memory and family history. Yet, amid cultivated mistrust, recriminations, fears, and political hatreds, the interactions we witnessed signal the possibility of a different symbolic order.

Unsettling empathy is part of our responsiveness toward each other. "[H]istory, like trauma, is never simply one's own," Cathy Caruth writes in *Unclaimed Experience*. Rather, "history is precisely the way we are implicated in each other's trauma" (1996, 11, 24). When communicating across cultural and historical divides, we reach beyond one-sided national narratives and narrow-minded large-group identifications in order to seek cross-cultural understanding and empathy.

Notes

1. When groups of Israelis and Palestinians officially meet in the West Bank without an international organization, permission needs to be granted by the Palestinian Authority and the Israeli security.

2. The term *second Generation* for Germans born after 1945 is analytically imprecise, for it assumes similarity of experiences across many generational cohorts. Elsewhere, I suggest differentiating between the different "political cohorts" of 1968, 1979, and 1989 (Krondorfer 2006). The 1968ers (born 1937–1953) constitute the first German postwar cohort that vehemently protested against their German parents during the Vietnam War era. The 1979ers (born 1954–1966) constitute the second German postwar cohort, marked by medialized encounters of the Holocaust (such as the 1979 German release of the American TV series *Holocaust*) and insufficient Holocaust education in school. The 1989ers (born 1967–1976) constitute the third postwar cohort, which learned about the Holocaust in school and was politically marked by the fall of the Berlin wall in 1989. I belong to the 1979ers.

3. In the 1980s, together with a Jewish friend I co-founded *The Jewish-German Dance Theatre* for American Jewish and non-Jewish German dancers and actors to confront communal, cultural, and personal memories of the Holocaust. We turned these explorations into a performance piece that toured for five years in the United States and Germany, including a show in the Jewish community of East Berlin in 1989, shortly before the wall came down. Later, I led educational Holocaust programs for Jewish-American and German university students; between 1989 and 2005, we organized four-week-long summer programs, where university students studied and lived together while traveling in the U.S., Germany, and Poland (Krondorfer 2013). Other programs I have facilitated include: a seminar in Weimar and the former concentration camp of Buchenwald for German Protestant and Catholic clergy and rabbis from the Chicago area; workshops on Jewish-German relations; interactive seminars on intergenerational issues for the Australian Jewish community in Melbourne and on German families' biographies in Germany; art installations with a Jewish-German artist residing in the United States, in which we explored our divergent European family roots through lithographs, artist books, prints, and sculptures (Krondorfer and Baldner 2013); and racial reconciliation retreats for American college students to probe and confront their ethnic, religious, cultural, and linguistic diversities.

4. The organization *Friendship Across Borders* (FAB) invited me conduct these seminars; http://www.fab-friendshipacrossborders.net/index.php/en/.

5. To put the Holocaust and the Nakba into some comparative frame remains a highly contested and politicized issue. See, for example, Bashir and Goldberg (2014); Shaw and Bartov (2010); the chapter on "The Palestinian Catas-

trophe (Nakba) versus the Holocaust," in Litvak and Webman (2009, 309–29). In terms of the seminar, the precise wording for "collective trauma" on the cards of the three national groups read:

ISRAELIS: (for themselves) Holocaust, hostile environment—wars—terrorist attack; (for Germans) 3rd generation conflict!? Accusations? Conflicts?; (for Palestinians) Nakba, life under occupation.

GERMANS: (for themselves) Collective guilt because of the 3rd Reich; (for Israelis) Antisemitism; (for Palestinians) Nakba.

PALESTINIANS: (for themselves) Nakba: dispossession & rejection, ethnic cleansing, disempowerment, internalized inferiority, media misinterpretation/dehumanization, family fragmentation, restriction of movement; (for Germans) Holocaust, guilt—racism—shame—separation; (for Israelis) Holocaust, rejection—victimization—fear/survival—dispossession.

6. "A group of people" can refer to "a tribe, a clan, a class, an ethnicity, a race, a nationality, a religion, or a political ideology" (Volkan 2013, 77).

7. A good and effective way to reach group consensus on how to proceed topically is to ask each participant to write on a notecard (anonymously) his or her first choice of a topic to be discussed in the group. The cards are collected, then distributed across the floor with enough space between them for everyone to walk around. Each participant steps on card that they prefer to work on first. In the first round, all those cards are removed that have no or only very few "takers." In the second round, the whole group walks around again and steps on one of the remaining cards. Usually, by the third round there is a clear "winner." This is how the 2015 participants chose the "collective trauma" card. There was no card resembling anything like "national glories."

8. The *Nakba* (Catastrophe) was followed by the 1967 war (the "Six Day War"), which is called by Palestinians the *Naksa* (Calamity). It led to the beginning of the military occupation of the remaining Palestinian territory. One can also mention the 1993 Oslo Peace Accords, which were to give to the Palestinians limited self-governance in the West Bank and Gaza, and resulted not in peace but in further entrenched separation between Palestinians and Israelis.

9. Irvin Yalom, in his extensive study on group therapies, helpfully distinguishes between the "front" and the "core" of different group therapies: "The *front* consists of the trappings, the form, the techniques, the specialized language, and the aura surrounding each of the ideological schools; the *core* consists of those aspects of the experience that are intrinsic to the therapeutic process—that is, *the*

bare-boned mechanisms of change" (Yalom 1995; emphasis in original). Similar to Yalom, I am interested in the "core" when describing and reflecting on the potential for change and transformation in reconciliatory processes with groups in conflict.

10. For a broader context, see also Litvak (2009).

11. In the field of trauma studies, Dominick LaCapra (2001) has developed the concept of "empathic unsettlement" to make a similar point. Speaking of "unsettling empathy," I am gesturing toward LaCapra's alike-sounding concept. They are, however, not identical. See Krondorfer (2015b); for another discussion of LaCapra, see Goldberg (2015).

12. The spiritual song *Kumbaya* has become a folk song with great popularity, especially in the 1960s. "Kumbaya" now refers to an artificial holding of hands in groups under the pretense of agreement while deep-seated discord remains.

13. See especially her chapter "Expanding our Sense of Time and History," in Boulding (1990).

14. The *Study Group on Intergenerational Consequences of the Holocaust* (formerly PAKH) invited me to lead this workshop. The group was founded in 1995 by Jewish and non-Jewish German members, most of them psychotherapists, with the aim of raising awareness of the impact of traumatic histories through personal confrontation, especially with respect to the Holocaust and World War II. http://www.pakh.de/EN/index.html.

15. For biographies of *Trümmerfrauen*, see Unruh (1987); for the genesis and historicization of the myth of *Trümmerfrauen*, see Treber (2014).

16. Recent historical scholarship has countered the myth of German women's innocence. See Lower (2013); Harvey (2003); Schwarz (1997); Ebbinghaus (1996).

17. Bar-On has used the "double wall" to describe the interactions between the German perpetrator generation and their children with respect to confronting the Nazi past. In postwar Germany, Bar-On observed, the parents build a wall "around their feelings about the atrocities" and the children a protective wall in reaction to their parents' past. "If those on one side try to find an opening, they encounter the wall on the other side" (1989, 328). Similar dynamics can be observed in group interactions between Jews and Germans. I have often encountered it when facilitating intercultural groups that are in tension or antagonism with each other.

Works Cited

Bar-On, Dan. 1989. *Legacy of Silence: Encounters with Children of the Third Reich.* Cambridge: Harvard University Press.

Bashir, Bashir, and Amos Goldberg. 2014. "Deliberating the Holocaust and the Nakba: Disruptive Empathy and Binationalism in Israel/Palestine." *Journal of Genocide Research* 16(1): 77–99.

Baumeister, Roy F. 1997. *Evil: Inside Human Violence and Cruelty*. New York: Freeman.

Berens, Claudia, ed. 1996. *"Coming Home" from Trauma: The Next Generation, Muteness, and the Search for a Voice*. Hamburg: Hamburger Institut für Sozialforschung.

Boulding, Elise. 1990. *Building a Global Civic Culture*. Syracuse: Syracuse University Press.

Brunner, Claudia, and von Seltmann. 2006. *Schweigen die Täter, reden die Enkel*. Frankfurt: S. Fischer.

Caruth, Cathy. 1996. *Unclaimed Experience: Trauma, Narrative, and History*. Baltimore: Johns Hopkins University Press.

Chaitin, Julia. 2011. *Peace-Building in Israel and Palestine: Social Psychology and Grassroots Initiatives*. New York: Palgrave Macmillan.

Ebbinghaus, Angelika, ed. 1996. *Opfer und Täterinnen: Frauenbiographien des Nationalsozialismus*. Hamburg: Fischer.

Edwards, Bruce. 1998. "History, Myth, and Mind." *Mind and Human Interaction* 9: 1–4.

Goldberg, Amos. 2015. "Narrative, Testimony, and Trauma: The Nakba and the Holocaust in Elias Khoury's *Gate of the Sun*." *Interventions: International Journal of Postcolonial Studies* (June): 1–14. DOI: 10.1080/1369801X.2015.1042396.

Govier, Trudy, and Wilhelm Verwoerd. 2002. "Trust and the Problem of National Reconciliation." *Philosophy of the Social Sciences* 32(2) (June): 178: 205.

Harvey, Elizabeth. 2003. *Women and the Nazi East: Agents and Witnesses of Germanization*. New Haven: Yale University Press.

Krondorfer, Björn. 1995. *Remembrance and Reconciliation: Encounters between Young Jews and Germans*. New Haven: Yale University Press.

———. 2000. "Afterword." In *My Father's Testament: Memoir of a Jewish Teenager, 1938–1945*, edited by Edward Gastfriend, with an afterword by B. Krondorfer, 173–87. Philadelphia: Temple University Press.

———. 2001. "At Ratner's Kosher Restaurant." In *Second Generation Voices: Reflections by Children of Holocaust Survivors and Perpetrators*, edited by Alan Berger and Naomi Berger, 258–69. Syracuse: Syracuse University Press.

———. 2002. "Eine Reise gegen das Schweigen." In *Das Vermächtnis annehmen*, edited by Brigitta Huhnke and B. Krondorfer, 315–44. Giessen: Psychosozial Verlag.

———. 2006. "Nationalsozialismus und Holocaust in Autobiographien protestantischer Theologen." In *Mit Blick auf die Täter: Fragen an die deutsche Theologie nach 1945*, edited by Björn Krondorfer, Katharina von Kellenbach, and Norbert Reck, 23–170. Gütersloh: Gütersloher Verlag.

———. 2013. "Interkulturelle Erinnerungsarbeit als offener Prozess." In *Handbuch Nationalsozialismus und Holocaust: Historisch-politisches Lernen in Schule, außerschulischer Bildung und Lehrerbildung*, edited by Hannsfred Rathenow et al., 481–97. Schwalbach: Wochenschau Verlag.

———. 2015a. "Notes from a Field of Conflict: Trilateral Dialogical Engagement in Israel/ Palestine." *Journal of Ecumenical Studies* 50(1) (Winter): 153–58.

46 Björn Krondorfer

———. 2015b. "Unsettling Empathy: Intercultural Dialogue in the Aftermath of Historical and Cultural Trauma." In *Breaking Cycles of Repetition: A Global Dialogue on Historical Trauma and Memory*, edited by Pumla Gobodo-Madikizela, 90–112. Opladen: Budrich.

———, and Karen Baldner. 2013. "From Pulp to Palimpsest: Witnessing and Re-Imagining through the Arts." In *Different Horrors, Same Hell: Gender and the Holocaust*, edited by Myrna Goldenberg and Amy H. Shapiro, 132–62. Seattle: University of Washington Press.

LaCapra, Dominick. 2001. *Writing History, Writing Trauma*. Baltimore: Johns Hopkins University Press.

Litvak, Meir, ed. 2009. *Palestinian Collective Memory and National Identity*. New York: Palgrave Macmillan.

———, and Esther Webman. 2009. *From Empathy to Denial: Arab Responses to the Holocaust*. New York: Columbia University Press.

Lower, Wendy. 2013. *Hitler's Furies: German Women in the Nazi Killing Fields*. Boston: Houghton Mifflin Harcourt.

Schwarz, Gudrun. 1997. *Eine Frau an seiner Seite: Ehefrauen in der "SS-Sippengemeinschaft."* Hamburg: Hamburger Edition.

Shaw, Martin, and Omer Bartov. 2010. "The Question of Genocide in Palestine, 1948: An Exchange between Martin Shaw and Omer Bartov." *Journal of Genocide Research* 12(3–4) (September-December): 243–59.

Treber, Leoni. 2014. *Mythos Trümmerfrauen: Von der Trümmerbeseitigung in der Kriegs- und Nachkriegszeit und der Entstehung eines deutschen Erinnerungsortes*. Essen: Klartext-Verlag.

Unruh, Trude, ed. 1987. *Trümmerfrauen: Biografien einer betrogenen Generation*. Essen: Klartext-Verlag.

Vetlesen, Arne Johan. 2005. *Evil and Human Agency: Understanding Collective Evildoing*. Cambridge: Cambridge University Press.

Volkan, Vamik. 2013. *Enemies on the Couch: A Psychopolitical Journey through War and Peace*. Durham: Pitchstone.

Yalom, Irvin. 1995. *The Theory and Practice of Group Psychotherapy*. 4th ed. New York: Basic Books.

2

Beyond a Dilemma of Apology

Transforming (Veteran) Resistance to Reconciliation in Northern Ireland and South Africa

WILHELM VERWOERD AND ALISTAIR LITTLE

Gerard Foster is a former political prisoner from an Irish Republican background. As a teenager from a tough Belfast, working-class, and "Catholic" neighborhood he became a member of the Irish National Liberation Army (INLA)—"because they were the most active in fighting the British Army in our area." During about five years in prison his political commitment to a "socialist, united Ireland" and the use of violence to help achieve this goal was deepened. Upon his release from prison he was faced with ceasefires from mainstream Loyalist (Protestant) and Republican paramilitary organizations and growing acceptance of the need for political negotiations (mid-1990s). He therefore withdrew in disgust from community-based political activism, believing at that time that "we lost the war . . . we should have *increased* violence!" Through a grassroots organization focusing on the needs of (Republican Socialist) political prisoners and a fledgling radical political party (the Irish Republican Socialist Party), he reengaged as a political activist from the late 1990s onward. This included being delegated to represent his "movement" at a series of behind-the-scenes political dialogues with (former) enemies.

Thus, Gerard became a participant—a very reluctant participant—in the "Glencree Survivors and Former Combatants Programme."[1] In the process, he slowly and pragmatically moved away from the current use of political violence while remaining passionate about the (exclusive) "right-ness" of his political beliefs—until a heartfelt engagement with elderly family members of British soldiers who were killed by Irish Republicans. Gerard recalls:

> For me the biggest thing was that weekend at Glencree . . . see-ing . . . for me, and I've said this before, genuinely seeing the hurt and pain of the enemy. Some of these people have lost their family members 30 years ago.
>
> It was really frightening. My dad is buried near the INLA plot in Belfast, so you can't go to one without the other. It was after that weekend at Glencree that I really felt the strong sense of betrayal. I was up at my dad's grave and they're feet apart, the INLA plot is near enough next to it. I was look-ing down at the names on INLA graves, most of the names I knew. I was thinking by myself "What would they think of me now; what would they be thinking of what I'm doing?" I felt "I let youse down, lads." That was a part that was really strong within me, that I am not only letting them'uns down. I am letting myself down. A real struggle, but I couldn't get past what I'd seen—it kept coming back to me what I'd seen that week end at Glencree.
>
> Just because of my background, there would be people who would see me as a terrorist, or whatever, and no matter [what], what I did was wrong and I should be seeking forgive-ness. But I will spin it round and say, "I don't want forgiveness; I don't need forgiveness . . ."
>
> Now what impact will that have on people who have lost loved ones? Will it reinforce that I'm the bad guy and I'm still heartless and I still don't care about their hurt and pain?[2]

Gerard's story is, unfortunately, not unique. In our personal and profes-sional experience we, Alistair Little and Wilhelm Verwoerd, have found that many politically motivated former combatants find it particularly difficult to say sorry or to ask for forgiveness.[3]

Such an apology would, they feel, amount to a betrayal of "us": of political cause, of comrades (especially those who died), of community, and of themselves. On the other hand, if they deny any wrongdoing and show no sensitivity to the human cost of their actions, there is a high risk of further wounding, of insult being added to the injuries of those directly and indirectly affected amongst "them" (Govier and Verwoerd 2002d, 71).

Many of these former combatants are actually committed to peace; they do not want further violence, at least for the sake of their children. But their reluctance to say sorry (motivated by loyalty to "us") can easily rub salt into the wounds of (former) enemies and thus, sadly, contribute to cycles of intergroup and intergenerational conflict. In other words, these former combatants are faced with a dilemma: If they do not apologize they might encourage retaliatory or revengeful reactions from "them"; if they do apologize they might well be rejected by "us," their own group, organization, or community. This tension between apology-as-betrayal-of-us and non-apology-as-further-wounding-of-them can be described as a "dilemma of apology."

This dilemma of apology—and the challenges of its transformation—has been a key theme that emerged from a recent "Beyond Dehumanisation" international research project that involved former combatant peacemakers from South Africa, Israel, Palestine, the U.S.A., and the conflict in and about Northern Ireland. We explain this project more fully later in this chapter.

Even though the challenge of moving beyond this "dilemma of apology" features prominently in this research project and resonates strongly with our personal and professional experiences over a number of decades, as far as we can gather it has not received enough attention in academic literature. For example, Nadler promisingly defines "socio-emotional reconciliation" as "a process of working through emotions and threats to identity that are the consequence of the pain and humiliation that parties had inflicted on each other" (Nadler et al. 2008, 6). However, Nadler views "the successful completion of an apology-forgiveness cycle" as "lying at the centre of socioemotional reconciliation" (ibid., 42). The critical role given to apology and forgiveness presupposes a clear distinction between the roles of "victim" and "perpetrator." We have found this distinction to be a problematic starting point in working with politically motivated ex-combatants/veterans and also problematic at a conceptual-ethical level (Govier and Verwoerd 2004). The necessity of apology within Nadler's understanding of "socio-emotional reconciliation" also derives from a "bilateral forgiveness" model in which apology becomes a *precondition* for forgiveness (Govier and Verwoerd 2002b; 2002c; Verwoerd 2007). Again, from practical and philosophical perspectives, this is too narrow a view of the connections between forgiveness and apology; it results, arguably, in undue and counterproductive stress on the need for "perpetrators" to ask for forgiveness.

Furthermore, we will defend our view in this chapter that neither forgiveness nor apology is essential for "reconciliation," especially when involving former combatants who have to "work through emotions and threats to identity" (Nadler et al. 2008, 6). Dan Philpott's *Just and Unjust Peace: An Ethic of Political Reconciliation* (2012) contains much that we can relate to in terms of the pitfalls of responsibility avoidance, the dynamics of further wounding as well as the complexity of forgiveness. However, his "political injustice" model again presupposes too clear a distinction between "victim" (V) and "perpetrator" (P). He recognizes that V and P are "Weberian ideal types" and admits to "greater complexity." He acknowledges, for example, "that parties can play gradations of each role and sometimes more than one role" (2012, 31). But he does not really address the dilemmas, especially regarding the "perpetrator side," that flow from this "greater complexity." Philpott does not grapple with the messiness of apology, in particular when "V" stands for "veteran," when "reconciliation" between former combatant enemies is involved, or when unconventional wars and "cycles of blood" have blurred conceptual and ethical lines—as is the case, in our experience, with the conflict in and about Northern Ireland.

Philpott's approach points to the limits of a reconciliation discourse that gives too central and uncritical a role to "apology" and "forgiveness" and to the accompanying presupposed clarity regarding wrongdoing.

Our response in this chapter consists of two main parts. The first part—"Toward Apologizing"—accepts the need for apology, but then continues to explore, (1) the need to take the reality of the above-mentioned dilemma more seriously, and (2) ways to reduce the sense of betrayal. The latter is done by highlighting options between being either *fully* right or *completely* wrong, by clarifying the distinction between *doing* wrong and *being* bad, and by stressing the *process* character of apologizing.

The second part—"Beyond Apology?"—consists of a more fundamental challenge to the need for apology. This challenge is fleshed out by exploring the promise and pitfalls of moral acknowledgment, of "saying sorry" without apologizing, and, more specifically, of compassion without "confession."

In the process, a more complex and, we believe, a more realistic picture is portrayed of the dynamics of genuine "reconciliation," which we broadly and currently understand in terms of the *cultivation of humanizing relations across conflict divides.*

As authors of this chapter, we hesitate to point out what we see as some of the widespread limitations of mainstream academic writing on reconciliation. We are particularly cautious to draw attention to a "dilemma of apology" and to question the central and necessary role of apology within the (re)humanization of relations between former political enemies. Given our personal conflict backgrounds and professional experience we are acutely aware of the pitfalls and further wounding potential of self-serving justifications, of moral blindness, and of self-deception.

We are not blind to organizational and community power dynamics, especially among those (who have been) directly and indirectly involved in political violence: how difficult it is to be really honest; how tempting it is to create half-truths that make one look more noble and righteous than one actually is; how often people lie, cover up, intimidate, bully, threaten, force, expel, and murder any opposition within to fight their wars and then find a way to convince themselves that all that was done was necessary; how a narrative is then created that must be adhered to within the group, party, or movement, with dissent silenced and unjust methods employed to maintain group think.

We have often come across the pervasiveness of the "magnitude gap" (Baumeister 1997, 18) between (expressed) political motivations and "good intentions" of those (directly and indirectly) responsible for violence and the harsh realities of dehumanizing consequences for those on the receiving end.[4] These pitfalls are explicitly addressed in earlier writing (Govier and Verwoerd 2002a; 2002d; Verwoerd and Little 2008). We are also busy with in-depth reflections on the "Beyond Dehumanisation International Research Project," which we hope to publish in the near future.

At this stage, we want to stress that the transformative purpose of our reflective practitioner work and writing is to make a humble contribution to humanization, ultimately, for the sake of those who have been or who might be on the receiving end of violence and injustice. In this chapter we argue specifically that underestimating a potentially genuine dilemma of apology might actually undermine lasting reconciliation; that a too one-sided insistence on apology may in reality increase further wounding and thus the continuation of cycles of victimization.

To further clarify our approach, the next section takes a closer look at the international research project on "Beyond Dehumanization."

Practical Wisdom of "Veteran Reconcilers"

Between November 2012 and May 2014, Little and Verwoerd (supported by Brandon Hamber and Louise Little) brought together small groups of former-enemy peace practitioners for a series of reflective workshops—four country/region-specific workshops (in Ireland, South Africa, Israel/Palestine, and the United States) as well as an international combined workshop that included a few participants from the workshops in South Africa, Israel/Palestine, and Ireland. In each context a few follow-up interviews were also held. The main purpose of the workshops and interviews was to gather and share practical wisdom around the tough challenges of humanizing and cross-cutting compassion in settings marred by political violence.

The focus of this project emerged from the real life challenges facing Alistair Little who was immersed in political violence as a teenager and over time became genuinely committed to an inner and outer journeying beyond dehumanization. The ongoing difficulties of this kind of personal and professional peacemaking also came to the fore in the "beyond Apartheid" trekking of Wilhelm Verwoerd as a white, Afrikaner South African and a grandson of Dr. H. F. Verwoerd, widely regarded as "the architect of Apartheid."

Thus, a key feature of the reflective process facilitated by us became a joint exploration of the promise and the pitfalls of widely used concepts such as love, forgiveness, apology, compassion, healing, and reconciliation within what can roughly be portrayed as humanizing processes.[5]

Our sensitivity to risks, difficulties, and challenges within these humanizing processes is, firstly, a reflection of what the above family of concepts has come to mean to us in our personal and professional practice of dealing with the legacy of violent conflict. Some of the questions we posed during the above-mentioned reflective workshops were: How do you have difficult, honest conversations with those that you have seen as your enemy? How do you have conversations with people who lost loved ones or who suffered and you may have belonged to an organization that was responsible for that suffering? How do we deal with issues of justice, truth recovery, and reconciliation, and what do these concepts *really* mean?

Secondly, the hope is that this focus on gritty and costly, though reachable, realities will also increase the likelihood of encouraging the transformation of resistance to life-giving, humanizing journeying, especially among those who have been hardened by conflict. We are under no illusion that those who are still intent on violence or many of those who have been involved in violence are likely to look for reasons *not* to listen when they hear people talking about "peace" or "reconciliation." We continue to face those (including our "young," militant selves) who see peacemakers as "soft, fluffy people who don't understand the realities of war" or as people "who haven't really thought through" what they are advocating.

The reflective process furthermore focused on "veterans" in two senses of the word. The more general sense refers to people with *significant experience* as participants and facilitators of humanizing and relational work in settings linked with violent political conflict. The more specific meaning of "veterans" is the literal sense of involving mostly former combatants who have become committed to peace/reconciliation/humanization work.

Underlying the (literal) veteran focus is the conviction that many people who have been involved in violence and who have found ways to move beyond cycles of revenge have authentic, wide-reaching learning to share. We have also found that this hard-won practical wisdom of (politically motivated) veterans—often only described as "perpetrators" and thus dismissed—is relatively neglected in the fields of conflict transformation and peace studies.

A number of factors influenced our decision to mostly use the format of small group, multiday reflective workshops to gather the real life, practical, transformative wisdom we were looking for. We have experienced many times that it is in the interaction and discussion between committed and diverse participants that questions and insights come to the fore that transcend the wisdom of individuals reflecting on their own. Furthermore, our aim was to make the reflective process as real as possible, that is, carefully selecting participants in each country to ensure a diversity of conflict backgrounds. By allowing space for storytelling and dialogue during the workshops, we were often experiencing in the moment what we were reflecting on—the promise of mutual understanding and cross-border compassion, the riskiness of truly engaging with one's deeper, darker self, while genuinely facing the Other.

With this background and approach in mind we can now move on to look at some of the practical wisdom that emerged specifically regarding the realities and the transformation of a dilemma of apology. We have deliberately opted to include a number of extracts from the transcripts of workshops and interviews gathered through this research project.[6] We believe it is important to bring the voices of these veteran reconcilers into the room, since we are also committed to helping transform the typical, unproductive divide between academics and practitioners, especially in the fields of peace/reconciliation/conflict studies.

We Were Right

As noted before, the "Beyond Dehumanisation" project highlighted a dilemma of apology faced by many deeply committed, politically motivated ex-combatants. If they were to apologize they would first have to accept that "we were wrong." This acceptance of wrongdoing amounts to a betrayal of what often is seen as a long and noble tradition of fighting injustice. During the Ireland/Northern Ireland workshop, Gerry McMonagle, a former Irish Republican Army (IRA) prisoner and influential local politician-peace activist, strongly articulated this sense of betrayal: "From our perspective 'we took on the might of the British Empire' and we were right in doing that and it was noble. We didn't see nothing wrong with it. This is what we should've been doing. We were trampled on, we were treated badly, there was a lot of injustice and we had to stand up and fight." For someone like Gerry McMonagle to apologize for "fighting injustice" would therefore be dishonest and also boil down to self-betrayal.

On the other hand, if these former combatants hold on to their sense of (political and moral) rightness in their encounters with people who have "lost loved ones," then there is a high risk of causing "further damage"; if they are not willing to apologize, they easily may become responsible for further wounding: "Will it reinforce that I still don't care about their hurt and pain? I do believe there should be some sort of a relationship there [with those people], maybe. But if it's going to be damaging, then I accept I shouldn't get involved" (Gerard Foster, as quoted in the introduction to this chapter).

The tension between the horns of this dilemma can be reduced by taking a closer look at what appears to be morally exclusive and insensitive claims that "we were right." There are a number of ways to move beyond a simplistic choice between either "we were right" or "we were wrong." In the process it can be shown, on the one hand, that acceptance of at least some wrongdoing should not immediately be equated with disloyalty and betrayal-of-us. On the other hand, recognizing understandable, human reasons behind resistance to repentance can counter a tendency to quickly interpret this resistance as "moral indifference" and thus reduce further wounding potential.

Some participants suggested the need for critical, difficult self-examination when it comes to claims that "we were right"; they were prepared to raise the uncomfortable question, "Were we *really* right?" A clear illustration of this kind of cautious introspective questioning—witnessed by former enemies—can be seen in the following exchanges between Republican ex-prisoners Gerard Foster, Gerry McMonagle, and Bríd Duffy at the regional Ireland/Northern Ireland workshop:

> BRÍD: . . . you know something, it's easy to think. . . . As you said [Gerard], it's easy to think we're right. . . .
>
> GERARD: "We were right"—that's what keeps coming back.
>
> BRÍD: Yeah, but that thought can justify everything that went on.
>
> GERRY: For thirty years we isolated ourselves, you know, we isolated ourselves for thirty years. I mean "we are right, everybody out there is wrong." Everything that we had round us were telling us, "You're one hundred percent right; you're one hundred percent right!"
>
> GERARD: And even if we did something wrong, it was their fault. If they hadn't been here, we wouldn't have done that.

There is, of course, a risk that those who hold on to a sense of rightness with regard to past political actions are actually avoiding the challenges of dealing with painful feelings of guilt, of making practical amends, or of taking real, shared responsibility.[7] Any romanticizing of some aspects of a conflict, no matter what side it comes from, can also create resistance to believing that an apology is genuine and not simply politically expedient. It can also reinforce the demonization of the figure of the "unrepentant perpetrator."

However, for the sake of reconciliation the need remains to allow some breathing space, some room for movement, around a strong sense of rightness and therefore a deep resistance to apology. As is the case with pressurized forgiveness, any enforced apology will be counterproductive for everyone involved.[8] In this regard, the "Beyond Dehumanisation" reflective process brought a number of important distinctions to the fore. These distinctions can be helpful to support veterans (and other political

activists) on journeys beyond a defensive, wounding, unqualified justification of, as Bríd put it, *"everything* that went on" (emphasis added).

We Were Not *Always* Right

The following extracts from the same workshop demonstrate that "we
were right" cannot be used to "justify everything that went on"; not every
apology automatically becomes a betrayal. In fact, things were done that
undermined the rightness of "engaging in a war against injustice"; not
to apologize for terrible acts would actually betray the integrity of one's
commitment to what was genuinely believed to have been a moral struggle:

> GERRY: I was talking at lunch time to Bríd in relation to the
> people who were "disappeared" by the IRA [Irish Republican
> Army], who were taken away, shot and buried on a hillside.
> As a member of the IRA at the time, I was appalled when I
> heard that. It was admitted then by the IRA that "yes, people
> were taken away, and they were disappeared and now we're
> trying to find them." But still, to me that there was a terrible
> act. And it's something that we need to, you know, apologize
> for and make good. I mean, find these people who were taken
> away and buried. We need to find the remains and return them
> to their families, for closure.
>
> And it's the same with people who are saying to us, "You
> need to apologize for some of the hurt. Or recognize that
> you caused hurt." We need to be big enough to stand up to
> that—recognizing that we caused hurt. Yes, of course, we were
> in a war; people died; people were badly injured.
>
> Alright, you're bound then to say, "Oh, we're very, very
> sorry for doing that there." But, then, what are you doing?
> Are you saying that you were wrong, that the whole thing, the
> contextual side of being involved in this conflict was wrong? I
> certainly would not be in a position to do that. And I wouldn't.
>
> GERARD: And it's not just an IRA thing. I know even within our
> own organization [INLA]. But it's about qualifying it in terms
> of, "We're sorry for the hurt and pain, but not the struggle."

The same distinction came to the fore through the experience of a former African National Congress (ANC) youth activist, Themba Lonzi. During the South African and International workshops, Themba remained clear about the rightness of the "struggle against Apartheid," but at the same time he recognized the need for forgiveness and "self-forgiveness"[9] for some of the actions that he was involved with.

This willingness to at least recognize some wrongs, to live with some tension, complicates the wounding picture of former activists/combatants being morally insensitive and indifferent to the consequences of (some of) their actions.[10] In this way there is some movement beyond that conditioned certainty of absolute rightness that Gerry McMonagle referred to: "Everything that we had round us were telling us, 'You're one hundred percent right; you're one hundred percent right!'"[11]

We Were Right *Then,* but *Now?*

In some contexts there has been a widespread shift from a historical sense of rightness to a retrospective sense of wrongness, such as for those who fought in the Vietnam War or for many of those who fought in support of the Apartheid system. In an interview following the USA workshop, Vietnam veteran and experienced peace activist Wayne Smith articulated the importance of the distinction between a historical belief that "we were right" and the painful, retrospective acceptance that "the war was wrong":

> I believed in this country. As tragic as it is for me to say, I believed when I took that oath to swear to defend the constitution of this United States. . . . I believed that by being a combat medic I was going to help the Vietnamese people. I wasn't there to kill. I wanted to help them. I wanted them to have some of the freedom that we were trying to have in this country. I really believed that, as did most of the men that I know and served with.
>
> And it's very painful to realize that was a lie. That those fifty-eight thousand-plus names on the wall—why did they die, if not for the reasons that we believed, to help those people?
>
> So it's not a repudiation of their death. It doesn't diminish their death at all. Rather, I think it's an affirmation that

we soldiers, we individuals, did what we thought was right. But now recognizing, history is proving time and time again, it was a wrong war. It was unnecessary. We should not have been there as a country. And sadly, countries don't say, "I'm sorry." Countries don't acknowledge their wrong. It is left to ordinary individuals.

If an apology is seen as "repudiation" or "diminishment" of the death of fallen comrades it is understandable indeed that this kind of apology will be resisted. However, Wayne embodies the possibility that with the benefit and wisdom of hindsight it is conceivable to accept wrongdoing while continuing to respect the genuine, though tragic sense of rightness in the past. In this way, the transformation of a sense of apology-as-betrayal-of-comrades can be supported.

During the international reflective workshop, Bríd made a similar point: "So everybody wants everybody to say they're sorry—'I'm sorry, I'm sorry.' But it's not just a word. It's an acknowledgment of what you did was wrong. Now you may have not realized that at the time. But it was wrong. It hurt somebody. It's wrong. And how can I make that right?" During the same International workshop, Themba put this kind of plea for contextual understanding and historical respect (without justification, without denial of wrongdoing) as follows:

I think the best step for me has been about acknowledging that there were wrong things that I did. And I think, for me, the fact that I'm able to acknowledge that, I am kind of in the right path. Because for me the most difficult thing is when we don't acknowledge your part in the madness. And yes, I'm sure; I'm very clear that we had good reasons to do what we did. And that doesn't mean that the things that we did were right. There were good reasons. And having good reasons doesn't mean that those things were right. They were wrong. You know.

A closely related, fundamental distinction also emerged, namely, between the wrongness of (past) actions and the badness of the person who acted, an important issue to which we are now turning.

We Were Wrong, but We *Are* Not Bad

The vital importance of decoupling *doing* wrong from (fully) *being* bad came strongly to the fore in especially the reflective workshop in the USA. In response to the perception amongst former combatants that acceptance of wrongdoing amounts to betrayal (especially of fallen comrades), Wayne offered the following important reflection:

> I think we have to decouple that. Years ago, after the war in Vietnam, when this country . . . the American people, many who had been "Rah rah, go to Vietnam! Yeah, Yeah, go defeat communism, help the Vietnamese!" [early, the majority of the American people supported the Vietnam War] . . . when they saw it was wrong, when they saw the reality on TV, they said, "Oh no, sorry . . . maybe we shouldn't be there. . . ." And they said, "Wrong war, bad war."
>
> They saw the killing of civilians, which happens in every war, but what they didn't do: they never separated the war from the warrior; the war from the individuals. It was, like, "bad war, bad people." And many of us kind of brought that into our being. We believed that.

If the "war" is not separated from the "warriors," and if "wrongness" is equated with "badness," then it becomes very tempting for previous supporters of the war, such as the "American people," to jump to the conclusion that "wrong war" equals "bad war" equals "bad warriors." The problem is that former combatants themselves may follow the same faulty line of reasoning: "It was, like, 'bad war, bad people.' And many of us kind of brought that into our being. We believed that."

Now, if the acceptance of past wrongdoing is also interpreted as consent to *being* bad, then it is no wonder that there is resistance to apologizing. If morally saying "No" to what I *and* we did during the war boils down to saying, "Yes, I and my comrades (and those who supported us) are bad people," then a sense of apology as betrayal is to be expected. For this sense of apology-as-betrayal to be transformed it becomes essential to guard against turning combatants into "terrible people" and making those with blood on their hands into monsters. By conveying the message that these inhuman monsters are *only* bad, this kind of demonization actually increases the likelihood that those involved in violence will react by holding on more tightly to an equation of "we were right . . . we are good." An exclusive focus on an all-pervasive badness of being makes it more difficult for the accused to acknowledge that at least some actions were wrong and some aspects of who they have been might be bad.

An important part of a creative response to the dilemma of apology is therefore addressing the underlying challenge of the transformation of demonization, of abnormalization. The human face of this challenge came to the fore in the following interaction between people from three different sides of the conflict in and about Northern Ireland: Alistair Little (Loyalist ex-prisoner), Gerry McMonagle (Republican ex-prisoner), and Rachel McMonagle (cross-community, Protestant youth worker).[12] Rachel's father had been a member of the UDR (Ulster Defence Regiment, former Northern Irish part of the British Army); as a child she witnessed numerous attempts by the INLA and the IRA to kill her father. Given their "on the ground" struggle with the seductive and still-pervasive dynamics of dehumanization, it is worth allowing some space for their interaction, which took place during the Ireland/Northern Ireland regional workshop:

> ALISTAIR: Gerry, there is something that you said about holidays and I keep coming back to it, about how we are on holidays. . . . What I actually hear you saying is, and you said it again there, "I am a father, a brother, a husband . . ." You were all of those things, and you would like to think that you were a loving person . . . and then the demonization.
>
> I think one of the most difficult things that I have found is that people who say that conflict has nothing to do with them—and that's questionable—or, that they were not actually directly involved in the fighting, is that they don't consider those things (father, husband, et cetera), because we (former combatants) cannot be normal. We have to be abnormal—those who were engaged in the fighting, as combatants. "To be able to do those things, you cannot be like the rest of us, you cannot be normal, something has to be wrong with you as a human being." And for those not directly involved the most difficult thing to accept is that people like me and Gerry are normal people. Why would people be surprised that you, Gerry, are a loving father? There is almost a resistance to accept that because

it doesn't fit. Like someone said earlier about the conditioning, "These people have to be monsters."

Now, I think that would be easier if we [former combatants] were "monsters." I think what is more difficult is that we are not! That we are just ordinary people that were caught up in a conflict and may have been involved in terrible things in terms of the human perspective of loss of life and injuring and all of that, but we're normal people.

GERRY: That's why I think the context is important, "Why did you become involved in a conflict?" I don't believe that I am a bad person or (that) a lot of the people who would have been involved with me, in the IRA, are bad people. . . . So you have to contextualize the reason why they became involved in conflict, why they would go out and shoot British soldiers or UDR or RUC and blow up places. . . . You have to ask, "Why are they trying to overthrow the state?" "Why are they trying to wreck the community?" And that's why I think it is important the storytelling aspect of things—that people can put in context why they were involved in conflict.

RACHEL: I just want to go back to the whole abnormal-normal thing and what you [Gerry] says whenever you mention my father, just when you mentioned that word, you know that you were a "father," I felt myself getting emotional. I need to say that, because that's what I felt whenever I heard you saying that.

And that takes me back to a place whenever I was in South Africa, two years ago. And there was a member of our group who was a former IRA member, and at that time it was much easier for me to just label him as an "IRA member" and not to look beyond that.

It wasn't until we moved into the wilderness aspect of the [Journey through Conflict] process—where we were completely and utterly stripped away from the whole outside world and we were in a place where we all were there as a team and we were all there to work together—that I saw a different side and humanity to Sean. I almost saw him like a father figure! That was very, very hard to deal with, because it was like a contradiction of anything I grew up with. And me and him had talks about that.

It was funny because you were woken up in the morning and Sean would've had a cup of tea sitting ready for me as I woke up. Me and him would have sat, chatting on the rock. I really . . . I struggled with that for the first day that we were there, but as time went on, and we were cooking together and we were looking after one another, and you were going to the toilet, as you know you went with your trowel [chuckling], and he always used to say "If you are not back in fifteen minutes, I'll come and look for you!" and stuff like that.

It is almost about being true and being real to yourself. Once somebody shares something with you, you can't pretend that you didn't hear it, you can't pretend that you didn't feel empathy for them. And I did. I saw him as something other than just "an IRA man" at that time. I saw him "normal" (I don't like to use that word).

This kind of "normalization" of people who might have been "involved in terrible things in terms of the human perspective of loss of life and injuring" is more challenging to accept than abnormalization (demonization), especially for those who have not directly been involved in terrible things. For the implication is that any one of us, any normal person is capable of getting human blood on our hands. This humanizing, humbling recognition leaves little room for morally superior finger pointing. Instead, it gives more space for honest (self-) examination regarding "terrible actions." As Pumla Gobodo-Madikizela[13] powerfully put it during the South African workshop:

> There is a tendency among scholars in general (other people as well), that suggest that people can't change. That people who either apologize or experience remorse, that it's staged remorse, they're acting, they're not serious. Why didn't they, you know, feel remorse then?
>
> And what people forget is that we are really products of our time, *all* of us. And that there is no way of knowing how we would have behaved had we been in the shoes of those people in their contexts. Unless we were tested ourselves, been in those people shoes, confronted with their dilemma,

we can't say we are morally superior, because we don't know how we would have behaved. Really working with Eugene de Kock[14] helped me to confront this fact, because I realized, What would I have done if I were in his shoes? I don't have to answer all those questions. But I can't say I would have done better, because I don't know.

And therefore, when people open up and reach out and say, "For this past I feel terrible," we should embrace that and understand what led them—because this is really the lesson— what led people to commit these terrible things. That's where the teaching is. The teaching is not to place ourselves on a higher moral level and say they are that and we are better, because we really have no certainty.[15]

In this context of Pumla's heartfelt call for inclusive humility, it is important to note that the "Beyond Dehumanisation" reflective process drew attention to the possibility that forgiveness can be "used as a weapon" (Themba), that is, when destructive moral pressure is placed on someone to forgive. Without Pumla's attitude of moral humility and uncertainty a similar risk applies to any insistence on apology. If an apology is seen to require the acceptance of wrongdoing *and* of being bad, and if there is a morally arrogant demand for such an apology, then the specter of humiliation and public shaming looms large. During the workshop in South Africa, Wilhelm rang this warning bell as follows:

It's not about beating people with a moral *sjambok* [whip], like my one cousin was saying: "You know, I don't want to talk about the past; I'm tired of being beaten by a moral *sjambok*." And another person in Northern Ireland saying, "I will take a physical beating . . . but I don't want to go into a room . . ." You also said that, Alistair. "I don't want to go into a room with victims, because that kind of beating is worse than get-ting a physical beating." So if our encounters are about that kind of going into a space where you know you're going to be beaten morally and spiritually, why would people go there?

Using that language [of moral beating] is of course problematic because now they [those responsible for violence] become the "victims." But there's something there about it not being a space where people are invited and encouraged, becoming creative and becoming more human in the process.

Bearing in mind the pitfall of inappropriate victimhood, it is important to guard against apology being employed as a humiliating moral and emotional weapon. Humbly maintaining the distinction between "terrible actions" and "ordinary people" helps to transform a sense of apology as a betrayal-of-comrades: To apologize for what "we did" does not mean "we are (only) bad." Carefully decoupling "bad war" from "bad people" can also help to prevent dehumanizing self-betrayal. For to bring "'bad war, bad people' . . . kind of into our being," as Wayne said, in effect boils down to a betrayal of the inalienably tender, beautiful, good, and innocent part of ourselves.[16]

Maintaining the distinction between the wrongness of action(s) and the badness of the actor is also fundamental to the possibility of forgiveness of a person for what they have done. Forgiveness of a person, despite evil wrongdoing that appears to be without any potential for goodness, is possible because these "terrible things" do not necessarily turn a person into an irredeemable "Prime Evil," as Eugene De Kock had been called in the South African media.

The important point of this subsection is that resistance to "we were wrong" (and therefore aversion to apology) can be lowered by stressing that the acknowledgment of some wrongdoing does not imply the acceptance of an all-pervasive badness of oneself or one's comrades, community, and family.

There is a further distinction that is critical to encourage at least the start of a journey beyond "You're one hundred percent right; you're one hundred percent right!' Elsewhere, we stress that forgiving is a process rather than a one-time event (see Little and Verwoerd 2016; Govier and Verwoerd 2002b). If this same distinction is applied more fully to apologizing, then there will be a larger scope for transforming the initial reaction of apology-as-betrayal.

Journeying through "We Were Right"

The "Beyond Dehumanisation" reflective process highlights the challenging need for a consultative process in terms of collective, public apologies to ensure that the spokespeople or leaders in fact convey the apology or acknowledgment on behalf of the group or organization (see Govier and Verwoerd 2002a). As Gerard put it during the Ireland/Northern Ireland workshop:

> You know, do you have a right to apologize as an organization? I mean, when Declan Kearney brought this up, the Sinn Fein chairman, I think in March of this year. . . . One of the things that I queried was, "Where do you get the right to apologize?' First of all, where's the consultation? People who were in the IRA in the seventies, eighties, nineties, a lot of them have nothing to do with the IRA now. You know yourself people went to prison and came out, and for one reason or another, got on with their lives. And there must have been thousands of people. What if people who were involved in the seventies turn around and say, "Whoah! Whoah! What are you doing? Don't be apologizing on my behalf, I've done nothing wrong"?

The process character of apology or acknowledgment at this collective, institutional level is pretty obvious in principle, though hard to implement. However, our sense is that the process character of apology at the individual level has not been adequately appreciated, either in theory or in practice.

The foregoing discussion of retrospective acknowledgment of wrongdoing began to draw attention to the intrapersonal journey that is needed for genuine apology, if only in the form of sincere recognition of human suffering. In this subsection, the process character of acknowledgment and apology at the individual level is fleshed out a bit more. For example, during the International workshop, the following reflections were offered:

> Bríd: But it's not just a word. It's an acknowledgment of what you did was wrong. Now you may have not realized that at the time. But it was wrong. It hurt somebody. It's wrong. And how can I make that right? And that's what I want to do. And I hope I get the opportunity to do that and to continue to do that, but also to talk and try and help other people reach that particular place.

> Themba: Part of the challenge is to work with others who haven't taken the process of healing or began the process

of dealing with the stuff they have inside them. I think it's basically the lesson of being patient with other people who have not reached the point that I'm at. It's about having an understanding. But it's not an easy journey to take. For some people, it's quite scary. And I know from experience that it's not an easy step to take, to confront issues that have shaped your life, especially issues that are connected to pain. It's really not an easy process.

But saying that it's not easy doesn't mean that it's impossible. I believe in the possibility we can coexist as people and live with one another. But definitely I believe we need to work together on this process. We need spaces, like these spaces, like this one created together here, for us to have a much deeper reflection and to learn from the different contexts from how people have responded to very difficult experiences.

So it's been a learning process for me in terms of my struggle with forgiveness.

Themba's appreciation of the need for "spaces" to support a self-confronting process that is "really not easy" resonates deeply with our own personal and professional journeys. We continue to struggle with this question: How does one really support a former combatant when genuinely exploring his/her past actions? And where will this leave a person afterward?

This honest self-examination is much more difficult than for someone to go to the bar and reminisce about the past with former comrades in an attempt to numb oneself or to have the rightness of one's actions reinforced by others. In the process, this person continuously falls into the trap of avoidance. In our experience there is a huge lack of resources to support individuals (especially non-state combatants and former political prisoners) who have been involved in political violence and who are honestly trying to make deep sense of it all. There is no trust in statutory therapists, because they are required to report potentially incriminating information. Someone struggling emotionally and morally with what they have been involved with cannot talk to a professional therapist about anything relating to the conflict, especially if it falls outside any actions for which they have already been convicted. The result is often that these ex-combatants deny that they are struggling with feelings of shame, guilt, or even regret; they are less likely to engage in reconciliation work in any deep and meaningful way.

Some people also try to discredit those who do express very real human feelings of regret and guilt and who are acknowledging wrongdoing. Such human expressions put the spotlight on those who claim to have no regret and who refuse a basic acknowledgment of possible wrongdoing.

In the context of political conflicts, former combatants who are willing to question the rightness of their actions also need to reckon with the potential political and media consequences of apologizing. There are those within the political establishment and the media who might welcome an apology as a positive move toward reconciliation; but others might use it to further criminalize the very people who say they are sorry, highlighting that they themselves now admit being criminals through their acknowledgment of wrongdoing. This further complicates individual (and group) journeys toward peace and rehumanization.

The above complications, in combination with the dynamics of betrayal already mentioned, underline why the journey from violence to nonviolence can be so challenging and slow. If this journey involves a painful, lonely, soul-searching transformation, then we may better understand why it might take so long before someone is ready to apologize. Much of this kind of difficult inner journeying would be hidden from the public eye, but is a necessary part of a *process* that will hopefully culminate in a visible apology. What appears as moral indifference on the surface might, at least in some cases, not be the real story. In these cases it would be appropriate to shift the emphasis from condemnation of a "lack of apology" to finding constructive ways to support someone on the difficult inner journey that makes a genuine expression of apology possible. Themba highlighted another important though tricky aspect of this apology-as-process during the International workshop:

> So it's been a learning process for me in terms of my struggle with forgiveness. I mean, I know I've asked forgiveness from my own parents, because of things that I did and how I disappointed them. And I did that through writing a letter and posting it. I mean, I'm living with them. I couldn't sit down and talk to them because really the communication lines in my family were not that open. Even during Apartheid, our parents never told us what was happening. We got to learn

about it outside our home. So I know our parents were scared about how we were going to respond. But there was no way of hiding what was happening.

Themba's reference to writing a letter of apology to his parents rather than speaking directly to them points to the need of approaching apologizing carefully, even indirectly. The type of process that might best enable an actual, sincere expression of apology and/or forgiveness can be portrayed, in metaphorical terms, as a "candlelight" rather than a "spotlight."[17] Yet, it is often the quiet and gentle candlelight approach that is easy to snuff out, to silence, or to isolate as a lone person's guilt that is not reflective of the majority of wider society.

There are no easy answers or process recipes. There is obviously more to be explored and analyzed in terms of which kind of process might be more likely to enable "real" apologizing/forgiving. The promises and pitfalls of processes such as storytelling, deep dialogue, and participatory facilitation that, in our experience, tend to encourage journeys beyond dehumanization and beyond betrayal are worthy of more in-depth reflection.[18]

A core challenge underlying these processes is how to encourage those who have been hardened by violence to be touched by the pain of those who had suffered and been victimized, without former combatants being abused or destroyed by this pain. As participatory facilitators, we try to support processes that are honest and real without perpetuating the extremely tempting dehumanization, demonization, and hatred that come with political violence. This humanizing process also requires a willingness to explore the possibility of moving beyond apologizing as a promising route to transform the dilemma of apology. The key appears to be an acknowledgment of *their* suffering. It may reduce the risk of further wounding without pushing former combatants into too tight a moral corner.

Acknowledging *Their* Suffering: Between Apology and Indifference/Justification/Denial

During the International workshop, Themba stressed the key difference between knowledge and acknowledgment. He accentuated the potential of acknowledgment to help prevent and transform further wounding, thus becoming an enabler on the journey of forgiveness.

I think forgiveness is not something on the table because sometimes . . . my experience back in South Africa. . . . I think a lot of people haven't acknowledged that the damage caused by Apartheid. A lot of people are in denial. A lot of people want us to move forward very quickly. They say why do you always talk about the past? Let's move on. And I think those sentiments are not helpful because *they are making the pain worse* because I think at that point what I only need is for people to acknowledge.

You know, there's a difference between knowledge and acknowledgment. That people know certain things have happened but if they are not acknowledged, you feel. . . . I always say that I want to buy these people a T-shirt and print "In Denial" on the front. Because people are, for example, denying that horrible things have happened.

And I think part of the problem is that those who have done bad things to us are somehow responsible for the struggle for me to walk towards forgiveness, because if there's so much denial; if there's so much lack of acknowledgment; how does that enable me to walk a journey towards forgiveness and reconciliation?

I think what can become an enabler towards this journey of forgiveness, it is the acknowledgement. I think for me that's important, that more than anything else, acknowledging past wrongs can enable us to walk a journey towards forgiveness, perhaps.

In the above quotations, Themba still talks about acknowledgment of "past wrongs," coupled with the language of forgiveness. This explicit sense of moral rather than politically expedient acknowledgment can indeed be seen as the heart of apology (Govier and Verwoerd 2002d; 2002a). But Themba also uses acknowledgment in a wider sense that goes beyond the strong connection between apology and particular wrongful actions. During the same workshop he also stated:

[Forgiveness is] a challenging process and I think in the face of denial; in the face of inequalities and poverty, it's a challenging thing. I'm not angry against anybody but I believe that when moments of forgiveness happen, there is a liberating effect.

And I believe when people are able to come to you and say, "We're very sorry for what you experienced. We're very sorry for how your life has unfolded.'" So those things have a positive effect on you as an individual.

The following example from the USA workshop illustrates how Wayne also uses the language of being sorry and of acknowledging suffering in a way that does not neatly fit into an apology. Notwithstanding the fact that it is not clear why American veterans would apologize to Japanese veterans who were widely seen as aggressors in the context of World War II, Wayne shared the following story:

I saw, years ago, an example that really brought me to tears. And that was when American marines who had fought in World War Two at the battle of Iwo Jima. They went back to Iwo . . . I think it was the fortieth anniversary. Japanese soldiers who had fought against these American marines, some of them hand to hand combat . . . we're talking tens of thousands of casualties here . . . one of the American marines who went back had captured a Japanese battle flag with the names and symbols of the men who fought under that flag, most of them dead; bodies not recovered. And a very simple gesture of this marine to give that flag to one of the Japanese survivors and to say that "I'm sorry." And to hug one another. They cried together. That was the lesson to me as an adult, as a veteran. That it's simply not enough to have peace between governments, but we as individuals must take responsibility for our actions and work for peace and understanding.

In the International workshop a similar humanizing, reconciliatory sense of acknowledgment transpired:

RACHEL: I think for me, personally, to come back to what you said earlier on, Bríd, about sorry is not just a word; it's something more than that, something around that acknowledgment. And for me personally, the acknowledgment factor is a big part of my own journey—acknowledgment to be heard, but also the acknowledgment that I was willing to be there and undertake a journey where I was willing to hear people from the other side as well.

During the South African workshop Pumla formulated this kind of acknowledgment as follows:

> [O]verwhelmingly, the reason that people are in pain—and what you have been saying so many times, I mean, so much here—is that there is no acknowledgment from white people in South Africa. . . . Then of course when it happens, people say, "Oh, that's not enough." So, you know, it's the action. When I think of acknowledgment as knowledge in action . . . that really it is action. And that action does something to people. I've seen it.
>
> Some people may think it's little, but really this sense of hope, it changes people's lives. Because it makes people feel they are worth something. Someone walked from, or drove, or came to us to make us feel like human beings. And that opens up a whole lot for people who have a deep sense of hopelessness. That opens up a flood of feeling a big sense of worth that people have never experienced. Which is why their lives are kind of . . . not big lives, but they are really destroyed lives. And now there is that turning point where they look forward to someone say over and over again, "You matter. Your story matters. I know you're suffering and I can relate and it moves me. I have nothing to give you but all I have to give you is just . . . my eyes and seeing your pain." And that goes a long way. I have seen it.

These wider meanings of acknowledgment provide useful background to begin to make sense of Gerard's advocacy of a third type of response to "*hurt and pain you'd caused.*" During the Ireland/Northern Ireland workshop he expressed what might be seen as a middle way: between apology-as-betrayal and indifferent, wounding denial of wrongdoing:

> GERARD: By maybe coming to an understanding that the hurt and pain you'd caused, and recognizing it, it didn't mean it was going to change your politics or your beliefs.

Now, it could change your way of thinking about conflict, and it certainly changed my way of thinking about conflict, because up to that point I hadn't seen . . . of course we'd seen funerals on television, but somehow as I said you either ignored it, or you'd seen the parents of the wife crying and thought, "Well, what did you expect, in for a penny, in for a pound . . . she knew who he was when she married him." Whether that was rationalizing to yourself or whatever, I don't know. Seeing the hurt and pain, but you didn't feel it, or weren't interested, or they deserved it.

Turning to Ralph—the elderly father of one of the last British soldiers killed on duty in Northern Ireland, whose tears have remained very shallow in his eyes over the years of participating in the Glencree Survivors and Former Combatants Programme—Gerard continued:

But to see it in your face like that, Ralph, was the biggest struggle to come to terms with—the hurt and pain that we inflicted. By recognizing that, what was it going to take away from me? I was frightened about political thinking, but I realized, no it doesn't matter, just because you are seeing their hurt and pain it doesn't mean that you are going to depoliticize yourself or say, "We were wrong and everything we did was wrong." Sometimes it is not even easy today when you are dealing with people who have lost loved ones, and trying to explain and trying to talk at that level, at the human level. "Yeah, I can recognize your hurt and pain and I am sorry about what happened"—but still hold on to what your beliefs are.

Strong resistance to apologizing for the overall "struggle" (for example of Irish Republicans against the British state on the island of Ireland), while being willing to acknowledge the human suffering resulting from this violent conflict, was also clearly articulated by Gerry McMonagle at the Ireland/Northern Ireland workshop:

GERRY: [W]ould that do any good if I was to say, "I'm sorry for being involved in the IRA and being involved in the conflict." If I'm being truthful, that would be telling a lie. I'm sorry for *having* to be involved in the IRA and *having* to be involved in conflict. I'm seriously sorry about that; I'm seriously sorry about people having to die as a result, but I wouldn't apologize for carrying out them operations.

ALISTAIR: Am I hearing you say there's a place for acknowledging the suffering and the hurt, which is different from saying sorry for being involved, or apologizing?

GERRY: Yeah, personally and collectively, we've done that acknowledgement. You know, as I say, personally, I would be very sorry that I was involved in a conflict that went on for so long and that I was involved in operations during that conflict, that I had to be involved in that type of stuff or I was brought into that. Of course you are. You weren't born to do those things . . . of course you're sorry that so many people had to die and of course you're sorry that you had to get involved in the conflict. The reasons for why that conflict took place, the reasons why them people died—you're sorry for that.

This type of acknowledgment of suffering without apologizing also came to the fore in terms of "us"-as-family, during the International workshop:

GERARD: [F]orgiveness isn't all about the victims here, that's one thing we need to keep in mind. There are other people suffering in different ways apart from those who have lost loved ones. We've spoken about it earlier . . . certainly about suffering because of imprisonment. My family suffered because of my actions: the home being wrecked, my brother being tortured because of me and beaten; and stuff like . . . all these wee things that are easily forgotten about. And you actually do forget about them as you go on with your life. And me and my brother . . . I sometimes wonder, I wonder how that impacted on them? Because I know at the time it terrified them.

So there are all these things. At that level, I can turn around and say, "I'm sorry about what happened." They [my family] might look at me and go, "You're nuts! Sure we knew the sort of stuff they [the British] did.""You know what I mean? So there are parts of me that say, "There are some things I need to talk to people about." But it seems to be the ones close to me that I brought hurt and pain to, rather than the ones at a distance, which, again, comes back to the contradictions that we're trying to live with within ourselves.

The question is whether Gerard's third option, that is, acknowledgment-without-apology, is not also a contradiction that he is trying to live with. How would the people respond who lost loved ones at the hands of his organization? Does it really make sense to say "I am sorry" and, in the same breath, continue to deny wrongdoing? Is this perhaps a kind of avoidance, an attempt to wriggle out of a hole? Does this third option mirror an inner struggle of finding a way of saying sorry without undermining one's former cause and comrades?

I'm Sorry, but We Were Right

Again, there are no easy answers. The promising third option of acknowledgment-without-apology comes with its own pitfalls, especially when the language of "I am sorry" is employed in interpersonal settings.

The potential for sending a confusing message to those who have lost loved ones, and thus potentially increasing the risk of a second wounding, was highlighted during the Ireland/Northern Ireland workshop when Alistair faced Gerard McErlane, an "ordinary Catholic" from West Belfast, whose two brothers died at the hands of the Ulster Volunteer Force (UVF), the organization that Alistair had belonged to. The immediacy and very personal nature of the interaction between these two men portrays the real-world challenge of steering a middle way between apology-as-betrayal and indifference:

> ALISTAIR: [I]t wouldn't make sense to me if I, coming from the UVF, went up to you, Gerard, and said to you, "I am sorry that your two brothers died. But it was the right thing to do." That would make absolutely no sense to you. In fact, it would be more damaging. Not only would that be an insult, it would add more pain. Because there's no way you can make sense of that.

But I could see me coming to you and saying to you, for whatever it's worth, "I think that that was wrong and that it shouldn't have happened. And I just want to acknowledge that to you."

So, I think it's about being clear when we're saying sorry. I think you were clear, Gerry [McMonagle], when you talked about saying sorry to those people who had been killed who weren't combatants, who were innocent, or got caught up, and the killing wasn't intentional, and wanting to say sorry for those deaths and that suffering.

But then, if you believe that you're involved in a war and you believe that your war or your cause was right, I don't think it's possible to say sorry for the deaths, but at the same time say it was the right thing to do. This is personal for me.

I think a place one may come to is by saying: "This is difficult. There was a war and we felt that fighting that war was the right thing to do. But I want to acknowledge that, as an organization, we're responsible for acts of violence where people lost their lives and which caused great suffering and pain. And we just want to acknowledge as an organization that we were responsible for that suffering." What you're actually doing is taking responsibility onto yourself, as opposed to saying, "We're not going to acknowledge anything. There was a war. People die. So what, move on."

So I do think there is a place for words. It's about how it's said and how we understand what's being said.

A key point regarding the promise of acknowledgment-without-saying-sorry is to move beyond a cold-blooded, hard-hearted, and rubbing-salt-in-wounds phrase such as, "There was a war. People die. So what, move on." The willingness to acknowledge responsibility for suffering is dependent on the ability to see beyond conditioned hardening that was necessary during violent conflict. To "become tender again," as Themba put it, is part of the challenge. This difficult kind of open-heartedness toward (former) enemies can be described as a journey of *compassion*—slowly, hesitantly transforming indifference toward "them," and, perhaps, the former pleasure in the suffering of "them," into inclusive, cross-cutting compassion (see also Gobodo-Madikizela 2008; Halperin and Weinstein 2004; Krondorfer 2015).

Compassion without Confession

If the story behind acknowledgment is a growing, expanded sense of sensitivity to suffering beyond the boundaries of ethnic belonging, then it might be less confusing to practice a language of compassion rather than trying to distinguish between sorry-as-apology and sorry-as-acknowledgment. It might be clearer to talk about compassion-for-them without feeling forced into a confession box and without sending what can easily become a contradictory, wounding message to survivors.

A clear example of this kind of tension-filled compassion-without-confession came to the fore during the South African workshop. One of the participating peace practitioners was Ginn Fourie.[19] Her daughter Lyndi was one of the people killed in an Azanian People's Liberation Army (APLA) attack in the early 1990s. This attack was ordered by Letlapa Mphahlele. Years later and after a difficult process, Ginn and Letlapa founded the Lyndi Fourie Foundation. They started to work together for conciliation in South Africa and abroad, even though Letlapa has never apologized.

> GINN: In South Sudan, when Letlapa and I were there now in April, we showed the five minute clip of "Spear Cleansing." And one of the leaders, in fact the Vice President's wife, at a gathering, said how profound it was for her that Letlapa could acknowledge and take responsibility for what he had done and ordered and at the same time feel compassion and—she didn't use the word *love*—for the people that he had injured. So for them, and for her, it was holding both of those together.
>
> So Letlapa was saying, "We could do no other. We had to fight. We couldn't just be oppressed forever. We had to fight. I did it. If I was pushed to that place again, where there was no other way, I might respond the same way, but I would try everything in my power not to do the same thing first. And at the same time, I'm deeply affected by the sadness in people's lives that resulted."

On Tragic Choices and Moral Dilemmas

Letlapa's ability to "acknowledge and take responsibility for what he had done and ordered and at the same time feel compassion for the people that he had injured" echoes what Alistair suggested during the Ireland/Northern Ireland workshop as a way to express acknowledgment-without-apology:

> This is difficult. There was a war and we felt that fighting that war was the right thing to do. But I want to acknowledge that, as an organization, we're responsible for acts of violence where people lost their lives and which caused great suffering and pain.

In the course of trying to hold together a sense of rightness about "our cause" and compassion for "their pain," Gerry McMonagle used a very important word, namely "tragic," during the Ireland/Northern Ireland workshop:

> I am [sorry] . . . for the people who did get killed and all that there. It is *tragic.* I am very sorry for that—that people had to get killed, that there was a situation there, a war that materialized. Because when you sit here now and look at it, you can say, "This could have been prevented." But this is the whole thing about putting the conflict in a historical context. For years, they tried to sort it out through talking, through peaceful protests, through all them avenues. And all them avenues were closed. People were left with no option. And they took up the gun and then . . . things just spiraled out of control. For a long time nobody seen nothing but the barrel of a gun.

During the South African workshop Pumla Gobodo-Madikizela also talked about "tragic pasts": "And then the question is, in the absence of a truth commission, for example, what are we finding about effective ways of responding to these tragic pasts that don't seem to go away. And how people who carry the guilt, how they themselves work through the guilt and the memory of what they did now that they're outside of that original context." The language of "tragic pasts" or a "tragic" absence of choice opens up the huge specter of moral dilemmas, pointing toward the messy reality of violent conflict where someone rarely has the luxury of choosing between what is clearly right and what is clearly wrong. The choice is more often between the lesser of two evils. Awareness of moral dilemmas encourages one to avoid and go beyond two mutually exclusive extremes, highlighted in the apology-as-betrayal part of this chapter:

rather than holding on to either a blinkered "we were right" or a simplistic condemnation of "you were wrong" one needs to explore creative,
humanizing ways to transform the dynamics of betrayal.

Sensitivity to the element of the tragic and interpreting past actions
in terms of tragic choices encourages moral humility in judging those
with "our blood on their hands." This humility, in turn, creates space for
someone to be open and vulnerable to the suffering of former enemies.
Thus, approaching acknowledgment with a sense of the tragic and framing
acknowledgment in terms of cross-border compassion for human suffering
cannot only help to transform apology-as-betrayal but also reduce some of the
potential confusion surrounding "saying sorry" in the absence of an apology.

Concluding Remarks:
Transforming Resistance to Reconciliation

The "Beyond Dehumanisation Project" can be seen as an attempt to
provide a constructive "veteran peacemaker" response to what Appleby
described as a "formidable obstacle to peace":

> Linking forgiveness to reconciliation and both to lasting peace
> does not guarantee that politicians and peacemakers will be able
> to overcome the disparate historical memories and heritages
> of each side in a conflict, the different moral vocabularies, and
> underlying disagreements about language itself. *Such points of
> dispute stand behind the exclusive self-definitions of combatants* in
> the Balkans, South Africa, the Middle East, Northern Ireland,
> and elsewhere. They remain a formidable obstacle to peace.
> (Appleby 2000, 203; emphasis added)

This chapter identified a dilemma of apology as an underestimated
contributing factor to the "exclusive self-definitions of combatants." As
authors and facilitators, we faced a "dilemma" in highlighting the dilemma
of apology. Given our backgrounds as a former combatant and as a former
supporter and ongoing beneficiary of Apartheid, our plea for a cautious
understanding of apologies might come across as being too "perpetrator
friendly," thus becoming another source of further wounding. Yet, we
are taking this risk because we believe that by uncritically accepting the
central role typically given to apology we would deny key realities of our

personal and professional experiences with veterans and former combatants. If we were to choose not to reflect critically on apology this choice might actually make us complicit in building higher and thicker walls around the "exclusive self-definitions" of former combatants.

We forthrightly admit that breaking down these walls is indeed a formidable obstacle. But part of the problem might be that the hard-won practical wisdom of those who are breaking through these walls from the *inside* has too often been neglected. Former combatants who have become bridge builders humbly suggest that the murky realities of resistance to the acceptance of wrongdoing are ignored at everyone's peril. They point to the need for a greater appreciation of the intra- and interpersonal dynamics of betrayal, which typically accompanies a serious questioning of "We were right." Thus, they encourage more sensitivity to apology as a *process*. And they expand and re-prioritize our moral vocabulary to help reduce resistance to reconciliation.

In the interest of transforming those exclusive and destructive self-definitions (Appleby), we are suggesting that in much reconciliation discourse there might be an (unintended) exclusive focus on "apology" and "forgiveness," especially in situations where politically motivated former combatants are included. By honestly struggling with saying sorry, former combatant peace workers can actually enrich the vocabulary and processes of reconciliation.

Notes

1. This program included Alistair (first as participant and later as co-facilitator) and Wilhelm (co-facilitator). For more detail see www.glencree.ie.

2. Transcripts of Ireland/Northern Ireland workshop and International workshop. For more information, see International "Beyond Dehumanisation" Research Project in Section 2 of this chapter. This project was partly funded and supported by The Fetzer Institute, USA, and delivered in partnership with INCORE, University of Ulster. The project facilitated reflective, region-specific workshops with former-enemies-peace-practitioners in Ireland/ Northern Ireland, South Africa, Israel/Palestine, and the United States. There was also one culminating International workshop bringing together a few participants from Ireland/Northern Ireland, South Africa, and Israel/Palestine. Gerard Foster was a participant in both the Ireland/Northern Ireland and the International workshops. The transcripts of these workshops are not publicly available, but quotations will make it clear which workshop transcript is referred to.

3. Alistair Little and Wilhelm Verwoerd are directors of *Beyond Walls* (www. beyondwalls.co.uk). Little has twenty-five years of experience as a former-combatant-peace-practitioner, and since 2001 Little and Verwoerd have worked together with former combatants and survivors, mostly regarding the conflict in and about Northern Ireland, but also in South Africa and Israel/Palestine. On their personal journeys, see Little (2009) and Verwoerd (1997).

4. See also the subsection on the "problem of perspectives" in chapter 7, volume 5 of *Truth and Reconciliation Commission of South Africa Report* (TRC Report), 271–73. The whole of chapter 7 (259–303) provides relevant background material.

5. For more background and a specific focus on our caution with regard to (public) forgiveness, see Little and Verwoerd (2016).

6. The methodology that allowed us to focus on specific themes for the current writing stage of the reflective process included the following steps: transcribing the country-specific and international reflective workshops and most of the interviews; editing transcripts to improve readability (reduce repetitions and grammar mistakes, clarify where necessary), while staying as close as possible to what was said; systematic working through hundreds of pages of these transcripts and allocating themes and subthemes on a page by page basis; identifying the main themes and grouping relevant material from transcripts together under these themes and subthemes.

7. Discussed in chapter 5 of the *Beyond Dehumanisation Report* to The Fetzer Institute. This four hundred–page report is forming the basis for our current reflective work and thus not available to the public.

8. See the pitfall of moral pressure regarding forgiveness, in Little and Verwoerd (2016).

9. The promise and pitfalls of "self-forgiveness" is addressed in chapter 4 of Project Report.

10. See the basic "just war" distinction between justness *of war* and justness *in war*. This distinction is relatively clear in theory, but gets blurred in practice—morally and emotionally, as clearly argued by Robert Meagher in his book *Killing from the Inside Out* (2014).

11. From a factual, historical point of view, this statement is very likely not correct. It might be how one would want to remember those times, but it is clear that not literally "everyone" supported the violence. Many opposed it or, if not, at least chose not to engage in it. We aim to address some of the larger, complex questions around historical remembrance and reconciliation in our further writing on the reflective workshop material. See also Verwoerd (2007) and Verwoerd and Little (2008).

12. Rachel is not related to Gerry.

13. Former TRC Commissioner, psychology professor, participant in the South African workshop.

14. Notorious covert hit squad commander under Apartheid regime, nick-named by colleagues "Prime Evil."

15. See TRC Report, chapter 7, Vol. 5. The overview of social psychological literature in this chapter supports Gobodo-Madikizela's "situationalist" approach to someone such as Eugene de Kock, versus the seductive tendency to use individual pathology as the main explanation for horrific human behavior.

16. In chapter 3 of the *Beyond Dehumanisation Report* the key theme of "restoring tenderness" as part of a process of rehumanization of hardened ex-combatants is explored.

17. More on these metaphors in Little and Verwoerd (2013).

18. See Little and Verwoerd (2013). These process-oriented reflections are also the focus of chapter 7 in the *Beyond Dehumanisation Report*.

19. See www.lyndifouriefoundation.org.za.

Works Cited

Appleby, R. Scott. 2000. *The Ambivalence of the Sacred: Religion, Violence, and Rec-onciliation*. New York: Rowman and Littlefield.

Baumeister, Roy F. 1997. *Evil: Inside Human Violence and Cruelty*. New York: W. H. Freeman.

Gobodo-Madikizela, Pumla. 2008. "Trauma, Forgiveness, and the Witnessing Dance: Making Public Spaces Intimate." *Journal of Analytical Psychology* 53(2): 169–88.

Govier, Trudy, and Wilhelm J. Verwoerd. 2002a. "Taking Wrongs Seriously: A Qualified Defence of Public Apologies." *Saskatchewan Law Review* 65: 153–76.

———. 2002b. "Trust and the Problem of National Reconciliation." *Philosophy of the Social Sciences* 32(2): 178–205.

———. 2002c. "Forgiveness: The Victim's Prerogative." *South African Journal of Philosophy* 21(2): 97–111.

———. 2002d. "The Promise and Pitfalls of Apologies." *Journal of Social Philosophy* 33(1): 67–82.

———. 2004. "How not to Polarize 'Victims' and 'Perpetrators.'" *Peace Review* 16(3): 371–77.

Halperin, Jodi, and Harvey M. Weinstein. 2004. "Rehumanizing the Other: Empathy and Reconciliation." *Human Rights Quarterly* 26(3): 561–83.

Krondorfer, Björn. 2015. "Unsettling Empathy: Intercultural Dialogue in the Aftermath of Historical and Cultural Trauma." In *Breaking Cycles of Repetition: A Global Dialogue on Historical Trauma and Memory*, edited by Pumla Gobodo-Madikizela, 90–112. Opladen: Budrich.

Little, Alistair, with Ruth Scott. 2009. *Give a Boy a Gun: From Killing to Peace-making*. London: Darton, Longman and Todd.

Little, Alistair, and Wilhelm J. Verwoerd. 2013. *Journey through Conflict Trail Guide: Introduction*. Bloomington, IN: Trafford Publishing.

———. 2016. "Public and Private: Practitioner Reflections on Forgiveness and Reconciliation." In *Reasonable Responses: The Thought of Trudy Govier*, edited by Catherine Hundleby, 148–73. Windsor, Ontario: University of Windsor.

Malešević, Siniša. 2010. *The Sociology of War and Violence*. New York: Cambridge University Press.

Meagher, Robert. 2014. *Killing from the Inside Out: Moral Injury and Just War*. Eugene, OR: Cascade Books.

Nadler, Arie, Thomas E. Malloy, and Jeffrey D. Fisher. 2008. *The Social Psychology of Intergroup Reconciliation*. Oxford: Oxford University Press.

Philpott, Daniel, 2012. *Just and Unjust Peace: An Ethic of Political Reconciliation*. Oxford: Oxford University Press.

Sen, Amartya, 2006. *Identity and Violence: The Illusion of Destiny*. London: Allen Lane.

Truth and Reconciliation Commission of South Africa Report. 1998. "Causes, Motives and Perspectives of Perpetrators." Volume 5, 259–303. Cape Town: Juta.

Verwoerd, Wilhelm J. 1997. *My Winds of Change*. Johannesburg: Ravan Press.

———. 2006. "Towards Inclusive Remembrance after the 'Troubles': A Philosophical Perspective from within the South African Truth and Reconciliation Commission." In *Explorations in Reconciliation*, edited by David Tombs and Joseph Liechty, 103–22. Aldershot: Ashgate.

———. 2007. *Equity, Mercy, Forgiveness: Interpreting Amnesty within the South African Truth and Reconciliation Commission*. Leuven: Peeters.

———, and Alistair Little. 2008. "Towards Truth and Shared Responsibility after the Troubles." In *Stories in Conflict*, edited by Liam O'Hagan, 97–111. Derry: Towards Understanding and Healing.

3

Societal Reconciliation through Psychosocial Methods

The Case of Zimbabwe

Joram Tarusarira

Conflict and violence generate negative psychological beliefs, perspectives, emotions, attitudes, and identities between antagonists (negative psychological repertoires), which stand as barriers to reconciliation. In this chapter, I discuss how negative psychological repertoires developed in the postcolonial Zimbabwean conflict, and how violence can be transformed in pursuit of societal reconciliation. The objective is, thus, to discuss psychological legacies and consequences of intractable conflict, how they can be barriers to societal reconciliation, and how they can be addressed using the case study of Zimbabwe. I propose psychosocial methods as tools that can unlock the negative psychological gridlock to pave the way for societal reconciliation.

To demonstrate my argument, I suggest a particular psychosocial methodology known as Training for Transformation (TfT), developed from Paulo Freire's psychology of critical consciousness, and based on my experience of deploying it in development practice to facilitate creative and self-reliant communities. Through TfT, actors engage in a dialogical problem-solving approach through which they deepen their reflection on their own experienced reality, both at the cognitive level of ideas and, more importantly for societal reconciliation, at the level of feelings.

Much of the interest in the pursuit of reconciliation after violent conflict focuses on reform of political and economic systems and structures, such as the media, police, army, and internally displaced persons, inter alia, sidestepping transformation of conflicting parties' minds and hearts, which are at the center of societal reconciliation. Accordingly, this chapter argues that negative psychological emotions, beliefs, and attitudes constructed during conflicts need to be deconstructed and positive ones constructed. This is necessary to facilitate restoration of relationships, especially in conflicts after which people continue to live in close geographic proximity as neighbors.

This chapter is divided into three major parts. First, I contextualize the discussion through key vignettes of violence in Zimbabwe since independence in 1980. Second, I articulate the psychosocial conceptual framework in relation to conflict, violence, and reconciliation. Lastly, I concentrate on my proposal to apply psychosocial methods to reconciliation using the TfT methodology.

The topic of reconciliation is of prime importance and urgency in Zimbabwe because of underlying tension that exists between the Shona and the Ndebele-speaking people as a result of *Gukurahundi* massacre (which I discuss in more detail later). This massacre continues to threaten the stability of Zimbabwe as evidenced by emergent demands for cessation from some of the Ndebele people as well as to the relationship between the people themselves in everyday life. The contest for power between political parties, which has often degenerated into violence upon and between citizens, prompted my interest in understanding Zimbabwean politics and processes of violence. I have also worked on politically contentious issues with a faith-based organization called Silveira House, a Social Justice and Development Centre founded in 1964. Before Zimbabwe's independence, Silveira House focused on the struggle for freedom and provided basic organizational methods in rural and urban communities. After independence, it concentrated on building up capacities for development on a broad front. In the 1990s, it got involved in studying the Economic Structural Adjustment Program (ESAP) and its effects on poor Zimbabweans. Today, the organization engages with the new struggles in an independent nation, such as violence (Silveira House 2005). The organization's vision is to see emancipated people with critical minds working for positive change. It aims to assist people to develop their own potential to engage in the struggle to improve their situation. Its mission is to promote integrated human development through a participatory process of empowering communities with matters of justice, human rights, democracy, peace, reconciliation, health, and skills for self-sustainability. Its values are: respect for life, options for the poor, team spirit, justice, honesty and integrity, self-reliance, and respect for local languages and culture.

Violence in Zimbabwe: 1980 to the Present

Outlining some vignettes of violence in postcolonial Zimbabwe offers contextual background to why and how I propose psychosocial methods as tools for reconciliation. In 1980, the Zimbabwe African National Union-Patriotic Front (ZANU PF) came into power, led by Robert Mugabe. Two years after independence, in 1982, Robert Mugabe suspected the opposition party, the Zimbabwe African People's Union (ZAPU), of threatening ZANU PF's stability and hold on power. As a result he unleashed a violent attack in Midlands and Matabeleland provinces where ZAPU dominated. Within weeks, North Korean–trained 5th Brigade soldiers massacred thousands of civilians and tortured thousands more. An estimated twenty thousand people died (Catholic Commission for Justice and Peace 1997). "Massacres, mass beatings and destruction of property occurred in the village setting in front of thousands of witnesses" (Eppel 2005, 45; Catholic Commission for Justice and Peace 1997). When the atrocities were committed, victims were told "they were being punished because they were Ndebele and that all Ndebeles supported ZAPU and all ZAPU supporters were dissidents" (Eppel 2005, 45). This resulted in hatred between the Mugabe regime and the Ndebele people. Since Mugabe's government and the 5th Brigade were Shona-dominated, the hatred by the Ndebele people also extended to the Shona people. In other words, the Ndebele people developed negative psychological repertoires toward the Shona. This tribal divide remains unreconciled to this day, to the extent that secessionists want the Matabeleland province (the region where Ndebele-speaking people are found) to become an independent state. In my research in 2012, an interviewee said:

> I feel we as Ndebele people were robbed, we feel we need somebody coming and apologizing. That issue wasn't addressed. It wasn't solved. The majority of the guys are the Shona, and they don't see anything wrong in that, so you just cannot force those guys. They think everything is okay, especially if you start

talking about it, they think it's something that happened long
back, and why are you opening up old wounds. That thing is
done. (Jan. 14, 2012)

Even after more than thirty years, the wounds of the Ndebele people have
not healed, and the tribal cleavage emanating from this massacre is still
present. ZAPU saw the best way for itself and its people to join ZANU
PF in a Unity Accord of 1987 between ZANU and ZAPU. Despite this
move, the chasm remains alive.

The adoption of the Economic Structural Adjustment Program (ESAP)
from international financial institutions in 1990 resulted in a deceleration
of economic growth, a decrease in employment, and a rise in inflation,
among many other effects. This ultimately led to increased suffering of
the ordinary person, loss of jobs, reduced incomes, and the crumbling of
social services. The decline of workers' incomes led to a series of nationwide strikes by the labor movement (the Zimbabwe Congress of Trade
Unions; ZCTU), especially between 1996 and 1998. Demonstrators were
beaten up by the police, whose operations were occasional reinforced by
the military.

The ZCTU and a civic organization called the National Constitutional Assembly (NCA) traced the socioeconomic and political problems
to a faulty constitution; they thus spearheaded the crafting of a new
national constitution. Campaigns were held nationwide, which forced the
government to set up its own constitutional commission (CC) in 1999.
At the ZCTU's National Working People's Convention in February 1999,
the creation of a new party was mooted, resulting in the birth of a new
labor-based political party, the Movement for Democratic Change (MDC),
in September of the same year (Raftopolous 2004; Masunungure 2004).
Since independence in 1980, the MDC has posed an unprecedented threat
to the ruling party ZANU PF. The NCA successfully mobilized people
to reject the government-sponsored draft and demanded a people-driven
new constitution. This was the first government defeat since 1980, posing
a threat to the elections that were to follow.

Subsequently, ZANU PF responded by unleashing violence. White
farmers who were accused of sponsoring the MDC suffered retributions.
War veterans invaded their commercial farms in the name of a land reform
program, which remained ZANU PF's rhetorical source of mobilization
(Dorman 2003, 848). The process was called *jambanja* (chaos). Unruly gangs
occupied the land, destroyed crops, confiscated livestock and equipment, and

forced farm owners and their workers to flee during the preludes to the elections of 2000, 2002, and 2005. Subsequent elections were characterized by the banning of the MDC from campaigning, electoral violence, and state-sponsored militias, which harassed, intimidated, raped, and murdered MDC candidates and supporters (Bratton and Masunungure 2011, 23–24). This was done under the *Third Chimurenga* project. It is uncontested that local people were evicted from productive land in the 1890s. Though the majority of Zimbabweans supported the land reform program, they were against the violent method that was used to redistribute the land. Commenting on how *Third Chimurenga* operated, Muponde notes:

> [*Third Chimurenga*] is a virulent, narrowed down version of Zimbabwean history, oversimplified and made rigid by its reliance on dualisms and binaries of insider/outsider, indigene/stranger, landed/landless, authentic/inauthentic, patriotic/sell out. The net effect of operating these binaries is the institution of othering as a permanent condition of political and cultural life where "difference" translates unproblematically into foe. For the other to insist on being different is to invite the title of enemy of the state: it is to invite treason charges. (Muponde 2004, 176)

In August 2001, ZANU PF launched a national youth training scheme. The program used crude propaganda, violence, and intimidation to indoctrinate youth into thinking that their own impunity and abuse of power were part of the struggle to protect ZANU PF and Zimbabwe from foreign influence (Smith 2005). In the rural areas, youths and war veterans convened meetings where huge crowds sang and danced to revolutionary songs in support of ZANU PF. Suspected members of the MDC were beaten up and forced to renounce their membership. There was political education from the party cadres. In towns, party thugs were terrorizing people in high-density suburbs, attacking all suspected MDC supporters and abducting them to be tortured. Communities rose up against each other according to which political party they supported.

Due to the conflation of party and government, ZANU PF expected civil servants (teachers, nurses, the judiciary, etc.) to operate in accordance with ZANU PF party business and not to entertain any opposition members. When they did otherwise, violence was meted out on them. The police, who are supposed to protect every citizen, for instance, did not intervene in violence perpetrated on non–ZANU PF members; if they did, they were no less than ZANU PF enthusiasts (Hill 2003; Feltoe 2004). The military was not spared either. The ruling regime occasionally summoned the military to reinforce the operations of the police, resulting in what Rupiya (2004) called politicization of the military and militarization of politics. The police force and the army lost favor with the general people. The ruling party engaged in a "carefully orchestrated campaign of violence, intimidation, harassment, rape, assaults and even murder" (Masunungure 2004, 178).

In 2005, the government executed a violent operation code-named "Operation Murambatsvina/Operation Restore Order," which was implemented under the guise of cleansing cities of illegal business dealers and settlements, leaving seven hundred thousand urban Zimbabweans homeless (Tibaijuka 2005, 7). Sometimes people were forced to demolish their own dwellings or source of income. A major motive was political retribution against sectors of the urban population who had voted for the MDC as well as the desire to ward off possible urban uprisings (Sachikonye 2011, 27). Operation *Maguta* ("having enough to eat") transferred the management of food production to the army, partly to ensure that the troops themselves remained well fed (Bratton and Masunungure 2011, 26–27). Operation *Mavhoterapapi* ("for whom did you vote?") was launched after the presidential runoff in 2008.

Zimbabweans were to go to the presidential polls in 2008. Four presidential candidates, including ZANU PF's Robert Mugabe and MDC's Morgan Tsvangirai, entered the presidential race (Zimbabwe Electoral Support Network, 2008). According to the electoral commission results, Mugabe garnered 43.2 percent and Tsvangirai led the polls with 47.9 percent of the votes. Since all candidates had failed to meet the 50 percent plus one vote requirement, the Electoral Act required that a runoff be undertaken within twenty-one days (according to Section 110 of the Electoral Act, Chapter 2:13; see Zimbabwe Electoral Support Network 2008). A runoff was scheduled for May 15, 2008. Between the release of the delayed presidential results and the day of the runoff, intense nationalist propaganda and extreme violence continued against not only the opposition members but also the ordinary people. The Zimbabwe Electoral Support Network notes that "the run-up to the 27 June run-off degenerated into a run-over, leaving in its wake a trail of destruction, houses burnt down, many people displaced and homeless, orphaned and homeless children and communities torn asunder" (Zimbabwe Electoral Support Network 2008, 48). Morgan Tsvangirai of the MDC withdrew from the election, citing preelection violence against his supporters and the ordinary people. Mugabe proceeded to a one-man election and swore himself in as president. This forced the Southern African Development Community to appoint former president of South Africa Thabo Mbeki to mediate between ZANU PF and MDC. This led to the formation of the Government of National Unity GNU in February 2009.

When nationalist ideology fails to create a homogeneous identity, the elites resort to the use of violence. Arendt (1969) understands violence as an instrument or a means to power. She notes that violence appears when power is in jeopardy; every decrease in power is an open invitation to violence. When those who hold power feel it slipping from their hands, they will find it difficult to resist the temptation to reinforce it with violence. In the interest of regime security and under pressure from the citizens to deliver political goods in a context of economic instability, the state develops, invents, and promotes instrumentalist nationalism among the people. When instrumentalist nationalism fails, the state resorts to violence. Nationalism metamorphosed into ultranationalism, chauvinism, and racism with violent consequences, ripping through the tapestry of relationships responsible for social order. This created fissures within communities, and neighbors and relatives turned against each other. Frayed emotions, anger, hostility, misunderstanding, and suspicion found fertile ground. As a result, people could no longer live side by side. Displaced people were afraid to return home, including those in the diaspora. It is clear that the intrastate conflict created distorted identities and a negative collective psychological and emotional climate in the country.

Psychological Consequences of Violence and Societal Reconciliation

The net effect of the long experiences of violence has been a ravaged, polarized, and unstable society. Zimbabwe is confronted with divisions between Ndebele/Shona people, urban/rural populations, state/civil society, whites/blacks, communities/youth militia, and war veterans, police and army/civil society. Groups developed particular identities and harbored particular beliefs, attitudes, and emotions against each other. These attitudes, beliefs, and emotions do not change overnight; nor are they changed by signatures appended to a political agreement. The Unity Accord of 1978 and the Government of National Unity in 2009, which did not transform negative emotions, beliefs, and attitudes of conflicting parties, prove this point. These sentiments and mentalities have continued to inhibit the development of peaceful relations (Bar-Tal 2004).

Societal reconciliation is partially but importantly a psychological process and it strives toward an outcome of changing negative motivations, goals, beliefs, attitudes, and emotions of people in conflict. Since it involves unlocking people from psychological barriers, approaches that reach into the minds and hearts of people, such as psychosocial methods, can make a significant contribution to societal healing. Just as individual trauma calls for redress, so does societal trauma. "Rebuilding a ravaged society includes restoring or creating new opportunities for productive social functions . . . within the sphere of social reconstruction one encounters processes such as community reconciliation" (Gutlove and Thompson 2006, 187). Community reconciliation implies addressing the societal trauma in order to restore trust, hope, and love; it also increases community cooperation and strengthens the development of shared values and expectations.

Catastrophic events cause societal trauma. When the event is natural, humans accept it as fate, but when trauma is the result of war or conflict, as is the case of Zimbabwe, the situation becomes more complicated because of the continued presence of the former conflicting parties. Collective emotional orientations such as anger, fear, and hatred, which, in turn, can become part of a social ethos, emerged. State-controlled media in Zimbabwe were at the forefront of fueling such collective orientations. Since media have the power to continue fanning bad relations even after a violent conflict has ended, they create a barrier to reconciliation (Bar-Tal 1998; 2004). Efforts to bring about societal reconciliation should therefore include the unlocking of a negative psychological repertoire, which holds captive groups-in-conflict.

Resolving conflicts at a political level, as is the case with the 1987 Unity Accord and the Government of National Unity of 2009, is necessary but not sufficient for surmounting the political and psychological barriers that may foil the normalization and stabilization of peace (Bar-Siman-Tov 2004). "Peace accords are not solutions in content but proposed negotiated processes, which if followed will change the expression of the conflict and provide avenues to redefine relationships" (Lederach 2005, 46). Peace accords represent a process for continuing conflicts under new definitions (Mayer 2000). Political and economic cooperation and interdependence are important for reconciliation, but they cannot unilaterally unlock the negative societal beliefs that communities harbor. Societal reconciliation as a process, then, has the task to transform the nature of relationships through a course of action that intertwines psychological, social, and political dynamics (Rouhana 2004). Bar-Tal (2004) concurs that reconciliation is a psychological process that consists of a change of motivations, goals, beliefs, attitudes, and emotions of the majority of society members. Understood this way, reconciliation supports the objective of peace, the new nature of peaceful relations, and a positive view of the other.

Psychological changes take place through the process of information processing, unfreezing, persuasion, learning, reframing, recategorization, and formation of a new psychological repertoire. This can be a very slow process because the emotions, beliefs, and attitudes formed during a conflict are entrenched and upheld with high confidence by the parties in conflict. To foster change, therefore, is a complex, arduous, prolonged, and multifaceted task that needs to overcome numerous inhibiting factors. The psychosocial basis of reconciliation must be rooted in and responsive to the experience and subjective realities that shape people's perspectives and needs (Bar-Tal 2004).

Maoz defines reconciliation as a "cluster of cognitive and emotional processes through which individuals, groups and states come to accept relationships of co-operation, concession and peace in situations of former conflict" (2004, 225). What this suggests is that reconciliation comprises the forming of relationships that must accompany political and structural processes in the transition from conflict to peace. According to Maoz, there are, first, the emotional, spiritual, and psychodynamic components of forgiveness, reaching beyond past grievances and acknowledging or taking responsibility for harm done to the other in the past. Second, there are the cognitive aspects such as beliefs and attitude that need to change in order for individuals to cooperate and establish peaceful relations. The cognitive dimension refers to the subjective construal of the sociopolitical reality, which affects readiness for a peaceful relationship (reconciliation) with a former enemy. Societal beliefs are lenses through which the majority of society members look at their own society (Bar-Tal 2000); they foster the emotional repertoire through their epistemic role or explanatory function. The various groups that are part of the Zimbabwean conflict possess particular emotions and beliefs, which lead to certain perceptions of reality and of the other; this, in turn, determines actions and reactions.

In conflict situations, societies view opponents as threatening. ZANU PF supporters, for instance, delegitimized the MDC and its supporters, the urban population, farmworkers, the white community, and teachers by labeling them "sellouts" and allies of Western countries, especially Britain and America (who were allegedly bent on bringing back colonialism). The same regime held the view that the Ndebele people were dissidents who wanted to unseat the ZANU PF government. Consequently, the government delegitimized its opponents as a way to explain and manage the conflict. Delegitimization helps explain why the other is construed and perceived as a threat, supposedly predicting what this other may do in the future (Bar-Tal 2000). It has an epistemic function. "One condition of being human is our urgent need to understand and order the meaning of our experiences," writes Mezirow. "If we are unable to understand, we often turn to tradition, thoughtlessly seize the explanations by authority figures" (2002, 3). In Zimbabwe, rural communities and ordinary people tended to believe what authority figures and the ruling regime's elites articulated. They received information gullibly and uncritically. Delegitimization, therefore, provides the needed rationale to support one's beliefs and misperceptions of the other.

Lasting peace requires ongoing sensitivity, attention, and care for the needs and goals of the other group. It becomes imperative to adjust the way of looking at reality and facilitate openness and readiness to reconciliation. In changing societal beliefs, communities also change their identity by removing the negation of the other. By so doing, they revise their own identity enough to accommodate the other, and this removes negative elements engendered by the conflict within their own social identity. In the process of reconstruction of collective identities in post-conflict situations, parties reflect and enter into dialogue with those perceived as enemies. Because intractable conflicts make groups develop a monolithic identity, each side constructs its collective identity in opposition to the "hostile" other (Bar-On 2006; see also Dinur in this volume). The challenge in Zimbabwe for the Ndebele people, the rural community, the whites, and ordinary citizens is to deconstruct and accommodate the Shona people, the urban population, blacks, youth militia, the police, army, and war veterans; and vice versa. "As parties overcome the negative interdependence of their identities, they can build on positive interdependencies of their identities that often characterize parties living in close proximity to each other" (Kelman 2004, 120). In the process, they internalize new relationships, integrate them into their own identities, and develop new attitudes toward the other (Kelman 2004, 120; 2008). The way people interpret events, actions, and behaviors related to a conflict and the manner in which they transition from conflict to peace significantly influences how they form a cooperative relationship within a framework of reconciliation.

Maoz (2004) refers to the negative psychological emotions, beliefs, and attitudes as biases. He remarks that people come out of conflict with biases and that these biases need to be "de-biased" because they distort our judgment and inferences. The biases include negative images of the opponent and an in-group favorability bias (a group thinking positively about itself all the time). ZANU PF would interpret its violence as defending the gains of the liberation struggle, while calling similar activities by the MDC acts of terrorism. "Perceiving the other side in a negative, unidimensional way prevents developing more complex and multidimensional, less dichotomous perceptions of both self and the other which are fundamental to reconciliation" (Maoz 2004, 229). These negative images, stereotypes, and prejudices against the other side persist even after formal political agreements have been reached. Opponents continue to perceive each other as having evil intentions, as embodying low morality, and as marked by inferior traits. It is societal beliefs that provide the psychological, emotional, and social rationale to cope with a conflict (Bar-Siman-Tov 2004).

Lewin (1976) suggests three phases of changing parties coming out of a conflict's cognitive, emotional, and behavioral reaction. He suggests unfreezing, movement, and refreezing. Unfreezing involves opening up to new information, melting the current "quasi-stationery equilibrium state" or status quo. The change needed is to abandon beliefs about the former enemy, legitimize new images of the former enemy, and develop relatively unbiased relations. This implies the reframing of understanding the status quo and unsettling previous attitudes toward the enemy. For example, one can point to favorable characteristics of the enemy that were formerly neglected and one can acknowledge one's own biased perception of the enemy. To do so entails a major "mental earthquake" for former combatants (Bargal and Sivan 2004). The second stage is movement. This is the stage where construction of a new ethos begins. It consists of "societal beliefs about the utility of cooperative relationship. . . . It also involves changing stereotypes about the former enemy and humanising his (or her) image" (Bargal and Sivan 2004, 135; see also Dinur, this volume). The third stage is refreezing, which refers to "institutionalization of the change products," whether they are attitudes and emotions or concrete programs. In reconciliation, this means "enabling the former adversarial parties to coexist on the basis of mutual respect and tolerance" (Bargal and Sivan 2004, 136). This process requires facilitation. It cannot happen on its own.

Addressing the anger, grievance, resentment, and polarization left as the result of the conflict presents a challenge. To unlock and transform these emotions and beliefs requires a process that transforms the nature of relationships between societies through a course of action that intertwines psychological, social, and political dynamics (Rouhana 2004). Psychosocial processes are thus positioned to facilitate this transformation because they tap into the deep belief structures of individuals and societies and transform negative emotions, beliefs, and attitudes.

Freire's Philosophy of Critical Consciousness and the Training for Transformation Methodology

To transform the negative psychological repertoire in Zimbabwe, I propose psychosocial educational approaches such as the TfT methodology. My assumption in proposing psychosocial methodologies is that when people emerge from war and violent conflict they are stripped of their capacities to listen and express themselves nonviolently, making it difficult to engage in critical reflection and purposeful rationality. Life-shattering trauma can defy language and receptive capacities, the latter undermined by fear and guilt (Cohen 2006). Methods that address the psyche and emotions can, thus, immensely contribute to adjusting the motivations, goals, attitudes, and perceptions of conflicting parties.

The psychologist Erik Erikson was first to use the term *psychosocial* to refer to psychological developments in and interactions with a social environment (Slee 2002). Psychosocial support fosters the resilience of victimized communities and individuals and aims to ease the resumption of normal life. It facilitates affected people's participation in their own convalescence and prevents pathological consequences of potentially traumatic situations. After conflict and violence, psychosocial methods engage affected people with the aim of fostering new understanding and active participation in creating open relationships for reconciliation.

When looking at sociopolitical situations, Paulo Freire's theory of transformation might be helpful. Freire referred to this theory of transformation as conscientization. It is aimed at developing critical consciousness among individuals and groups through a series of workshops and study circles. Critical consciousness refers to the ability of individuals and communities to analyze, pose questions, and take action on social, political, cultural, and economic factors that influence and shape our lives. Based on my experience with the Paulo Freire–based TfT methodology in development and civic education, I propose it as a tool to facilitate societal reconciliation. It can reach into people's inner beings, a necessary process for individual and societal transformation. TfT as a psychosocial method is a dialogical and people-engaging exercise that aims to develop a person's critical capacity. To this end, it facilitates creating critical awareness through experience-based learning such as sharing through discussions (problem posing), reflecting on people's own situations of life and finding out what to do about its inadequacies (analysis), acting in order to change the situation (implementation), and assessing failures and successes (evaluation), which in turn leads to a plan of action for improvement on people's actions (Mulura 2005, 157).

At the heart of the psychosocial method is not only dialogue but also reflectivity, that is, the ability for an inner dialogue (Bar-On 2006). Monological and interpersonal dialogue are complementary aspects to overcoming silence and silencing. Violence in Zimbabwe silenced the acts and responsibilities of perpetrators and the suffering and shame of victims. Dialogue, thus, does not allow one side to dictate the pace and content of the process to the other or deposit blame one-sidedly onto the other. This resonates with what Freire described as the "banking method" in education, where the other person is perceived as a *tabula rasa,* a clean slate upon which information or data are to be imprinted. As an alternative, Freire proposes "a process of active dialogical and stimulating method, based on the notion that there is nothing like total ignorance or absolute wisdom" (1973, 45).

In peacebuilding and reconciliation workshops, the facilitator's role is to animate the discussion, ask problem-posing questions, and present problem-posing materials with which to stimulate the learner. He or she does not bring ready-made answers to the participants. Rather, the participants discover the answers for themselves through dialogue and critical reflection (see also Krondorfer, this volume). Sustainable societal reconciliation is contingent on the involvement and ownership of the process by all parties to the conflict. Top-down approaches should be avoided because real reconciliation is a voluntary process that can only be encouraged but cannot be forced. The failure of the Organ for National Healing and Reconciliation, which was established under the Government of National Unity and housed in the president's office in Zimbabwe, illustrates the limitations of top-down approaches to reconciliation.

Community workshops allow participants to analyze how social structures shape and influence the way they think about themselves and the world. Critical consciousness provides an opportunity to name the world and in so doing construct the meaning of the world (Dirkx 1998). It also refers to a state of mind where individuals are aware of the forces around them and have the capacity to think of ways to address them. To be fully conscious, "we must emerge from it and inspect what we have absorbed, question what we have accepted, and scrutinise what we have been taught" (Wren 1986, 5). In the context of the conflict and violence in Zimbabwe, this means reflecting on what instrumentalist nationalism, through its various machinations, has led people to believe in. It will be a chance for the estranged parties, communities, and individuals to reflect on concepts that have saturated the public space during the conflict—patriotism, sovereignty, independence, and socialism. Transformative workshops, aimed at raising people's critical consciousness, allow parties to a conflict to inspect what they have absorbed, to question what they have accepted, and to scrutinize what they have been taught with respect to the other, the alleged enemy.

Freire (1970) believed that an oppressed people lack critical consciousness of the forces that control their lives; lacking that consciousness, they are powerless to redress the oppression that dominates them. This is more the case when a people have suffered subjectivation, as is the case with political enthusiasts who have been indoctrinated with political party ideology that guides their actions and reactions. Critical consciousness submits causality to analysis and represents things and facts as they exist empirically in circumstantial correlation. For Zimbabweans to emerge from intractable conflict, constructing a new world by critically reflecting on the past conflict and violence is imperative. The uniqueness of critical consciousness is that "it is situated in a critical perspective that stresses the transformation of relations between the dominated and the dominant within the boundaries of specific historical contexts and concrete cultural settings" (Giroux 1983, 227). Applied to societal reconciliation, it would stress the transformation of relations between (former) conflicting parties, between victims and perpetrators of violence: the Shona and the Ndebele, the rural and the urban, ZANU PF and MDC supporters.

Advancing Freire's philosophy, Jack Mezirow and Patricia Cranton developed the concept of transformative education, understood as a process by which previously uncritically assimilated assumptions, beliefs, values, and perspectives are questioned and thereby become open, permeable, and validated (Cranton 2005). For societal reconciliation in Zimbabwe, this implies engaging the conflicting communities in a process of revisiting and reflecting on societal beliefs that foster negative emotions such as fear, anger, hatred, and revenge, most of which people have assimilated uncritically. Many ideas were assimilated during the violence period by Zimbabweans without critically analyzing them. Instead, political party supporters, communities, and individuals were subjected to subject formation, resulting in fundamentalist mindsets. Fundamentalism often creates subjects who espouse a mind fixated on certainty and black and white worldviews. A case in point is ZANU PF's rigid distinction between its supporters and those who oppose them. Reconciliation thus implies redefining the past and reinterpreting past discourses and experiences in a manner that eases the intensity of feelings of hatred and bitterness against those deemed to be the other.

Making meaning from our experiences through critical reflection is central to transformative learning. Mezirow (2002) called it "perspective transformation." Sets of beliefs, values, and assumptions that have been acquired from previous experiences make up perspectives; they are lenses through which to read the world. While perspectives organize and make sense of the world, they can also distort and limit how people are able to understand and reality. Transformative learning produces individuals who are more inclusive in their perceptions of the world, able to differentiate its various aspects, open to other points of view, and able to interpret differing dimensions of their experiences into meaningful and holistic relationships (Dirkx 1998). This is what reconciliation is about: the ability to have open and inclusive relationships.

In post-conflict Zimbabwe, transformative education workshops and other such programs present an opportunity for parties to the conflict to revisit and modify taken-for-granted frames of reference. For instance, the MDC and its supporters were perceived as sellouts (often broadcast by the media) and ZANU PF was seen as party of thugs by MDC supporters. Conflicting parties can now focus on how to negotiate and act on their own purposes, values, feelings, and meanings rather than those uncritically assimilated from political elites. Transformative exercises help the groups to gain greater control over their lives as socially responsible, clear-thinking decision makers. They help conflicting parties to be aware of how they come to their specific knowledge and how their values lead to their perspectives (Mezirow 1978). With respect to the negative repertoire among conflicting parties in Zimbabwe, we can ask: "What happened? (content reflection); How did I/we come to think this way? (process reflection); and, Why is this important? (premise reflection). The last question can lead to transformation of habits of mind or frames of reference" (Cranton 2005, 631).

TfT is a participatory methodology through which communities and individuals are gradually taken into a process of critical reflection, rationality, and consciousness. In times of conflict and violence in Zimbabwe, there was little reflection, rationality, and consciousness as conflicting parties were guided by ideologies bent on denigrating and demonizing their opponents. In fact, the information was meant to develop instrumentalist sentiments that favored the ruling regime and subsequently justified violence against the opposition elements. Propagandist and particularistic media jingles were repeated over and over in both electronic and print media. An estimate made at the height of the violent fast-track land reform program in 2003 regarding one music jingle titled *Chave Chimurenga* ("It's now war") showed that four radio stations played the jingle approximately 288 times a day, which amounts to 8,640 times per month. On TV, it was featured approximately 72 times a day, which amounts to 2,160 times a month (Sibanda 2004).

In TfT, the facilitator leads the group through a series of steps in analyzing what is called problem-posing material also known as codes, the latter addressing issues from the times of conflict and violence. The steps are: (1) description of the code/problem using material; (2) first analysis, where the initial "why" questions are asked; (3) application to real life; (4) identifying related problems; (5) second analysis, where participants look for root causes that go beyond symptoms (this is the heart of conscientization, when participants reach the critical reflection stage); and (6) action planning (Hope and Timmel 1984).

The TfT method breaks down abstract philosophical language and professional jargon into simple useful language and exercises without distorting key ideas. It takes the actors through a process that reaches their psychological selves without forcing or rushing them. When conflicting Zimbabwean parties engage in this process they become open to the other and this enhances possibilities of apologizing for wrongdoings, forgiving where possible, and developing a vision for reconciliation. Only then will they transform their motivations, goals, and attitudes and dislodge psychological barriers to reconciliation.

At the center of TfT's process are the voices and experiences of the participants, who begin to think for themselves based on their experiences. Slowly, they unlock their minds and begin to read reality anew.

Participants begin to unmask myths about reality. The facilitator takes them through generative themes, understood as those issues that are immediate and relevant to the participants and for which they hold strong feelings of joy or anger (Hope and Timmel 1984; Freire 1973). Generative themes touch their lives. They cannot afford not to talk about them. They generate energy, thereby getting the participants into action.

In my experience with the Silveira House TfT program, we aimed to create communities that are responsible for themselves in various areas, ranging from food security, politics, and conflict to leadership. The program developed the critical consciousness of individuals and groups to influence changes within communities, to challenge unjust systems, to start self-help projects and influence self-reliance, to organize workshops, community meetings, and "look and learn" programs, where communities coexist and visit each other to learn from one another (Tarusarira and Kori 2008).

The communities could not do these initiatives prior to TfT workshops because they were locked in a culture of silence, apathy, and docility. They exhibited a dependency syndrome. They were not responsible for their own lives, in the same way parties to a conflict can be locked in anger and hatred. Negative emotions, beliefs, and attitudes are mental prisons from which conflicting parties need to be liberated. Given that TfT empowers people to actively participate in and take responsibility for their lives, the content of reconciliation workshops in Zimbabwe could include: developing greater understanding between people across different political divides in local communities; developing awareness and exploring key community, religious, cultural, political, and social issues; raising awareness; empowering participants to be actively involved in the practice of reconciliation within local communities; promoting the practice of equity, diversity, and interdependence between the traditions; and enabling participation in the building of an integrated and inclusive civic society through the practice of active citizenship. Importantly, mutual misperceptions and myths developed during the conflict will have to be unmasked.

Conclusion

By applying psychosocial methods, a shift is made from a culture of seeing things as polarized, dichotomized, and unconnected to a world where things are interrelated and complementary. Instead of things being simply black or white, right or wrong, a greater complexity is recognized where difference is not necessarily wrong but simply different. Freire's method suggests interdependence rather than compartmentalization, cooperation rather than competition. This is what is needed between the various parties in conflict in Zimbabwe. This is what constitutes reconciliation. Through mutual exploration of common values and aspirations, it is possible to transcend and transform negative emotions, beliefs, and attitudes and to negotiate a shared future based on love and respect for human dignity. Conscientization does not only raise awareness of oppressive forces but also of possible alternatives of coexistence (Kester 2007, 7). These constitute important steps toward societal reconciliation.

Works Cited

Arendt, Hannah. 1969. *On Violence*. London: Allen Lane the Penguin Press.

Bargal, David, and Emmanuel Sivan. 2004. "Leadership and Reconciliation." In *From Conflict Resolution to Reconciliation*, edited by Bar-Siman-Tov, 125–48. Oxford: Oxford University Press.

Bar-On, Daniel. 2006. "Reconciliation Revisited—Part III: The Concept of Reconciliation Revisited, the Testing Parameters." http://www.newropeans-magazine.org/en/2006/03/16/reconciliation-revisited-part-iii-the-concept-of-reconciliation-revisited-the-testing-parameters/.

Bar-Siman-Tov, Yaacov. 2004. "Introduction: Why Reconciliation?" In *From Conflict Resolution to Reconciliation*, edited by Bar-Siman-Tov, 3–10. Oxford: Oxford University Press.

Bar-Tal, Daniel. 1998. "Societal Beliefs in Times of Intractable Conflict: The Israeli Case." *The International Journal of Conflict Management* 9: 22–50.

———. 2000. *Shared Beliefs in a Society: Social Psychological Analysis*. London: Sage.

———, and Gemma H. Bennink. 2004. "The Nature of Reconciliation as an Outcome and as a Process." In *From Conflict Resolution to Reconciliation*, edited by Bar-Siman-Tov, 11–38. Oxford: Oxford University Press.

Bloomfield, David, Teresa Barnes, and Luc Huyse. 2003. "Reconciliation: An Introduction." In *Reconciliation After Violent Conflict: A Handbook*, edited by David Bloomfield, Teresa Barnes, and Luc Huyse, 10–18. Stockholm: IDEA.

Bratton, Michael, and Eldred Masunungure. 2011. "The Anatomy of Political Predation: Leaders, Elites and Coalitions in Zimbabwe, 1980–2010." DLP Research Paper 9. http://www.dlprog.org/news-events/new-paper-on-the-anatomy-of-political-predation-in-zimbabwe-.php; accessed June 7, 2012.

Catholic Commission for Justice and Peace in Zimbabwe. 2008/1997. *Gukurahundi in Zimbabwe: A Report on the Disturbances in Matabeleland and the Midlands, 1980–1988*. New York: Columbia University Press.

Cohen, Cynthia. 2005. "Creative Approaches to Reconciliation." In *The Psychology of Resolving Global Conflicts: From War to Peace* (vol. 3), edited by Mari Fitzduff and Chris E. Stout. Westport, CT: Praeger.

Cranton, Patricia. 2005. "Transformative Learning." In *International Encyclopedia of Adult Education*, edited by Leona M. English, 10–18. New York: Palgrave Macmillan.

Dirkx, John M. 1998. "Transformative Learning Theory in the Practice of Adult Education: An Overview." file:///C:/Users/p274963/Downloads/Dirkx1998.pdf.

Dorman, S. 2003. "NGOs and the Constitutional Debate in Zimbabwe: From Inclusion to Exclusion." *Journal of Southern African Studies* 29(4): 845–63.

Eppel, Shari. 2005. "'Gukurahundi': The Need for Truth and Reparation." In *Zimbabwe: Injustice and the Politics of Reconciliation,* edited by Brian Raftopolous and Tyrone Savage, 43–62. Harare: Weaver Press.

Feltoe, Geoffrey. 2004. "The Onslaught against Democracy and the Rule of Law in Zimbabwe in 2000." In *Zimbabwe: The Past is the Future*, edited by David Harold-Barry, 193–224. Harare: Weaver Press.

Freire, Paulo. 1970. *Pedagogy of the Oppressed.* New York: Continuum.

———. 1973. *Education for Critical Consciousness.* New York: Continuum.

Giroux, Henry A. 1983. *Theory and Resistance in Education: A Pedagogy of Oppression.* South Hadley, MA: Bergin and Garvey.

Gutlove, Paula, and Gordon Thompson. 2006. "Using Psychological Healing in Post-Conflict Reconstruction." In *The Psychology of Resolving Global Conflicts: From War to Peace, Vol. 3: Interventions*, edited by Mari Fitzduff and Chris E. Stout. London: Praeger Security International.

Hill, Geoff. 2003. *The Battle for Zimbabwe: The Final Countdown.* Cape Town: Zebra Press.

Hope, A., and Timmel, S. (1984) *Training for Transformation: A Handbook for Community Workers.* Books 1–3. Gweru: Mambo Press.

Kelman, Herbert C. 2004. "Reconciliation as Identity Change: A Social-Psychological Perspective." In *From Conflict Resolution to Reconciliation*, edited by Bar-Siman-Tov, 111–24. Oxford: Oxford University Press.

———. 2008. "Reconciliation from a Social-Psychological Perspective." In *The Social Psychology of Intergroup Reconciliation*, edited by Arie Nadler, Thomas E. Malloy, and Jeffrey D. Fisher, 15–36. New York: Oxford University Press.

Kester, Kevin. 2007. "Peace Education: Experience and Storytelling as Living Education." *Peace and Conflict Review* 2(2): 1–14.

Lederach, John P. 2005. *The Moral Imagination: The Art and Soul of Building Peace.* Oxford: Oxford University Press.

Lewin, Kurt. 1976. "Frontiers in Group Dynamics." In *Field Theory in Social Science: Selected Theoretical Papers by Kurt Lewin,* edited by Dorwin Cartwright, 188–237. Chicago: University of Chicago Press.

Maoz, Ifat. 2004. "Social Cognitive Mechanism in Reconciliation." In *From Conflict Resolution to Reconciliation,* edited by Bar-Siman-Tov, 225–38. Oxford: Oxford University Press.

Masunungure, Eldred. 2004. "Travails of Opposition Politics in Zimbabwe since Independence." In *Zimbabwe: The Past is the Future,* edited by David Harold-Barry, 147–92. Harare: Weaver Press.

Mayer, Bernard. 2000. *The Dynamics of Conflict Resolution: A Practitioner's Guide.* San Francisco: Jossey-Bass.

Mezirow, Jack. 2002. "Learning to Think Like an Adult: Core Concepts of Transformation Theory." In *Learning as Transformation,* edited by Mezirow and Associates, 3–33. San Francisco: Jossey-Bass.

Mulura, Francis. 2005. "Paulo Freire's Development Education Methodology." In *Social and Religious Concerns of East Africa: A Wanjibu Anthology,* edited by Gerald J. Wanjohi and G. Wakuraya Wanjohi, 155–64. Washington, DC: The Council for Research in Values and Philosophy.

Muponde, Robert. 2004. "The Worm and the Woe: Cultural Politics and Reconciliation after Third Chimurenga." In *Zimbabwe: Injustice and the Politics of Reconciliation,* edited by Brian Raftopolous and Tyrone Savage, 176–92. Harare: Weaver Press.

Raftopolous, Brian. 2004. "Current Politics in Zimbabwe: Confronting the Crises." In *Zimbabwe: The Past is the Future,* edited by David Harold-Barry, 1–18. Harare: Weaver Press.

Raftopoulos, Brian. 2004. "Nation, Race and History in Zimbabwean Politics in Zimbabwe." In *Zimbabwe: Injustice and the Politics of Reconciliation,* edited by Brian Raftopolous and Tyrone Savage, 160–75. Harare: Weaver Press.

Rouhana, Nadim N. 2004. "Identity and the Power in the Reconciliation of National Conflict." In *The Social Psychology of Group Identity and Social Conflict: Theory and Practice,* edited by Alice H. Eagly, Reuben M. Baron, and V. Lee Hamilton, 173–87. Washington, DC: American Psychological Association.

Rupiya, Martin. 2004. "Contextualising the Military in Zimbabwe Between 1999 and 2004 and Beyond." In *Zimbabwe: Injustice and the Politics of Reconciliation,* edited by Brian Raftopolous and Tyrone Savage, 79–98. Harare: Weaver Press.

Sachikonye, Lloyd M. 2011. *Zimbabwe's Lost Decade: Politics, Development, and Society.* Harare: Weaver Press.

Sibanda, Maxwell. 2004. "Zimbabwe: Complete Control—Music and Propaganda in Zimbabwe." http://freemuse.org/news/zimbabwe-complete-control-music-and-propaganda-in-zimbabwe/.

Sibanda, Tichaona. 2009. "ZANU PF Militias Back in Action in Rural Areas." http://www.africafiles.org/article.asp?ID=21189.

Slee, Phillip T. 2002. *Child, Adolescent, and Family Development.* Edinburgh: Cambridge University Press.

Smith, Antony D. 1986. *The Ethnic Origins of Nations.* Oxford: Blackwell.

Smith, Richard. 2005. "Fear, Terror and the Spoils of Power: Youths Militias in Zimbabwe." http://www.csvr.org.za/media-articles/latest-csvr-in-the-media/2319-fear-terror-and-the-spoils-of-power--youth-militias-in-zimbabwe.

Tarusarira, Joram, and A. Kori. 2008. *Opening Eyes: Community Empowerment through Training for Transformation.* Harare: Silveira House.

Tibaijuka, Anna Kajumulo. 2005. *Report of the Fact-Finding Mission to Zimbabwe to Assess the Scope and Impact of Operation Murambatsvina.* UN Special Envoy on Human Settlements Issues in Zimbabwe. New York: United Nations.

Wren, Brian. 1986. *Education for Justice.* London: SCM Press.

Zimbabwe Election Support Network. 2008. "Report on the Zimbabwe 29 March Harmonised Election and 27 June 2008 Presidential Run-off." akcampaign.files.wordpress.com/2012/02/report-on-the-zimbabwe-29-march-2008-harmonized-elections-and-27-june-presidential-run-off.pdf.

4

Bringing Faith into the Practice of Peace

Paths to Reconciliation of Bosnian Muslims

ZILKA SPAHIĆ ŠILJAK AND JULIANNE FUNK

In this chapter we explore the role of Muslim believers in peacebuilding and reconciliation and their struggle to challenge the imposed ethnic and religious divisions in the postwar, secular Bosnian and Herzegovinian society. Most faith-based initiatives in Bosnia and Herzegovina (BiH) began to flourish only in the last decade. In a context where ethnic identity is colored by religion, a small number of faith-based peacebuilders are counteracting the results of ethnic cleansing. Their reconciliation work arises from personal faith that provides not only vocation, but also unique techniques and methodologies.

Such reconciliation work from within religious communities is needed in BiH because the war in the 1990s utilized religions as the prime ethnic contents distinguishing the three warring parties. Currently, the conflict continues, pursued through politics, where Serbian Orthodoxy, Croat Catholicism, and Bosniak (or Bosnian) Islam—as traditions and institutions—are intertwined with their nations' legitimacy. In the postcommunist context, the religious communities have experienced not only a resurgence of collective belonging, but also individual devotion. In this environment, where religion colors each "ethnic tent" (Volkan 1998), a small and relatively invisible number of faith-based peacebuilders are doing what they can to counteract the results of ethnic cleansing, bridging the now-segregated communities and addressing the distrust, prejudice, suffering, and trauma. Since some of the most visible and active "religious peacebuilders" are Muslims (Funk Deckard 2012), we consider primarily the role of Islam in their peacebuilding efforts as a personal faith and key component to the implementation of their work.

The examples in this chapter come from the authors' own experiences as faith-based peacebuilders in BiH. Zilka Spahić Šiljak's activism started during the war in 1993 with Medica Zenica's trauma-healing work and continued after the war at the University of Sarajevo, where she combined religious studies with gender equality education; the latter she continues to pursue via her TPO Foundation. Julianne Funk, who is Christian, has been engaged with Bosnian Muslim peacebuilders for the last decade through research as well as her work with the local organizations Small Steps, the Center for Peacebuilding, the Ecumenical Women's Initiative, and currently the TPO Foundation.

The term *peacebuilding,* more than reconciliation, has become popular in BiH in the postwar period, corresponding roughly with the emergence of the peacebuilding concept within the UN from 1992 onward.[1] Peacebuilding conceptually encompasses the many and various efforts that seek to build a sustainable and "positive peace" (Galtung 1996). In BiH, peacebuilding was primarily associated with activities of postwar reconstruction, from the rebuilding of infrastructure and the democratization process to the facilitation of internally displaced persons and the return of refugees. These are all elements of "traditional" peacebuilding. In the late 1990s, John Paul Lederach challenged this conception of both peace theory and practice. He pointed out the truism that "standardized formulas" with mechanical solutions do not work in divided societies with direct experience of violence and trauma. In conflict situations "characterized by deep-rooted, intense animosity; fear; and severe stereotyping," the peacebuilding "framework must address and engage the relational aspects of reconciliation as the central component of peacebuilding" (Lederach 1997, 23–24). Lederach sees reconciliation as both as focus on relational aspects of conflict, but also a locus or place, "the point of encounter where concerns about both the past and the future can meet" (27). For us, too, reconciliation is a relational approach to peacebuilding, but also the practical experience of encountering other conflict parties with acknowledgment of experiences of suffering (truth), open ears and a compassionate heart (mercy), concern to right wrongs (justice), and respect and security for all (peace).[2]

Therefore, in our chapter peacebuilding and reconciliation overlap significantly, but that is less true for traditional peacebuilding practice.

In BiH, the challenge of conflict attitudes of and relations between different parties obstruct the resolution of issues (which is the usual focus of peace interventions). While official reconciliation projects have been initiated by well-funded actors in BiH, they have tended to focus on bringing people together with or without a change in their attitudes, and then proceeded to call the result "reconciliation." They may have created spaces for reconciliation, but not the sufficient conditions for the activity and ongoing process of reconciliation. Due to these associations with the term *reconciliation,* most BiH peacebuilders today tend not to use the term. Instead, trust, restored relations, and social cohesion are the qualities of reconciliation that are goals of the faith-based peacebuilders considered in this chapter.[3]

Religious actors have generally been neglected or avoided in international relations, diplomacy, and peace intervention in conflict situations despite or because of the fact that conflicts today often have a religious angle or are ethno-religious in nature as in BiH. The marginalization of religious actors from peace-seeking initiatives is due, at least in part, to the Western notion of secularity as a divide between public, state activities and the private realm of nonstate actors. There is also a widespread conviction, based on plenty of evidence, that religions tend to be divisive rather than bridgebuilders. But religiously justified violence is just one part of the picture; the less-visible part is religious actors committed to their faith's instructions to work for peace and reconciliation. Scholarship in the last twenty years has pointed to the potential and suitability of these religious actors to influence intractable situations (Appleby 2000; Gopin 2000; Helmick and Petersen 2001; Johnston and Sampson 1994; Little 2007). "Such persons are often better equipped to reach people at the level of the individual and the subnational group—where inequities and insecurities are often most keenly felt—than are most political leaders who walk the corridors of power. They are also better attuned to dealing with basic moral issues and spiritual needs" (Johnston and Sampson 1994, 4).

In this chapter, we look at the work of faith-based peacebuilders who are active on the ground in BiH. Our focus is on Muslim peacebuilders, with a few additions of interfaith peace efforts. The Muslim peace activists we have worked with and whom we describe in this chapter do not officially represent their religious institution (the Islamic Community of BiH). They do, however, have influence on the local level and they represent their faith in the global community. They are part of the lesser-known but no less active religious "militants for peace" throughout history (Appleby 2000). Our claim is that, contrary to general opinion among postwar peacebuilding initiatives, integrating faith-based agents into peacebuilding projects has potential to produce a more stable country and more sustainable social conditions. Engaging all involved in conflict brings the various social sectors and groups into an explicit relationship, which then may provide spaces for reconciliation to occur.

Religiosity and Secularism in BiH

BiH as a multiethnic and multireligious country has a history that includes both eruptions of violence and periods of coexistence. This is true for the last war (1992–95) as well as the current segregated and dysfunctional state. Given the many commonalities among its three main ethnic communities, religion has been the key differentiation for identity formation. After the fall of the Ottomans in the late nineteenth century, these Muslims were faced with life under non-Islamic law and governance. Regional nation-state projects at the end of the nineteenth and the twentieth centuries entangled the national and religious communities and also greatly affected Bosnian Muslims. The intermittent process of secularization limited the Islamic institution mostly to matters of the family, marriage, and inheritance. After World War II, Shari'a law was abolished and religious schools were shut down (Karčić 2008, 21). The responses of the Islamic Community to these challenges of "modernity" were mostly aimed at adaptation and integration into the new social and political contexts (Karić 1998).

BiH experienced each of Casanova's (1994) three dimensions of secularization during Socialist Yugoslavia: the differentiation of religious and state spheres; the decline of religious beliefs and practices; and the relegation of religion to people's private lives. After World War II, the country was marked by a structural differentiation of religion and state as well as assigning religions a marginal role limited to family life, especially in the first twenty years of communism, which emphasized South Slavic commonalities while suppressing religious differences. Nonreligious socialist secularism facilitated the overarching Yugoslav collective identity, which many accepted, especially former partisan families and the new intellectual elite (*inteligencia*).[4] The three major ethnic groups nurtured their religious beliefs, practices, and identities in the early years of Yugoslavia in the family or local neighborhood, mostly through cultural traditions. These differences, however, were not yet politically significant. During the

1970s and 1980s, with the decentralization of the federal state and a new constitution guaranteeing "Muslims" an ethnic designation (i.e., political representation), religions again began to flourish in Socialist Yugoslavia. However, Muslims were the only group in the former Yugoslavia to use a religious designation for ethnic identity. Religious schools and cultural institutions were reopened and many mosques and churches were built, while the intellectual work remained controlled by and limited to those in the Communist Party. In the 1980s, religious thinkers began to speak cautiously about religion's role in society, though limited to "establish[ing] a baseline of religious knowledge in Bosnian [language]" (Alibašić 2014). The late 1980s saw rising nationalistic ideologies and the great-state projects of Serbia and Croatia. When ethno-national parties won the first democratic elections in the 1990s, Muslim religious intellectuals spoke openly about the role of religion in public life. Religion became a powerful tool in national awakening and for ethnic mobilization and homogenization, although it was not accepted by all. Notably, this alignment of religion with nationalism also became one of the greatest obstacles to faith-based peacebuilding.

It is important to note that in the former Yugoslavia "religion did not disappear, but instead retreated from the view of the official socialist state" (Spahić Šiljak 2013b)—Casanova's second and third types of secularization. Religion was practiced more as a cultural tradition and folklore, and these were not considered a threat to the socialist regime because they did not necessarily divide communities. The tradition of *komšiluk* (neighborly relations) operated, for example, according to an unwritten code of conduct and duties (Sorabji 1989; Bringa 1995; Funk 2013; Spahić Šiljak 2015b). Bridging ethnic and religious boundaries, neighbors commonly acted as godparents (*kumovi*) for each other. They celebrated religious holidays together, and all three groups followed a *narodni kalendar* (people's calendar) marking shared agricultural and life-cycle rituals (Hadžić 1941; Fabijanic 1966). These traditional cultural practices still characterize religion in BiH today (though rarely bridging ethnicity as it did previously), which makes it all but impossible to separate religion from culture.

With the breakup of Yugoslavia and the end of communism, the entire Balkan region experienced desecularization—as Peter Berger (1999) described the contemporary world. This new world is "as furiously religious as it ever was" (Berger 1999, 2), with religion claiming a greater place in public life alongside the reaffirmation of ethno-national identity and "modern" democratization. The vast majority of residents (97 percent, according to the 2013 census) associate themselves with a religion or claim a faith, and attendance at churches and mosques is much higher than during communism. Since the 1990s, therefore, it is less relevant to measure the type or degree of secularization in BiH than the "character of the national religious communities" (Abazović 2006, 103). Powerful ethno-national and ethno-religious elites enabled religious communities to play important political roles.

> Religious organizations had put on political hats and they took over important roles of influence in . . . society on many different levels: as moral guards of the nations (each religion for its own), as educators (by becoming a part of the regular schooling), and as a mobilizing agency for all the different kinds of political goals one could have imagined on the territory of ex-Yugoslavia at the end of the twentieth century in Europe. (Ognjenović and Jozelić 2014, xviii)

Interestingly, in the midst of the 1990s war, when the three ethnic groups could agree on absolutely nothing, religious leaders worked together to introduce confessional religious education in the public school system (Popov and Mette Ofstad 2006). As major sources of political legitimacy for their communities during this period of upheaval, this was one visible way of securing their public presence.[5] Although today the BiH state is considered secular, with civic legislation accompanied by a set of international human rights norms and standards (BiH Constitution, Annex I, 1995), the revived religious heritage now enjoys prestige and protection under democratic rule. This experiment continues to provoke a heated debate due to its divisive character among the already divided society, and it remains one of the arguments for religion being relegated back to private life or "individual faith," as Fikret Karčić envisions it for Bosnian Islam (Bougarel 2007).

What stands out about the Muslim peacebuilders is their own struggle as human beings who suffered and who feel compelled to counteract their own and their group's feelings of anger and hate toward the "other." They rely on the resource of Islamic exhortations to peace—for example, the Qur'anic call to forgiveness as a better way than fighting back in defense. Since these individuals do not represent the Islamic Community of BiH, they have more space and freedom to negotiate their loyalties.

Faith-Based Activism in BiH's Postwar Civil Society

The initial postwar peace and reconciliation efforts in the hands of human rights initiatives were supported and funded by international organizations. This resulted in NGOs becoming big business and what some called "projectomania" (Fischer 2006, 17). NGOs became caught in a dependency trap, "develop[ing] their agendas according to donors' expectations instead of responding to social needs" (ibid., 17). At the same time, the international community was delegitimized via their perceived intent to "civilize" society via nongovernmental organizations (Belloni 2001). Despite this compromised start, the secular engagement of the international community was the key condition for faith-based peacebuilding to arise.

One Sarajevo faith-based activist, Amra Pandžo, reflects upon the early years, when peace activists were pioneers and experimented with approaches in response to the ever-present suffering, war trauma, and psychological and emotional devastation of the entire society. They had no methodology or expertise but simply responded to the social priority of rebuilding human life from the inside. When this priority necessitated addressing ethno-national divisions or administrative challenges, they did this as well. Later, education for peacebuilding was introduced to BiH by international nongovernmental organizations, such as the UN. Vahidin Omanović, another faith-based actor from Bosnia's Northwest Krajina and from the Center for Peacebuilding, remembers how "we didn't have a clear model developed, but we knew that the ultimate goal was to bring [people] together [across ethnic lines] and have them work as peacebuilders in the community."[6]

Peacebuilding and human rights activism during the first five postwar years in BiH (1996–2000) were not motivated by and did not engage religion (Spahić Šiljak 2014; Merdjanova and Brodeur 2009, 108–24). Instead, secular human rights organizations gathered people "who generally did not strongly identify with ethno-national politics or religion" (Spahić Šiljak 2014, 290). Religion was shunned because of its role in ethno-national partisanship. The international community and donors who supported democratization projects simply ignored religious communities and faith-based organizations. Amra Pandžo explains:

> The civil sector was separated from anything that was this ethno-national mainstream. In other words, these were the

organizations that mostly inherited some of the socialist and
communist and atheist ideas. Everything related to nationalism or, God forbid, religiosity was removed from civil society.
(Quoted in Spahić Šiljak 2014, 290)

In addition to both the complicity of religion in the segregation of
nationalist identities and the disinterest of secular international organizations in religion, another major challenge to the development of religious
peacebuilding in BiH has been the general lack of interest among the
religious communities themselves. The Islamic community, for example,
has no program or department on peacemaking, nor does it have trained
imams or teachers in this field.[7] Besides a general disinterest, we have
observed other excuses for this lack of engagement. Some argue that
since Muslims were the main victims during the war, they should not
take the first steps in peacebuilding; others argue that being a Muslim is
the same as a peacemaker because Islam means peace; yet again others
claim that since they were not personally involved in violence, they are
not responsible for reconciliation.

Serbian Orthodox peacebuilders are facing an institutional church
that has created an additional obstacle to their work: a special blessing
(blagoslov) is required from the religious authorities in order to officially
link their peace activities with their faith tradition. Practically speaking,
therefore, religious peacebuilders must be in line with the church's position,
a position that does not promote peacebuilding and reconciliation with
the enemy. This is different for Muslim peacebuilders: the decentralized
nature of the Islamic Community allows them to be freer agents, neither
hindered nor supported by their own community. This is most likely the
reason why there are more explicit peacebuilders among Muslims than
among Serbian Orthodox in BiH.[8] It must be also noted that Franciscans
have been the most vocal faith-based peace activists in BiH (Spahić Šiljak
2015a), perhaps due to their historic position of unity with other BiH
residents (Gavran 2001).

Despite this barren ground, faith-based peacebuilding managed to
develop. Five years after the end of the war, from 2000 onward, there
was a definite shift in capacity and vision for peace work. Some Muslim
peacebuilders contributed to dialogue and reconciliation through individual
civil society initiatives or as imams in their mosques. Others joined secular civic initiatives, while some secular organizations accepted faith-based
actors to work together. One Muslim peace activist said that she tried

for years to get involved with civil society initiatives, but upon arriving at an event (e.g., a human rights workshop) wearing her *hijab,* she was told "this is not a religious event," meaning she was not welcome. As she persisted in attending and involving herself in such activities, perceptions of her attendance changed and secular actors eventually understood that the *hijab* did not disqualify her interest in human rights activism. With the establishment of the BiH Interreligious Council in 1997,[9] and pressure on international funders, faith became recognized as a missing element in the peacebuilding process. It is now more acceptable to hear religious voices. The international community and donors seem to realize that religious actors can play a role in peace and reconciliation (Appleby 2000; Johnston and Sampson 1995),[10] and that the exclusion of faith-based activists can actually produce additional polarization, mistrust, and division.

Raising awareness among believers that they also belong to civil society contributed to the advent of faith-based peacebuilding. For many people in BiH, including peacebuilders, the idea of combining faith with working toward relational reconciliation is unprecedented. While many "secular" peacebuilders actually adhere to some religious belief, most do not use religion as an argument or explicit motivation for their work. With a few rare exceptions,[11] religious peacebuilding in BiH was therefore initiated within secular international organizations, which involved and trained local people in this activism. There has generally been little consideration of the suitability of faith to aspects of peacebuilding. The insight that the spirit or psyche can assist in becoming aware of inherent prejudice, in recalling traumatic experiences, or in re-encountering the other is not yet present in these organizations. As we see in the following section, the inclusion of religious stories, values, and teachings do, however, resonate strongly among many who identify as believers.

Given the compromised role of religions in BiH during and after the war, which furthered the political divisions and assisted nationalist agendas, the process of building a positive and sustainable peace requires that it is necessary to address even the most destructive aspects of the conflict. If religious violence is to be changed for the long term, religious actors must themselves address their capacity and inclination to do violence (Funk Deckard 2012). This is what religious peacebuilders seek to do—to work from the inside at a core aspect of the conflict rather than avoid it as too provocative. What makes the Bosnian faith-based peacebuilders unique is their explicit and crucial tie to a faith tradition, both with respect to motivation (vocation) and the actual implementation of their work.

Bosnian Muslim Peacebuilding

We have intentionally talked about Muslim peacebuilders rather than Islamic peacebuilding because the activities of individuals we have observed do not *originate* in Islamic teachings. Rather, these Muslim actors utilize their secular training and tools while personally reconciling their work with Islamic faith, principles, and inspiration. To combine faith with peace activities is thus mostly a result of an internal negotiation for the individuals involved, revealing the particular nature of Bosnian Islam as a religious culture and tradition. In many ways, these individuals adopt peacebuilding as a vocation. The Tanenbaum Center's study of religious peacemakers, *Peacemakers in Action* (2007), explains religious vocation for peace and reconciliation work as a deep "commitment toward making peace a living reality." The Muslim peacebuilders we know in BiH exhibit a "clarity of purpose" evident in all aspects of life and to everyone they encounter that "helps them to influence others, and helps explain their personal and spiritual charisma" (2007, 8).

Zilka Spahić Šiljak's peace and reconciliation work is informed both by her faith and her human rights activism. Raised in a traditional Muslim family that lived the Abrahamic tradition of hospitality and adhered to the Prophet Muhammad's tradition of mercy, and with her training in Islamic studies, Zilka has been motivated to deal with violence, trauma, and reconciliation from the very beginning of the recent war in BiH.

Julianne Funk's faith commitment to her reconciliation work arises primarily from her Mennonite heritage, a historic Peace Church with a tradition of nonviolence and social justice (Funk 2015a). She sees her role model, Jesus, as an example of radical love for the other and reformer of the standard order that relies on violence as a method. She shares her Muslim colleague's (Amra Pandžo) sentiment that faith is not only a "deep motivation and strength," but also that peace activism is actually "the path to be saved." Such an orientation to peace work can be called a "vocation" and a "sacred duty" (Tanenbaum Center 2007, 9), arising from a personally lived faith. For Pandžo as a Muslim, the key principle of Islam is *tawheed* (God is one), which includes all of creation. In her eyes, *tawheed,* as revealed reality, requires inclusive behavior and respect for each creature: not only for "us" but also for "others."

Another colleague, Omanović, calls "Islam and the revelation . . . our main source, our main motivation for our peace work"; Rahmanović says that it is the "engine" of their work.[12] Omanović and Rahmanović are co-directors of the Center for Peacebuilding and both are trained as imams. For Rahmanović, being a peacebuilder is even more important than being an imam: "Today Islam is seen more as a faith of violence and fighting, of hatred. In the western world this is the mainstream [idea]. People are afraid when they hear '*Allahu akbar*,' but for me, when I hear this, I feel peace and safety. . . . So this is my call, to show what Islam is really about."[13]

A key element of vocation, according to Max Weber (2015), is not (primarily) "living *from*" one's professional occupation, but more importantly "living *for*" it. This characterizes well our own constant struggle as well as those of other Muslim peacemakers: we are committed to the task, because we believe that peace does not have alternative. Funk's commitment to activism in BiH, for example, means she has chosen to work only part time in her current home in the West in order to maintain her engagement and work in BiH. For Zilka, after her wartime *pro bono* NGO work, she worked for the government, a most coveted employer due to life-long job security and a stable salary. However, she chose to resign in order to continue her peacebuilding and reconciliation work both in NGOs and academia, despite the loss of state benefits.[14]

While vocation is key to the identity of Bosnian Muslim peacebuilders, combining that faith explicitly into peacebuilding activities is crucial so as not to avoid one of the provocations of the conflict: interethnic relations. This may also be the most creative part of the work, since Bosnian Muslim peacebuilders start with their secular conflict resolution/transformation methodologies and then add the component of faith. For example, when working with young people, it is important to address the content and nature of national/ethnic and religious identities, precisely because these are often unquestionably combined. In line with Lederach's idea of conflict transformation as the goal of peacebuilding (1997; 2003), we understand this work as facilitating safe spaces for encounter, healing, and reconciliation, but with the additional component of faith. Faith can be an added value insofar as many recipients of this work in BiH are themselves believers; connecting with their faith can increase their own capacity for transformation. The Mennonite peacebuilders Randy and Amela Puljek-Shank write about their work in BiH that

> their faith has helped them . . . to recognize the presence of God in those who were their enemies. This process is a deeply spiritual experience that truly transforms tragedy into

a source of strength . . . developing a new sense of meaning for their own lives, a way to find something good amidst the difficult thing that happened to them. . . . These individuals have become wounded healers, where they carry their wounds with them but do not inflict them on others. They are fully aware of their pain and losses but there is something strong within them that pushes them to heal and through this healing process they carry [the] burdens of others (even their former enemies) and enable them to heal. (Puljek-Shank and Puljek-Shank 2008, 180)

When wounded healers become peacebuilders, they open further transformative platforms for reconciliation. "The other has been given the gift of entering the sphere of transformed trauma, into the realm of recovery, as if the subject has opened a door. This is a powerful demonstration of the way faith can enhance the transformative platform" (Funk Deckard 2012, 182). Religion has the capacity to change psychologically disabling contradictions:"Rather than encouraging denial, religion promotes reinterpretations of negative events through a sacred lens" (Pargament et al. 2005, 481). As such, the faith-based peacebuilder's focus on personal and relational transformation, rather than following a simple conflict resolution model, means that "deep cultural and religious aspects of identity and life can be valued, understood and reworked" (Funk Deckard 2012, 183).

Faith in Practice:
Religious Peacebuilding Techniques and Methods

The Tanenbaum Center for Interreligious Understanding has categorized some of the key techniques or methods of faith-based peace actors, as summarized below (see also Funk Deckard 2012, 183ff):

1. Incorporating religious texts into peace work

2. Preaching/public instruction ("the power of the pulpit")

3. Using and adapting existing religious and cultural rituals to traditional ways

4. Using religion in discussion/debate and finding common ground

5. Peace education as a foundation for transforming conflict and building peace within and between religious believers and communities

6. Religious peacemaking through communication skills

7. Creating philosophies of nonviolence and zones of peace

8. Interfaith mobilization for peace

9. Awakening the global community

10. Adapting secular and Western peacebuilding practices to religious peacebuilding

Using our personal experiences and working with Muslim peacebuilders, we want to illustrate some of these techniques in the particular situation of postwar BiH.

USING AND ADAPTING EXISTING RELIGIOUS AND CULTURAL RITUALS TO TRADITIONAL WAYS (3)

This technique relates to the creative adaptation of religious rituals and traditions in bringing people and communities together. During and after the war, Zilka Spahić Šiljak worked with her colleagues at Medica Zenica, where they "were deeply enmeshed in the pain, suffering, and trauma" brought to them by the abused women who sought help (Spahić Šiljak 2013a, 21). Trained as a Muslim theologian, Spahić Šiljak with her colleague Sabiha Husić did their best to respond to essential religious concerns, such as: How to believe in a God who could allow rape and torture? Is it sinful to abort pregnancies as a result of rape? How to bear the shame of women's victimhood within the (often religiously supported) patriarchal gender regime in BiH? Since the male-dominated Islamic Community would not discuss such issues, "contextualized interpretations of Islam" were provided to address abused women's needs and to provide a foundation for healing and reconciliation with families and society.

A powerful example is the use of the Muslim naming ritual for a newborn child, something typically conducted by men. In this rite of passage to connect the baby with God, Sabiha Husić would recite the first call to prayer (*adhan*) in the baby's right ear and then the second call to prayer (*iqama*) in the left ear before calling the baby by its name three times. "The child is [then] passed from one person to another, so that this new human being, who belongs to this community, can be accepted as a gift from God" (Spahić Šiljak 2014, 25). Through this ceremony, Husić observed an inner change: "Emotions rise and those [family members] who yesterday were against the baby and could not see this baby as their grandchild, would suddenly change their opinion" (quoted in Spahić Šiljak 2014, 24).

Another example of the method of combining religious rituals and cultural traditions is the annual communal *iftar* meal during Ramadan hosted by the Center for Peacebuilding (CIM) in the town of Sanski Most in northwestern BiH. Sanski Most's Muslims make up the vast majority of the town's inhabitants, and each year the feast grows in size, filling the central town park with carpets spread on the ground for sitting and food shared by all. CIM also personally invites the leaders and members of the Christian communities—Orthodox, Catholic, and Protestant—to attend regularly. This reflects the traditional practice of *suživot* (coexistence or mutual life) in BiH, especially before the war, when friends and neighbors of different faiths would celebrate holidays together (see Funk 2013; forthcoming).

USING RELIGION IN DEBATE AND FINDING COMMON GROUND (4)

Funk has been engaged in implementing this method of faith-based peacebuilding in different contexts, using the common phenomenon of faith to provide discussion space across different traditions. She was involved first in an interfaith dialogue on the topic of Mary, the mother of Jesus, organized by CIM in Sanski Most in 2011. Together with a Swiss Roman Catholic nun and a Bosnian Muslim woman, Julianne Funk (a Protestant Christian) discussed the meaning and understanding of Mary in each of their traditions in an open panel, explicitly engaging different belief systems and values as well as the roles of women in religions. Since women in BiH, especially in the religious communities, are subject to a patriarchal system, in which their voices and value are generally diminished, these discussions were unusually stimulating.

In a second instance, Funk was asked to share her personal encounter with Islam in BiH to a mixed group of women (Serbs and Albanians) from Kosovo. Her testimony recalled being welcomed into a Muslim community and simultaneously respected for engaging with them as a Christian. Implicitly, Funk proposed that one can worship with another religious community without feeling threatened and without losing one's own tradition and faith, which surprised the women. The cross-border (BiH-Kosovo) project also took the women to visit each other's religious sites, further empowering the women with real information about these sites, thus breaking with stereotypes about the other. One of the basic anxieties of believers when engaging in interreligious dialogue concerns the imagined pressure to convert to another faith. However, the purpose of interreligious encounter "is to increasingly understand the other and her faith because this breaks down stereotypes and prejudice (negative conceptions) so that a human picture of the other can grow. This fosters respect of all human persons as well as other religions" (Funk Deckard 2012, 191).

> Typically, when engaged between believers with strong foundations in their own faiths, this experience reveals as much about the other religion as one's own, because one begins to see her own religion through new eyes. "Each participant gives the best of who she/he is as a religious believer and part of a particular religious community." (Funk Deckard 2012, 191)[15]

Topics that emerge in interreligious dialogue and understanding are critical to peace and reconciliation between members of religious communities; secular civic initiatives are unlikely to address these.

PEACE EDUCATION AS A FOUNDATION FOR TRANSFORMING CONFLICT AND BUILDING PEACE WITHIN AND BETWEEN RELIGIOUS BELIEVERS AND COMMUNITIES (5)

The Tanenbaum Center for Interreligious Understanding notes that many faith-based peacebuilders use education "in one form or another . . . to empower and encourage new understandings that lead to peace" (2007, 13). Spahić Šiljak's endeavors in this direction were significant in her initiation and leadership of the Religious and Gender Studies Program at the University of Sarajevo, where she taught courses on gender and religion and gender and human rights. She also edited the textbook *Three Monotheistic Voices* (Spahić Šiljak and Abazović 2009) as complementary material for religious education in public high schools. The textbook was a result of the collaborative work of scholars who created the teaching materials to connect three religious traditions as well as nonreligious worldviews. In BiH, students are ethnically/religiously divided and attend religious study classes only for their own faith tradition; hence, they do not know much about their neighbor's faith. The textbook aimed to help them to learn about other worldviews and traditions; it also aimed at showing them that believers and nonbelievers share the same universal values of human dignity, freedom, justice, and equality.

Another important part of Spahić Šiljak's peace education work is the TPO Foundation's project on reconciling religious and secular human rights approaches by addressing gender equality. The book *Women Believers and Citizens* (Spahić Šiljak and Anić 2009), with an accompanying manual, was used for training civic activists from women's NGOs, primarily to empower them to use the channel of religion and local cultural tradition to counter gender stereotypes and discrimination. Women from secular NGOs who follow their own faith traditions were eager to relieve uneasiness over the secular–religious divide regarding gender equality, which is not supported by many religious traditions today in BiH.

Amra Pandžo has also worked extensively on religious peace education within her own Muslim community with her *Manual for the Teachers of Islamic Religion on the Peaceful Dimensions of Islam* (2008). She has traveled across the country to distribute it and train the nine hunred-plus public school teachers of Muslim religious education in how to use the manual. Amra hopes to expose Bosnia's youth to a "peaceful interpretation of the sacred text of Islam . . . result[ing] in healthy individuals who understand faith as a bridge to others" (Pandžo 2010, 5).

RELIGIOUS PEACEMAKING THROUGH COMMUNICATION SKILLS (6)

Within the TPO Foundation in Sarajevo, Spahić Šiljak designed the project "Countering Violence with Dialogue" (Spahić Siljak and Husić 2011) in an attempt to gather women from Muslim, Catholic, and Orthodox Christian villages and discuss issues of family violence. Since family violence is still a taboo, and many do not want to speak about it publicly or be associated with it, Spahić Šiljak and her team used the channel of interreligious dialogue to open the floor for women to discuss family violence. Women learned that violence happens in all communities, that it is not an exceptional case, and that religion does not support violence (despite the fact that representatives of religions sometimes use it when, for example, they pressure women to stay in a violent marriage for the sake of family). Many women reported that they felt relieved because they were not alone in their communities. Realizing that one is not alone with one's suffering helps to remove the shame and taboo around this topic. This realization also assured women that it is not God who wants them to suffer, but that domestic violence is rooted in patriarchal interpretations of religion. Women begin to see that religious teachings actually uphold women as equal human beings with their own dignity.

INTERFAITH MOBILIZATION FOR PEACE (8)

A unique interfaith mobilization is CIM's annual Peace Camp with youth from all corners of BiH, representing all ethnicities. Through this week-long event, set in an isolated and safe space in the countryside, CIM has trained more than three hundred youths to act in their own local communities. Peace Camp is a space of personal transformation; the workshops and activities provide young people a chance to expand their knowledge and perspective on BiH's current affairs and people of different faiths. These workshops help to break down prejudice and teach nonviolent communication methods. The young people are supported in designing and implementing their own follow-up dialogue and peace initiatives at home in order to develop the same capacity within the broader society (CIM Team 2015). Directors travel the country supporting these youth as they implement their plans in their home locations.

One of the ways to mobilize religious women for peacebuilding is the EPIL project run by Sabiha Husić at Medica Zenica. This transnational program gathers women from several European and Middle Eastern countries to show "that women of different religions can be together, listen to one another [and] exchange experiences" thereby "contribut[ing] to peace in their own countries and eliminat[ing] stereotypes and biases."[16]

Sabiha managed to motivate young women of different faiths to learn from one another and to pursue peace in their communities with interreligious knowledge. She envisions a future in which women are acknowledged and promoted, hoping that with the growing affirmation of their social equality, these women of different faiths can focus their efforts on competing in good deeds (Qur'an 5:48).

AWAKENING THE GLOBAL COMMUNITY (9)

Funk, as a Peace Ambassador of CIM, has participated in CIM's annual International Peace Week, which gathers the community and also hosts international delegations of activists, experts, and young people to learn about the situation in BiH. Each year the event attracts more international guests as it also grows in popularity in the local community. The connection made between locals and internationals is an important part of awakening the global community for peace and reconciliation by "creating a global network of peace builders . . . [where i]nternational guests and scholars [are provided] with opportunities to learn about what peace building looks like in Bosnia today" (CIM Team 2016). During this week, young people can learn from international experts and activists, receive peacebuilding training, and participate in local interreligious dialogue. Funk is one of those internationals who teaches and participates each year and takes the message of peacebuilding in BiH to audiences outside the region.

Conclusions

The peacebuilders in this chapter clearly and explicitly see their work toward social reconciliation as a faith-based activity and vocation. Their links to religious communities and traditions are generally personal rather than characterizing their nongovernmental organizations as faith-based. These faith-based initiatives for peace are slowly becoming accepted as legitimate in BiH society; the donor community too has recently begun to recognize the role of faith-based activism in civil society. In practice, therefore, neither is the faith of these activists relegated to the private sphere nor is it fully public. Imposing a strict code of secularism to separate the private/public and religious/secular domains does not do justice to the lived experience in BiH. Rather, it misrepresents the richness of lived faith (Funk 2015b). This insight is relevant to the hard work these actors are trying to pursue against the flow of public opinion. Misunderstanding the complexity of religions is dangerous, as we see today with the stereotyping of all Muslims (especially refugees and immigrants) as extremists or terrorists.

Most faith-based activism still happens within secular NGOs rather than being offered by religious institutions. Official religious institutions are not yet open to the idea of dialogue between religious and nonreligious worldviews. This could be an important next step in the evolution of religious or faith-based peacebuilding in BiH, especially if it were informed by the established initiatives of individual actors such as those represented in this chapter.

Notes

1. *Reconciliation* may be considered more fitting than *peacebuilding* with regard to the efforts described in this article. However, the authors are not the first or the last to avoid this term with regard to these efforts in BiH because of the stigma the term has gained through activities of the international community, which do not reflect a proper definition of reconciliation as the rebuilding of trust in relationships (see also the contribution of Heleen Touquet and Ana Milošević in this volume). For definitions of peacebuilding, see Boutros Boutros-Ghali's "An Agenda for Peace" (1992) and the 2000 United Nations' "Brahimi Report."

2. Lederach's "Meeting Place": http://www.colorado.edu/conflict/transform/jplchpt.htm.

3. In 2006, UNDP/ORI found that only 7.2 percent of people in BiH think "most people can be trusted," a significant reduction in social trust from 26.9 percent in 1998 (UNDP 2009, 43).

4. Yugoslav partisan families (*partizanske porodice*) supported Tito and the Communist Party in their cause to fight fascism during World War II. These respected and often distinguished families became the new intellectual (*inteligencija*) elite who received special benefits for their contributions (Donia and Fine 1994).

5. Religious education is regulated by the "Law on Freedom of Churches and Religious Communities" (2004).

6. Skype interview with Vahidin Omanovic and Mevludin Rahmanovic (November 12, 2015).

7. The Islamic community did, however, participate in the BiH Interreligious Council. Recently, it also established "The Center for Dialogue—Vesatijja" (from the Arabic *wasat,* meaning middle) with the aim of promoting dialogue among cultures and the idea of an Islamic middle way, or moderate Islam (see also Zeina Barakat's contribution to this volume). http://rijaset.islamskazajednica.ba/index.php/uprave-1/uprava-za-obrazovanje-i-nauku/centar-za-dijalog-vesatijja.

8. This is based on the research finding of Funk's dissertation. She considered three elements for religious peacebuilding: (1) the actors (believers), (2) faith as a "meaningful framework" (Fox 2002) for determining how they see and interact with the world, and (3) peace work oriented toward nonviolent conflict transformation or the rebuilding of relationships.

9. Interreligious Council of BiH. http://www.mrv.ba.

10. E.g., Catholic Relief Service (CRS), the United Methodist Committee on Relief (UMCOR), the International Research & Exchanges Board (IREX), and the Organization for Security and Cooperation in Europe (OSCE).

11. The rare exceptions to this were IMIC Zajedno Sarajevo (which started in 1991) and Abraham/Ibrahim and Face to Face, which were each established after the war. In 2007, the Interreligious Council of BiH was created. The

international organization Mennonite Central Committee was also present and active.

12. Skype interview with Vahidin Omanovic and Mevludin Rahmanovic (November 12, 2015).

13. Ibid.

14. Notably, when Spahić Šiljak resigned in 2004, people were shocked, and even the prime minister asked for a meeting to explain to him what went wrong. It was inconceivable that someone would choose to leave such a position.

15. Reference from Centar za Izgradnju Mira, "Notes from the Interreligious Dialogue Session," *Sanski Most*, September 15, 2010.

16. Personal Interview with Sabiha Husić (September 4, 2014).

Works Cited

Abazović, Dino. 2006. "Religijski Nacionalizam kako Prepreka Evropskim Inte-gracijama." In *Religija i Europske Integracije*, edited by Dino Abazović and Ivan Cvitković, 201–10. Sarajevo: Magistrat.

Alibašić, Ahmet. 2014. "Bosnia and Herzegovina." In *The Oxford Handbook of European Islam,* edited by Joselyne Cesary, 429–74. Oxford: Oxford University Press.

Appleby, R. Scott. 2000. *The Ambivalence of the Sacred: Religion, Violence, and Reconciliation.* Lanham, MD: Rowman and Littlefield.

Berger, Peter, ed. 1999. *The Desecularization of the World: Resurgent Religion and World Politics.* Grand Rapids: Eerdmans.

Bougarel, Xavier. 2007. "Bosnian Islam as 'European Islam': Limits and Shifts of a Concept." In *Islam in Europe: Diversity, Identity, and Influence,* edited by Aziz al-Azmeh and Effie Fokas, 96–124. Cambridge: Cambridge University Press.

Bringa, Tone. 1995. *Being Muslim the Bosnian Way: Identity and Community in a Central Bosnian Village.* Princeton: Princeton University Press.

Casanova, José. 1994. *Public Religions in the Modern World.* Chicago: University of Chicago Press.

CIM Team. 2015. "Peace Camp 2015." *Center for Peacebuilding* (September 7). http://unvocim.net/eng/peace-camp-2015/.

———. 2016. "CIM's 7th International Peace Week." *Center for Peacebuilding* (October 6). http://unvocim.net/eng/cims-7th-international-peace-week/.

Donia, Robert, and John V. A. Fine Jr. 1994. *Bosnia and Hercegovina: A Tradition Betrayed.* New York: Columbia University Press.

Fabijanic, Radmila. 1966. Narodne pripovetke i predanja iz Bosanske Posavine. *Glasnik zemaljskok muzeja* XX–XXI: 135–66.

Fox, Jonathan. 2002. *Ethnoreligious Conflict in the Late Twentieth Century: A General Theory.* Oxford: Lexington Books.

Funk, Julianne. Forthcoming. "Bosnian Diaspora Experiences of *Suživot* or Traditional Coexistence: Bosnian *Lonac*, American Melting Pot or Swiss Fondue?" In *Both Muslim and European: Diasporic and Migrant Identities of Bosnian Muslims*, edited by Dzevada Šuško. Leiden: Brill.

———. 2015a. "Mennonite Peacebuilding: Conflict Transformation as a Spiritual Practice." In *Nonkilling Spiritual Traditions*, edited by P. Dhakal and J. E. Pim, 195–219. Honolulu: The Center for Global Nonkilling.

———. 2015b. "Public Expressions of Bosnian Muslim Religiosity and Lived Faith: The Cases of Friday Prayer and Hijab." In *The Revival of Islam in the Balkans: From Identity to Religiosity*, edited by Arolda Elbasani and Olivier Roy, 204–21. Basingstoke: Palgrave.

———. 2013. "Women and the Spirit of Suživot in Postwar Bosnia-Herzegovina." In *Spirituality of Balkan Women: Breaking Boundaries: The Voices of Women of ex-Yugoslavia*, edited by Nadija Furlan Štante and Marijana Hacet, 171–84. Koper: Univerzitetna Založba Annales.

Funk Deckard, Julianne. 2012. *"Invisible" Believers for Peace: Religion and Peacebuilding in Postwar Bosnia and Herzegovina*. Unpublished PhD Dissertation, KU Leuven.

Galtung, Johan. 1996. *Peace by Peaceful Means: Peace and Conflict, Development and Civilization*. London: Sage.

Gavran, Fra Ignacije. 2001. *Fellow-Travelers of Bosnian History: Seven Centuries of Bosnian Franciscans*. Sarajevo: Müller.

Gopin, Marc. 2000. *Between Eden and Armageddon: The Future of World Religions, Violence, and Peacemaking*. Oxford: Oxford University Press.

Hadžić, Kasim. 1941. "Elementi staroslavenske tradicije u kulturi Bošnjaka." *Narodna Pravda* 32: 12.

Helmick, Raymond G., S.J., and Rodney L. Petersen. 2001. *Forgiveness and Reconciliation: Religion, Public Policy, and Conflict Transformation*. London: Templeton Foundation Press.

Johnston, Douglas, and Cynthia Sampson. 1995. *Religion, the Missing Dimension of Statecraft*. Oxford: Oxford University Press.

Karčić, Fikret. 2008. "Secular State and Religion(s)—Remarks on the Bosnian Experience in Regulating Religion and State Relations in View of the New Law on Freedom of Religion." In *Religion and Secular State. Role and Meaning of Religion in a Secular Society from Jewish, Christian, and Muslim Perspectives*, edited by Stefan Schreiner, 15–25. Sarajevo: European Abrahamic Forum and Interreligious Institute in BiH.

Karić, Enes. 1998. "Nase bosjnastvo i nase muslimanstvo." *Ljiljan* 6.264 (February 4): 20–22.

Lederach, John Paul. 1997. *Building Peace: Sustainable Reconciliation in Divided Societies*. Washington, DC: United States Institute of Peace.

———. 2003. *The Little Book of Conflict Transformation*. Intercourse: Good Books.

Little, David, ed. 2007. *Peacemakers in Action: Profiles of Religion in Conflict Resolution*. Cambridge: Cambridge University Press.

Merdjanova, Ina, and Patrice Brodeur. 2009. *Religion as a Conversation Starter: Interreligious Dialogue for Peacebuilding in the Balkans.* New York: Continuum.

Ognjenović, Gorana, and Jasna Jozelić, eds. 2014. *Politicization of Religion, the Power of State, Nation, and State: The Case of Former Yugoslavia and its Successor States.* New York: Palgrave Macmillan.

Pandžo, Amra. 2010. "On the Path to Peace." *Peace Office Newsletter* 40 (July–September): 4–5.

———, ed. 2008. *Manual for the Teachers of Islamic Religion the Peaceful Dimensions of Islam.* Sarajevo: Organization for Dialogue in Family and Society "Small Steps."

Pargament, Kenneth I., Gene G. Ano, and Amy B. Wachholtz. 2005. "The Religious Dimension of Coping: Advances in Theory, Research, and Practice." In *Handbook of the Psychology of Religion and Spirituality*, edited by Raymond F. Paloutzian and Crystal L. Park, 479–95. New York: Guilford Press.

Popov, Zlatiborka, and Anne Mette Ofstad. 2006. "Religious Education in Bosnia and Herzegovina." In *Religion and Pluralism in Education: Comparative Approaches in the Western Balkans*, edited by Zorica Kuburić and Christian Moe, 73–106. Novi Sad: CEIR.

Puljek-Shank, Amela, and Randy Puljek-Shank. 2008. "The Contribution of Trauma Healing to Peacebuilding in Southeast Europe." In *Peacebuilding in Traumatized Societies*, edited by Barry Hart, 155–83. Lanham, MD: University Press of America.

Spahić Šiljak, Zilka. 2015a. "Believers for Social Change: Bridging Secular Religious Divide in Bosnia and Herzegovina." *International Relations and Diplomacy* 3(10): 681–90.

———. 2015b. "Merhametli Peace Is Woman's Peace." In *Women and Peace in the Islamic World: Gender, Agency, and Influence*, edited by Yasmin Saikia and Chad Haines, 345–64. London: I. B. Tauris.

———. 2014. *Shining Humanity—Life Stories of Women Peace-builders in Bosnia and Herzegovina.* Newcastle: Cambridge Scholars Publishing.

———. 2013a. "Do It and Name It: Feminist Theology and Peacebuilding in Bosnia and Herzegovina." *Journal for Feminist Studies in Religion* 29(2): 178–86.

———. 2013b. "Women, Religion and Politics in Bosnia and Herzegovina." In *Religion, the Secular, and the Politics of Sexual Difference*, edited by Linell Cady and Tracy Fessenden, 121–36. New York: Columbia University Press.

Spahić-Šiljak, Zilka, and Dino Abazović. 2009. *Monoteističko Troglasje: uvod u judaizam, kršćanstvo i islam (Three Monotheistic Voices: An Introduction into Judaism, Christianity, and Islam).* Sarajevo: Rabic.

Spahić-Šiljak, Zilka, and Rebeka Jadranka Anić. 2009. *I Vjernice I Građanke (Women Believers and Citizens).* Sarajevo: TPO Foundation.

Spahić-Šiljak, Zilka, and Sabija Husić. 2011. *Countering Violence with Dialogue: Gender-based Violence and Multi-religious Dialogue.* Sarajevo: TPO Foundation.

Tanenbaum Center for Interreligious Understanding. 2007. "The Peacemakers in Action." In *Peacemakers in Action: Profiles of Religion in Conflict Resolution*, edited by David Little, 3–21. Cambridge: Cambridge University Press.

UNDP. 2009. "The Ties that Bind: Social Capital in Bosnia and Herzegovina." *National Human Development Report 2009*. Sarajevo: UNDP.

Volkan, Vamik. 1998. *Bloodlines: From Ethnic Pride to Ethnic Terrorism*. Boulder: Basic Books.

Weber, Max. 2015. "Politics as Vocation." In *Weber's Rationalism and Modern Society: New Translations on Politics, Bureaucracy, and Social Stratification*, edited and translated by Tony Waters and Dagmar Waters, 129–98. New York: Palgrave Macmillan.

5

Reconciliation in the Midst of Strife

Palestine

Zeina M. Barakat

While reconciliation is often understood as promoting peace and harmony in post-conflict situations (see Bieler et al. 2011; Bloomfield et al. 2003), this chapter explores reconciliation as it is pursued in the midst of strife/crisis/conflict, exemplified in the context of Palestine and Israel. I will argue that rather than waiting for an end to conflict, Palestinians and Israelis can get engaged with a reconciliation process that aims at building empathy, trust, and goodwill toward peace and coexistence. The model I employ adheres to the following ideal: creative and critical thinking opens the mind to a culture of balance and moderation, which in turn stirs the emotions of empathy, trust, compassion, and respect, ushering in cooperation and reconciliation; this, in turn, paves the way for negotiations in good faith and leads to a sustainable and peaceful resolution, political stability, and economic prosperity.

In the "Foreword" to Ralf Wüstenberg's *Political Dimension of Reconciliation*, Donald Shriver writes: "In the decade following the fall of the Berlin Wall in 1989, two countries—South Africa and Germany—attracted worldwide attention around the question: Can national societies, long riven with huge injustices and harms to their citizens, recover from these damages without repeating them under new regimes?" Shriver concludes: "What made world curiosity about Germany and South Africa so poignant was the apparent success of both countries in designing a political process for effecting 'reconciliation' between previously hostile, war-inclined groups of citizens" (Wüstenberg 2009, xii). The successful political transformation of South Africa in 1994, soon followed by the establishment of the Truth and Reconciliation Commission (TRC), enticed the introduction of the term *reconciliation* to other fields of inquiry, such as political science and social psychology. Frequently, the term *reconciliation* came to be applied to post-conflict states of affairs, be it after civil wars, genocides, mass killings, or other intractable conflicts (Bar-Simon-Tov 2004). In this chapter, I argue that reconciliation does not always have to be tied to post-conflict situations but can be inserted into ongoing conflicts.

Long associated with religion, reconciliation has become part of political idealism. Religion-based ethics mingled with political values and thus contributed to paving the way for concrete, nonviolent methods for effecting transitions from past civil alienation to present civil peace. The core meaning of reconciliation, held in the political field and in the religious arena, is moderation, coexistence, balance, justice, compromise, search for the golden mean, and taking the middle path (Covey 2011; Dajani Daoudi 2009).

Defining Reconciliation

Despite a recognizable core meaning, the term remains contested among scholars (Hamber and van der Merwe 1998). According to Arie Nadler, there is "definitional ambiguity." He writes: "While we all have concrete reconciliation-related memories, such as forgiving someone who has hurt us or apologizing to someone we have hurt, we do not have concrete memories of reconciliation. A second reason [for its ambiguity] is that the word 'reconciliation' describes both a process and an outcome, and authors have often used it without specifying whether they seek to define a reconciled intergroup reality or the way to get there" (Nadler 2012, 292).

The English term *reconciliation* has its etymological roots in the Latin *reconciliare*: *re-*/again combined with *conciliare*/make friendly. In most Germanic languages, the word for reconciliation—for example, the Swedish word *försoning*—has a Low German root, namely *sonen,* which means "to settle a strife." The *Swedish National Encyclopedia* defines *försoning* as "the re-establishment of peace and solidarity between divided peoples, in religion between deity and mankind" (Brounéus 2003, 4). Even though the Latin and German base words differ, they hold a similar meaning: the reestablishment of peace, friendship, or good relations. Thus, both refer to returning to a state that existed earlier, before a bond was broken.

Generally speaking, the word reconciliation is used to describe the process of creating good relationships between states, social groups, or individuals after incidents that destroyed normal relations between them. This can happen at the social as well as the political level (see contributions by Krondorfer and Tarusarira in this volume). Reconciliation can also be understood as the act of getting two things to be compatible with one another as well the reestablishment of civil relations after a conflict. We might have reconciliation with a former enemy, with our family, with our friends, or with ourselves. Some scholars have conceived reconciliation to mean "coming back together" or restoring mutual respect between two adversaries. Reconciliation is more than an ideal: it is both process and goal (Bloomfield 2003, 10–18). As a bottom-up process it also requires support from official institutions and strong leaders.

Daniel Bar-Tal defines reconciliation as "a psychological process for the formation of lasting peace" (2004, 11–12). In this perspective, past rivals come to mutual recognition and acceptance; they have vested interests and goals in developing peaceful relations and in establishing mutual trust, positive attitudes, sensitivity, and consideration for the other party's needs and interests. The transformation of beliefs, attitudes, and emotions regarding one's own group, the other group, and the relationship between them may take decades. "Reconciliation is not needed in all societies but only in those that have been subjected to protracted, intractable conflict; that is, conflicts in which the societies involved evolve a widely shared psychological repertoire that supports the adherence to the conflictive goals, maintain the conflict, delegitimize the opponent and thus negate the possibility of a peaceful resolution of the conflict and prevent the development of peaceful relations" (Bar-Tal and Bennink 2004, 4).

John Paul Lederach defines reconciliation as being constituted by both "a focus and a locus" (1997, 30). The focus of reconciliation is on building new and better relationships between former enemies. According to Lederach, relationships are both the root cause and the long-term solution of conflict. As a locus, Lederach argues, "reconciliation represents a space, a place or location of encounter, where parties to a conflict meet." In this place, the traumas of the past and the hopes for the future must be formulated and brought together by discussing issues of truth, forgiveness, justice, and peace. Reconciliation is often difficult, painful, and a thankless affair, as people attempt to overcome haunting memories of past atrocities.

It does not mean cheap peace or the giving up of rights, but necessarily includes truth and justice.

Johan Galtung defines reconciliation as "a theme with deep psychological, sociological, theological, philosophical, and profoundly human roots—and nobody really knows how to successfully achieve it" (2001, 4). Here, the question arises whether a political settlement must be reached first before reconciliation can take place, or whether reconciliation should be started in the midst of strive in order for trust and dialogue to emerge for conflict resolution. In the case of the the Arab-Israeli conflict, a political settlement had been reached at Camp David in 1978, but there was no real reconciliation on the human level between Egyptians and the Israelis. Moshe Sasson, the Israeli Ambassador to Egypt, who reflects on this issue in his book *Seven Years in the Land of the Egyptians* (1994), describes the difficult task of working as an Israeli diplomat in a hostile environment: though a political agreement had been reached, reconciliation on the ground remained elusive.

> [Reconciliation] applies to everyone. It is not just a process for those who suffered directly and those who inflicted the suffering, central though those people are. The attitudes and beliefs that underpin violent conflict spread much more generally through a community and must be addressed at that broad level. So, while there is a crucial individual element to reconciliation, there is also a community-wide element that demands a questioning of the attitudes, prejudices and negative stereotypes that we all develop about "the enemy" during violent conflict. This is because our definition of the enemy is rarely limited to a few politicians or fighters, but rather grows to encompass a whole community or a regime and all its supporters. Even those who have suffered or benefited little from the past absorb the beliefs of their community and their culture, and those beliefs can effectively block the reconciliation process if they are left unaddressed. (Bloomfield 2003, 13)

Reconciliation requires normalization of relations between people in conflict, and normalization, in turn, needs mutual recognition from all parties in the conflict, including the leadership and the people. As in the Egyptian-Israeli case of the Camp David agreement, it was not enough for the leadership to make peace without having the people on board.

Normalization cannot be understood as simply accepting a political settlement when the terms are unjust. For reconciliation and sustainable peace to take place it cannot demand a political settlement that favors only one side. In cases of power asymmetry, the more powerful party needs to take into consideration demands of justice and balance. Conflict over formation of memory of past tragedies and loss of loved ones, property, and identity render the conflict fiercer than traditional conflicts, where memories and narratives do not play such a central role (Mohanad Mustafa 2013). A case could be made that after World War I the victorious Allies overburdened defeated Germany with demands that eventually precipitated World War II. Reestablishing good relationships is hampered when a group's desires for justice are not addressed. The justice sought in reconciliation goes beyond retributive justice to include restorative justice (Tutu 1999).

Normalization does not imply accepting or rejecting the narrative of the other. It does, however, require that demeaning, demonizing, and stereotyping narratives should be discarded, particularly from the educational curriculum and the media, since such narratives are an essential component of the conflict that led to further escalation (Dajani and Barakat 2013). Civil society actors have a special role in achieving reconciliation between two parties because of their capacity to reach the hearts and minds of people on both sides. Bar-Tal (2000) emphasizes the significance of reciprocity in reconciliation systems: both parties to the conflict have to mutually recognize each other's interests and goals. Without reciprocity, reconciliation is meaningless. Since dialogue is a basic requirement for reconciliation, it is a two-way process. Otherwise, one group will dominate or impose on the other.

Some scholars distinguish between conciliation and reconciliation, such as Martin Leiner who makes a plea for a wider definition of reconciliation:

> As often political scientists and historians do, I would plead for a broad definition of reconciliation. Reconciliation in that broader sense is the reestablishment of "good" or at least "normal" relationships after a violent conflict like war, after mass atrocities like genocides, after crimes against humanity, or after other heavy injustices inflicted to one group by another. If there has never been a good relationship, I suggest using the term "conciliation." Conciliation requires learning more about the history and the culture of the others. Very often elements of reconciliation and conciliation have to be combined. (Leiner 2016, 31; see also Krog 1999)

Why Reconciliation?

Reconciliation has both symbolic and practical benefits: a spirit of good-will, trust, respect, and mutual recognition. The alternative is to remain in conflictual relationships or live in a hostile environment.

For society to function well, we must care for one another and try to understand one another. Reconciliation can be a spiritual path or a pragmatic choice. Regardless, it requires long-term efforts to create better relations between people after conflicts, and promises alternatives to continu-ing tensions, violence, and the destruction of lives through never-ending hostilities and bitterness. Demanding on both psychological and spiritual levels, I consider reconciliation in the midst of conflict a preferred option because it tries to bring peace at a time when it is most urgently needed.

As mentioned before, reconciliation is only possible if both conflict-ing parties are willing to reconcile. But there is no magical recipe that will make someone full of enmity easily switch to amity. Depending on the nature of the injury and its severity, reconciliation does not come without pain and agony. In some cases, angry people may not want to reconcile, and nothing that is said or done can change their minds. Hence, a basic desire to reconcile must be present among the conflicting parties, victims and perpetrators alike. This suggests that reconciliation is volun-tary; it cannot be forced on someone or imposed (Hamber and Grainne 2004). In other words, reconciliation requires cooperation and investment in improving broken relations.

Even third-party interventions will fail when there is no serious willingness to reconcile. For instance, in 2004 the majority of the Christian Greek-speaking inhabitants of southern Cyprus rejected a reunification with the Muslim pro-Turkish north. The European Union was inclined to accept as member state a reunified Cyprus, but the Greek Cypriots simply did not want it. Another example is the failed efforts of U.S. Secretary of State John Kerry to find some path toward reconciliation between Israel and Palestine.

One indicator for reconciliation is the restoration of trust. Having the capacity to start anew, human beings must be willing to close an old door if they want to open a new one. The future should be perceived as a positive option that is based on trust: trust in the beauty of life, trust in the coherence between word and action of the Other, trust in change, trust in moving ahead and leaving behind enmity and misgivings. There is no future without trust. What reconciliation has to achieve is *trust* between groups in conflict. A political process built on social trust is stronger and more effective than one lacking it. David Stevens (2004) observes that political institutions can only operate where there are relationships of trust. Trust, Putnam observes, is a virtue: "Virtuous citizens are helpful, respectful and trustful towards one another, even when they differ on matters of substance" (1993, 89). If voluntary associations are understood as sites to create conditions for community relations in a way that generates trust and cooperation between citizens, including high-level engagement between former protagonists in political processes, then they are conceptually and strategically positioned to facilitate post-violence transition and reconciliation (Tarusarira 2013). Reconciliation techniques shift the focus in two central ways: First, they take a grassroots approach, building agreement among the members of rival communities (and not only between leaders); second, they engage in a long-term view of dispute resolution (Bar-Siman-Tov 2004).

A Personal Perspective

As a Palestinian woman who has experienced the Palestinian/Israeli conflict firsthand, I have come to perceive reconciliation as a process of bonding, building trust, and bridging the gap between adversaries either in the midst of conflict or in post-conflict situations. Such a perspective ensures the sustainability of peaceful coexistence and avoids renewal of conflict. It is a way of enhancing understanding and rapport with the other, of renewing relationships so that people are able to coexist in peace and harmony.

I perceive reconciliation as a way of finding balance within oneself by moving ahead with life and leaving behind excess baggage of anger, bitterness, hurt, and resentment caused by others, whether on personal or national levels. It also includes, but is not limited to, forgiveness of those who have caused injury, pain, misery, and sorrow. Pierre Bourdieu's work has helped me to understand my experience of the conflict as one entangled within the gender field (a structured space with its own rules and schemes) and its accompanying habitus (a system of dispositions) and *doxa* (learned fundamental, deep founded unconscious beliefs and values) (Bourdieu 1990, 54). Like all societies, the Palestinian society has its own specific structures and rules. For example, it stipulates that women are subordinate to men (fathers, brothers, husbands, etc.), with a majority of women not even objecting to such mechanisms. Subordination, it seems, has been drilled into them. When men relate to women, they do so under the rules and schemes of the gender field, which are practiced every day and are imparted on men and women alike from childhood forward. Consequently, their dispositions toward each other are deeply rooted and perceived as fundamental. These schemes and rules have been absorbed and accepted to the extent of becoming foundational habits and frames of reference which are not inspected, questioned, or scrutinized.

As a young Palestinian woman, I often wondered what is worse: living under the constraints of a traditional and conservative society, which limits a woman's freedom and denies her personal rights, or living under the Israeli occupation, which denies Palestinians their human rights and to live in freedom and liberty with dignity, national identity, and statehood. Hence, I need reconciliation on both levels: between my people and me, and between my occupiers and me.

Having witnessed the first Intifada in 1987 as a five-year-old girl and the second Intifada in 2000 as a teenager, I have spent all my life living in an environment of enmity, hatred, violence, and bloodshed. Leaving home in the morning and heading to school, I had to cross checkpoints. Just going to classes was a traumatic daily experience. My heart was filled with anger, hate, and frustration against the Israeli occupiers: young army soldiers who imposed harsh measures and humiliation. Consequently, I never imagined I would be able to reconcile and reestablish normal relations with Israelis or Jews. My personal experiences were magnified by stories I have heard from my grandfather, my grandmother, other relatives, and my teachers regarding what they went through during the 1948 *Nakba* (Catastrophe) and the 1967 *Naksah* (Setback). Their stories of how they were deported from their homes in humiliation, how they lost their properties, and how they were deposed from their own precious land became my memories. Their narrative shaped my own perception in a way that made me blame and demonize the "other," perceiving the other as an inhuman perpetrator, occupier, and oppressor. Such a narrow prism of seeing the other dovetails with the societal creation of a negative psychological repertoire (Bar-Tal 2000).

In the Palestinian community, it was beyond the pale to consider peaceful options. Only a few had the courage to call for peace and reconciliation. The word *reconciliation* did not seem to exist in the Palestinian glossary. When I discussed politics with Israelis, it usually ended up in screaming matches and fights, believing at the same time that we engaged in dialogue. In reality, each of us practiced a monologue, with each side blaming the other for being insensitive to each other's feelings. We refused to hear the narrative of the other (Rotberg 2006). Neither of us had any intention to see things from the point of view of the other.

The secondary school I attended in Jerusalem left a significant impact on me. I was taught the Palestinian national collective narrative in our history classes, which focused on the Arab glories of the past and the Golden Age of the Islamic Empire. The textbooks narrated the struggle of our predecessors to regain our homeland, land of our forefathers and ancestors. The educational curriculum, at the time, taught us enmity and hatred for the other, depicting Israelis negatively as usurpers of the land and perpetrators of massacres. The lessons avoided introducing prospects of coexistence or living in harmony in peace with the other. Religious leaders in the community focused on how we should regain Palestine by *jihad* (fighting the occupier) in order to liberate our homeland.

I still recall when, in February 1994 during the holy month of Ramadan, I heard on the radio about the tragic massacre in the al-Ibrahimi Mosque in Hebron. The mosque houses the earthly remains of the religious patriarchs and matriarchs Abraham, Isaac, Jacob, Sarah, Rebecca, and Leah. In 1994, twenty-nine Palestinian Muslim worshippers were killed and more than a hundred others were injured when American-Israeli physician Baruch Goldstein opened fire at Muslim prayers. I was deeply moved. Pain crushed my heart, tears filled my eyes, and feelings of anger overpowered me. It felt as if I was exploding inside. How could such an atrocity be committed in one of the holiest places for both Jews and Muslims? A place where people worship, pray, and meditate? Why were people who did not commit any wrongdoing shot by an Israeli physician who had pledged in his profession to heal people and not to kill them? In that moment, I felt the urge to go out in the street and stab the first Israeli I would encounter. I was ready to do anything for revenge. Demonstrations and protests broke out everywhere in the country. I begged my mom and dad to go out and take part. They refused because they felt that as a young girl no one would guarantee for my safety.

At that moment, I felt I was doubly oppressed, both from the occupiers and my family. I hated being a woman since my brothers did not need to ask for permissions to do anything. Being a Palestinian, I needed permission from the Israelis to move around; being a woman, I needed permission from my parents to leave the house. I found myself asking: Why did God create me a woman? Why? Is it because I am a

woman that I cannot freely express my anger? Or is it that my parents
fear for my safety in case violence erupts? Yes, I was that girl ready to
fight, willing to sacrifice everything for the sake of my country Palestine.
Was this due to being a teenager full of energy, enthusiasm, passion, and
patriotism? Or had I been socialized to feel in a certain way by my sur-
roundings, the family, school, peers, and social media?

The issue of reconciliation remained blurred until I joined the
American Studies Master program at al-Quds University in 2003. The
liberal education I got there opened my mind and alerted me to the need
of balance in my search for truth. It made me question the accepted collective national narrative. As a student, and later as a teaching assistant at
the American Studies program, I began to realize that fighting violence
with violence is a vicious circle because violence only breeds violence. I
also came to believe that using violence would only give the colonizer a
pretext to perpetuate the occupation, to imprison innocent people without
trial, to confiscate more Palestinian lands, and to kill. I understood how
the asymmetry of power was used to the advantage of one people to
subjugate our people. I also learnt to broaden my understanding of the
psyche of "the other." This builds upon a line from the movie *To Kill a
Mockingbird* (1962). In the movie, Atticus Finch turns to his daughter Scout
and says: "You never really understand a person until you consider things
from his point of view. . . . Until you climb inside of his skin and walk
around in it." It is the same idea that the Japanese call *oyakudachi,* which
means, "walking in the shoes of the other." I learnt of the importance
of looking at the other person as if you are the other person. Only then
can you truly understand how that person feels and why they feel things
in particular ways (Barakat 2014).

In 2007, I took an active role in supporting the founding of the
Wasatia movement, which called for the promotion of moderation, reconciliation, balance, tolerance, acceptance of the other, justice, temperance,
and democracy. This introduced me to the Aristotelian Golden Mean and
to the idea of the Middle Way.

Embarking on joint Palestinian-Israeli people-to-people activities
was a deep learning experience for me. The *Seeds of Peace* at the camp
in Maine (USA) enriched my life and introduced me to the inspiring
work of its founder John Wallach and his book, *The Enemy Has a Face:
The Seeds of Peace Experience* (2000). As I continued my education in
other joint ventures, I became acquainted with the "other" when working with them as colleagues in academic projects. I benefited from the

liberal thinking of Israeli professor Eyal Winter from Hebrew University, where we cooperated on implementing a joint project on game theory. I also learned more about the "other" when I was the Palestinian coordinator of the American Democratic Partnership project, which was implemented during a period of three years. The project brought together fifteen Palestinian students from the American Studies graduate program at Al-Quds University, fifteen Israeli students from Tel Aviv University, and ten American students from Oberlin College in Ohio for three weeks of studying American democratic culture in Oberlin and Washington, D.C. The students arrived with preconceived ideas but left with memories of warmth and friendship.

I recall a discussion with a Jewish friend studying at Friedrich Schiller University in Jena, Germany, whose grandparents were Holocaust victims. He had lived his entire life in Germany (his land of birth). My friend said that Israel was once the land of his dreams that inspired him with ancient longings and promises. Recently, though, the daily news about ongoing atrocities, injustices, discrimination, and racism got him disenchanted with his dream. He was reminded of the injustices committed against Palestinians by the documentary film *Checkpoints*. He felt much anger and rage, asking himself, "Why do people become violent and how can we change that?" These thoughts kept haunting him for days.

The same thoughts have been haunting me for a long time. It is not easy for someone dreaming of the return to the land of milk and honey to see that his people have achieved their success at the expense of another people. The victims have become perpetrators, inflicting harm and injustice they themselves (or their families) had suffered during the Holocaust. I was asking myself: "Why do we do this to each other? Why don't we live as human beings in peace, harmony, and happiness away from all the violence?" I was thinking of life and death. It seems to me that every human being is entitled to have the opportunity to live a happy and fulfilling life. We live for a limited period of time, and at the end all we take with us to the grave are the good deeds we have done during our lifetime. My friend reminded me: "I am not an Israeli, and the terminology 'my people' is very difficult for me. . . . I am a human being: I love Jewish culture and Jewish religion; I love the Arabic culture and Islamic religion. But what I am seeing every day is that the people I love are destroying more and more the values I cherish and that I was raised to believe in."

His general point is supported by Scott Appleby's idea about "ambivalence of the sacred" (2000). He asserts that religion has the capacity to generate responses ranging from violent to nonviolent militancy. Appleby was influenced by the work of German theologian and philosopher Rudolph Otto. In *The Idea of the Holy* (1958), Otto presents the sacred as project-ing a numinous quality that inspires simultaneous dread and fascination in the subject. Rene Girard's *Violence and the Sacred* (2005) also supports the ambivalence thesis. He asserts that religion authorizes and restrains violence. It is ambivalent. It is a free-floating phenomenon (Beckford 1990), like a knife used to cut bread to eat or to stab someone to kill. Disenchanted with Israel, my friend also concurs with Aslan's critique that there is a need to reform certain elements of Islam that have been manipulated. "It took many years to cleanse Arabia of its 'false idols.' It will take many more to cleanse Islam of its new false idols—bigotry and fanaticism—worshipped by those who have replaced Muhammad's original vision of tolerance and unity with their own ideals of hatred and discord. But the cleansing is inevitable, and the tide of reform cannot be stopped. The Islamic Reformation is already here" (Aslan 2011, 292).

Before I started studying for my doctorate program at Ben Gurion University in Beer Sheva, Israel, I spent one year at Hebrew University in Jerusalem to learn Hebrew. At Ben Gurion University, studying with Israeli professors and students helped broaden my perspective about the "other" and transformed my way of thinking by deconstructing my stereotypes and demonized images. I moved from hate and enmity to reconciliation and cooperation. This is not to imply that I no longer felt strongly about my Palestinian identity or my national rights, hopes, and aspiration. If reconciliation is a focus, as Lederach argues, my focus changed in terms of a willingness to share the land in peace rather than continuing to live in conflict. In the midst of the conflict I began to be hopeful that small steps can be taken to reach out to the other, an idea that got strengthened when I encountered the *Hölderlin Perspective.*

The *Hölderlin Perspective*:
Reconciliation in the Midst of Conflict

Should the process of reconciliation begin at the end of a conflict? Or should it be initiated in the midst of conflict? Conventionally, reconciliation is viewed as possible only in the post-conflict phase. It is generally assumed that it occurs at the end of conflict and after a successful peacebuilding process. Since the Israeli-Palestinian conflict is generally perceived as not capable of being resolved anytime soon, reconciliation does not seem to be a realistic option for Israelis and Palestinians. However, learning about other conflicts in various regions of the world has given me hope that we can already start working toward reconciliation when we adopt the Hölderlin perspective as a conceptual tool.

Even in post-conflict situations, reconciliation is not an easy process, as can be seen in films such as *Long Walk to Freedom* (2013) and *Invictus* (2009), about South African leader Nelson Mandela's journey from being in jailed for twenty-seven years to being elected president of South Africa. Though he personally was able to overcome his strong feelings of revenge, hate, bitterness, and enmity, he faced the challenge to convince his people to believe in reconciliation and coexistence and to have the courage to call for an end to violent conflict.

When I joined the doctorate program at Friedrich-Schiller University in Germany, I was introduced to the Hölderlin Perspective—an approach in peace research named after the German poet Friedrich Hölderlin (1770–1843). In the last pages of his novel *Hyperion* he wrote, "*Versöhnung ist mitten im Streit und alles Getrennte findet sich wieder* [Reconciliation is in the middle of strife and all things separated find each other again]" (Hölderlin 1998, 760). Hölderlin calls for reconciliation in the midst of conflict (or strife) rather than restrict it to post-conflict peacebuilding situations.

For Palestinians and Israelis, this is a most ambitious endeavor. The challenge is how to apply this creative concept of "reconciliation in the midst of strife" to the Palestinian-Israeli conflict. How can we endorse reconciliation in the midst of the conflict at a time when enmity and hatred are high in both camps and a wall separates us? It is like swimming against the tide to convince Palestinians and Israelis to adopt the Hölderlin perspective. In a seminar on reconciliation at Friedrich-Schiller University, I was introduced to the documentary film *Pray Back the Devil to Hell* (2008). The film tells of the struggle in Liberia to end the civil strife, led by ordinary mothers, grandmothers, aunts, and daughters, both Christian and Muslim. Getting united and armed with the courage of their convictions, these women played a major role in achieving reconciliation between the factions fighting in the civil war. I was inspired by the dedication and spirit of those women who took on the warlords and the regime of the dictator Charles Taylor in the midst of a brutal civil war.

Amazingly, in 2003 they won a once unimaginable peace accord for their shattered country. In one memorable scene, the women barricaded the location of a meeting in which peace talks got stalled and they refused to move until a deal was reached. Their struggle culminated in Taylor's exile and the rise of Africa's first female head of state, Ellen Johnson Sirleaf. I asked myself: Could women tormented by conflict achieve the same results if we were to adopt similar tactics in the Israeli-Palestine conflict?

The film inspired me to create a group on Facebook entitled "Women for Peace and Reconciliation." Today, its membership has reached nearly two thousand Palestinian, Israeli, and international women calling for peace and reconciliation. As a Palestinian woman, I see reconciliation being hampered by the persistence of traumatic memories and resistance to reopening wounds of the past. Learning to forgive those who hurt us can help us manage anger, cut stress, and improve relations. Forgiveness, and a readiness to move on, can be powerful antidotes to hate and bitterness (Tutu 1999). We should not fear to forgive. South African psychologist Gobodo-Madikizela (2006) reminds us that the notion that some evil deeds are simply unforgivable does not capture the complexity and rich-ness of all social contexts within which gross evil is committed. There is a need to engage with the social context, in this case the Palestine/Israel context to dig out the possibilities of forgiveness.

Generally speaking, reconciliation is best when the luggage of the past is left in the past. It requires discarding injuries of the past in order to move forward. However, leaving the past behind does not mean to forgive and forget, but to forgive and remember. To remember does not mean to keep the grudge or the hate but to prevent new cycles of injury. In the midst of conflict, the past is integrated in the present.

As a Palestinian, I have reconciled with the idea that, politically, Israel as a Jewish state is here to stay; I also think that Israel must reciprocate by reconciling with the Palestinians and acknowledge the State of Palestine as an essential part in fulfilling the quest for Palestinian national identity. Such a reciprocal move would fulfill the United Nations 1947 Partition Resolution of creating two states, a Jewish state and an Arab state. The longer the Israeli occupation continues and Palestinian demands remain unaddressed, the more the ground continues to remain fertile for radical-ism and violence. Desmond Tutu asserts in *No Future without Forgiveness*: "True security would come when all the inhabitants of the Middle East, that region so revered by so many, believed that their human rights and dignity were respected and upheld, when true justice prevailed" (1999, 216).

True reconciliation is not cheap. It cost God the death of His only begotten Son. . . . People are not being asked to forget. On the contrary, it is important to remember, so that we should not let such atrocities happen again. Forgiveness does not mean condoning what has been done. It means taking what has happened seriously and not minimizing it; drawing out the sting in the memory that threatens to poison our entire existence. It involves trying to understand the perpetrators and so have empathy, to try to stand in their shoes, and to appreciate the sort of pressures and influences that might have brought them to do what they did. (Tutu 1999, 219)

As I argued earlier, reconciliation has practical elements. To create an environment for reconciliation, we need to work on improving the living conditions of the Palestinian people. The conflict has destroyed the livelihoods of many people. There is a need to secure basic human needs for families, including providing health insurance and adequate housing, and enjoying basic human rights. The high rate of unemployment among Palestinian youth has led to radicalization and to adoption of violence as a way of life. Without improving the dire economic conditions, hopes of reconciliation for the majority of the Palestinians remains dim and blurred, overshadowed by the daily struggle for survival. By opening the job market and reviving the economy, the majority of people will become productive and invest in their future, and thus will have no need for extremism. The political reality of the continuing occupation, however, will hamper daily economic activities by its strict control of exit and entry of goods and people. Economic growth goes hand in hand with the availability of human resources that provide knowledge, skills, and values to implement moderation, empathy, and justice in the midst of conflict. There is an urgent need to create an educational curriculum that teaches our children the skills for ethical thinking and acting. In *The Self beyond Itself*, Heidi M. Ravven addresses the educational issue of how to teach our children to be ethical. She focuses on helping young people understand the importance of ethical values and virtues, "developing young people of good character who become responsible and caring citizens" (2013, 6).

Ravven offers a simple example of how education can build up the moral character of the youth. In one particular school, students and teachers made a large colorful ceramic mural for the purpose of "building character," a line written in ceramic letters at the top. Embedded in the mural were the values that focused on the teaching and daily activities of the school. Thus, values representing the pillars of the community were inculcated at an early age, such as fairness, respect, responsibility, perseverance, honesty, helpfulness, patience, and good manners. Each month, students and teachers chose one of these values and planned activities around it. They read stories pertaining to the selected value and practiced it in their daily and school life.

As regards this kind of education, we cannot overlook the dimension of gender. As mentioned earlier, as a young Palestinian woman I found myself trapped between being a woman and being a Palestinian. Struggling with being a Palestinian, I also had to battle as a woman, rescuing myself from the social and cultural trappings that hindered my participation in the public sphere. My desire to play a part in the conflict was constrained by the social mores and cultural perspectives on what women are expected to do. Women, however, possess a lot of potential that can be harnessed for facilitating peace and reconciliation. Children in schools should learn this at a tender age so that girls and women are accorded space to contribute to such endeavors.

Another practical factor concerning reconciliation is improving the efficiency of various religious institutions, specifically the church, mosque, and synagogue. They must commit to and engage in transformational and reconciliatory activities by preaching on shared values and by raising awareness among their constituents that dialogue and cooperation rather than conflict should dominate interfaith relations. Religion possesses the capacity to generate peaceful responses to conflict.

Related to religious concerns is ethnicity. The film *Live and Become* (2005) documents how Israel brought Ethiopian Jewish emigrants to the Promised Land, the land of their dreams. Although they were told that they are now free and liberated, and they were provided with basic provisions such as food, shelter, schooling, and jobs, I could not help but observe that Israelis continued to view the Ethiopian newcomers as outsiders because of their color and ethnic background. Justice and human dignity were lacking, resulting in public demonstrations by Ethiopian Jews. The racism and discrimination they experienced within the Israeli community had started with disrespect to Palestinians and now spread to the Ethiopians—a virus that will no doubt continue to infect the whole society in the coming years.

Israeli novelist Amos Oz asks, "What is the right on the Zionist side?" He responds:

It is the right of tragedy of a drowning man who takes hold of the only available raft, even if it means pushing aside the legs of the people who are already sitting on it so as to make some room for himself . . . so long as he only asks them to move up, and does not demand that they get off the raft or drown in the sea. A Zionism which asks for a part of the land is morally justified; a Zionism which asks the Palestinians to renounce their identity and give up the whole land is not justified. I blame the Palestinian national movement for insensitivity to the suffering of the Jews, for callousness (it's a European problem which doesn't concern the Arabs) and for lack of imagination; but I do not blame them for refusing to welcome the Jews with a deferential bow and hand over the keys of the land. I blame the militant Zionists for disregarding the identity population; but I cannot blame the Jews for seeing the land as their last possible life-raft. All these considerations lead me to accept the moral (and not merely pragmatic) rightness of the idea of partitioning the land between its two nations. The task of fixing the borders of the partitioned land I leave to the politicians. (Oz 1994, 39)

What troubles the Palestinian people is, of course, not a unique fate. When I saw the film *Aghet* (2010; "catastrophe" in Armenian), which documents the Armenian Genocide of 1915, I was shocked to realize that while Americans and Germans were watching from balconies the drums of the war, 1.5 million people were murdered. This genocide may have inspired Hitler to adopt the same model against different people in the Holocaust, expecting that the memory of this genocide would fade away with time, just as it did in the case of the Armenian genocide. Genocide breeds genocide. To stop it, the moderate silent majority needs to stand up, defend what is right, and have the moral courage to speak out.

I like to share a personal moment. It pertains to the fond memory of my younger brother Fares. He passed away in 2007 due to a motorcycle accident. Everybody—my students, extended family, friends, and neighbors—came to share their condolences. At night, I received a call from my Israeli friends who were with me at the *Seeds of Peace* camp in Maine, asking me for my address and how to get to our house in Beit Hannina, a neighborhood of Jerusalem. I was stunned when, the next day, four of my Israeli friends came up the stairs of our house to give condolences to my family and me. Yes, I was shaken by their visit because, in my experience, Israelis usually avoid going to Palestinians neighborhoods out of security concerns. After that visit, I felt proud to say I have Israeli friends and to work for reconciliation in the midst of conflict. In the end, we are all human beings, and the only thing separating us is politics.

Fear, Trust, and Reconciliation

When Israelis hold maximalist positions, they fear that they may lose their basic sense of security, freedom, integrity, and a positive self-image. They may also fear to lose the "good life" if they allow Palestinians to enjoy their own good life. Any denial of basic needs makes peace elusive. It seems that both the Israeli and Palestinian societies have learned over time to adapt to and cope with an abnormal, violent, and insecure status quo through various social and psychological mechanisms.

In *Made for Goodness* (2010), Desmond and Mpho Tutu remark that Palestinians face Israelis across hopeless barriers of mistrust. From my perspective, I believe the same is true for Israelis. They fear that the Arab states may inflict on them the same harm that had suffered under Nazi Germany—and hence they have developed a "never again" attitude. But this mistrust, which divides both sides, makes progress toward peace difficult. Neither side is ready to put differences on the table and then move on to see clearly the realities on the ground and change them.

The collective memory of both peoples has created clashing narratives about their respective histories, which, in turn, affect emotions and decision-making capabilities. Their selectively constructed narratives have become framed as stories of victimization and dehumanization, including the stereotyping of the other. Such narratives are sustained and repeated in social institutions such as family, schools, the media, peer groups, friends, and places of worship. These narratives demand from their constituents conformity, loyalty, a readiness to make sacrifices, and positive emotions toward one's in-group while excluding, mistrusting, and disliking the out-group. When, on a rare occasion, Palestinian teachers and students have visited the Auschwitz concentration camp, they could experience the suffering of the other. These are difficult visits, and people who accompany such groups, such as Mohammed Dajani Daoudi, might not be well received by the public in Palestine; Daoudi, for example, was accused of brainwashing his students and labeled a traitor by members of his community (Tiffanie 2015).

The need for security creates fear, fear creates conflict, and conflict generates emotions of extreme mistrust that does not lead to negotiations to end conflict. "If a group chooses instead to follow a path of moderation, that is, if they are willing to cooperate and potentially accept solutions that grant concessions to their opponent, they may actually achieve a great deal more in terms of their own deep self-interests, however that may be measured" (Knoepffler and O'Malley 2016, 20). When Israelis and Palestinians choose to follow a path of moderation and reconciliation, they will be in a better position to end the long and seemingly intractable conflict than when they stay on the well-trodden path of fear and mistrust.

Concluding Remarks

Creating a moderate culture characterized by cooperation, understanding, tolerance, acceptance, temperance, rationality, and dialogue can help in ushering in a liberal, more open-minded setting that promises to resolve conflicts peacefully. Reconciliation in the midst of conflict helps to create an environment of trust and cooperation; it can engender people-to-people initiatives, move toward the humanization of the other, and allow expressions of empathy for the other. Practicing reconciliation in the midst of conflict is also a practicing of democracy, in which human rights and the rule of law are respected, replacing, hopefully, authoritarianism, anarchy, corruption, and nepotism with political stability, economic development, and social prosperity.

Palestinians must start where others have ended; not end where others have started. *Palestine of the past is part of the history of the past.* If we do not seek reconciliation, our hopes for the establishment of the State of Palestine will fade away. Israel should also build bridges across the Middle East by acknowledging the Palestinian suffering and their rights for self-determination and liberty. Those who cling to violence and extremism will have to become of lesser significance. Spreading a culture of moderation aims to promote a permanent shift in psychosocial thinking that it is conducive to social conflict transformation. The peace train is rolling (Abu-Sharif and Mahnaimi 1995).

Works Cited

Abu-Sharif, Bassam, and Uzi Mahnaimi. 1995. *Best of Enemies: The Memoirs of Bassam Abu-Sharif and Uzi Mahnaimi*. Boston: Little, Brown.

Appleby, R. Scott. 2000. *The Ambivalence of the Sacred: Religion, Violence, and Reconciliation*. Lanham, MD: Rowman and Littlefield.

Aslan, Reza. 2011. *No God but God: The Origins, Evolution, and Future of Islam*. New York: Random House.

Assefa, Hizkias. 2005. "Reconciliation, Challenges, Responses and the Role of Civil Society." In *People Building Peace 2, Successful Stories of Civil Society*. Published in association with the European Centre for Conflict Prevention, 637–45.

Barakat, Zeina. 2014. "A Palestinian Student Defends Her Visit to Auschwitz," *The Atlantic* (April 28). http://www.theatlantic.com/internatioal/archive/2014/04/a-palestinian-student-defends-her-visit-to-auschwitz/361311/; accessed October 2, 2015.

Bar-Tal, Daniel. 2000. "From Intractable Conflict through Conflict Resolution to Reconciliation: Psychological Analysis." *Political Psychology* 21: 351–65.

———, and G. H. Bennink. 2004. "The Nature of Reconciliation as an Outcome and as a Process." In *From Conflict Resolution to Reconciliation*, edited by Yaacov Bar-Siman-Tov, 11–38. Oxford: Oxford University Press. Also published in *Politika* 9 (2002): 9–34 (Hebrew).

Bar-Siman-Tov, Yaacov. 2004. *From Conflict Resolution to Reconciliation*. New York: Oxford University Press.

Beckford, James. 1990. "The Sociology of Religion and Social Problems." *Sociological Analysis* 51(1): 1–14.

Bieler, Andrea, Christian Bingel, and Hans-Martin Gutmann. 2011. *After Violence: Religion, Trauma, and Reconciliation*. Leipzig: Evangelische Verlagsanstalt.

Bloomfield, David, Tersa Barnes, and Luc Huyse, eds. 2003. *Reconciliation after Violent Conflict: A Handbook*. Stockholm: International IDEA.

Bourdieu, Pierre. 1990. "Structures, Habitus, Practices." In *The Logic of Practice*, 52–79. Stanford: Stanford University Press.

Brounéus, Karen. 2003. *Reconciliation Theory and Practice for Development Cooperation*. http://www.pcr.uu.se/digitalAssets/66/c_66768-l_1-k_reconciliation--theory-and-practice.pdf; accessed November 30, 2015.

———. 2007. *Reconciliation and Development*. http://www.researchgate.net/publication/23777948_Reconciliation_and_Development; accessed November 29, 2015.

Daoudi, Dajani M. 2009. *Wasatia: The Spirit of Islam*. Jerusalem: Wasatia Publishing.

———, and Barakat, Zeina. 2013. "Israelis and Palestinians: Contested Narratives." *Israel Studies* 18(2) (Summer): 53–69.

———, et al. 2016. *Teaching Empathy and Reconciliation in Midst of Conflict*. Jerusalem and Jena: Wasatia Press.

Galtung, Johan. 2001. "After Violence, Reconstruction, Reconciliation, and Resolution: Coping with Visible and Invisible Effects of War and Violence." In *Reconciliation, Justice, and Coexistence: Theory and Practice*, edited by Mohammed Abu-Nimer, 3–23. Lanham, MD: Lexington Books.

Girard, René. 2005. *Violence and the Sacred*. London; New York: Continuum.

Gobodo-Madikizela, Pumla. 2006. *A Human Being Died That Night: Forgiving Apartheid's Chief Killer*. London: Portobello Books.

Hamber, Brandon, and Hugo van der Merwe. 1998. "What Is This Thing Called Reconciliation?" *Center for the Study of Violence and Reconciliation, Reconciliation in Review* 1(1).

———. "After the Truth and Reconciliation Commission." Paper presented at the Goedgedacht forum, Cape Town (March 1998). http://www.csvr.org.za/articles/artrcb&h.htm.

Hamber, Brandon, and Kelly Grainne. 2004. *Reconciliation: A Working Definition*. http://cain.ulst.ac.uk/dd/papers/dd04recondef.pdf; accessed November 29, 2015.

Hölderlin, Friedrich. 1998. *Sämtliche Werke und Briefe*. Vol. 1. Edited by Michael Knaupp. Darmstadt: Wissenschaftliche Buchgesellschaft.

Knoepfler, Nikolaus, and Martin O'Malley. 2016. "Wasatia: A Way to Enduring Peace in Palestine." In *Teaching Empathy and Reconciliation in Midst of Conflict*, 19–27. Jerusalem and Jena: Wasatia Academic Institute.

Krog, Antjie. 1999. *Country of My Skull*. London: Vintage.

Lederach, John Paul. 1997. *Building Peace: Sustainable Reconciliation in Divided Societies*. Washington, DC: U. S. Institute of Peace.

Leiner, Martin. 2016. *Teaching Empathy and Reconciliation in Midst of Conflict*. Jerusalem and Jena: Wasatia Press.

Mohanad Mustafa, As'ad Ghanem. 2013. "The Israeli Negotiation Strategy under Netanyahu: Settlement without Reconciliation." *International Journal for Conflict Management* 24: 265–83.

Nadakarni, Mangesh V. 2011. *Ethics for Our Times: Essays in Gandhian Perspective*. New Delhi and Oxford: Oxford University Press.

Nadler, Arie. 2012. "Intergroup Reconciliation: Definitions, Processes, and Future Directions." In *The Oxford Handbook of Intergroup Conflict*, edited by L. R. Tropp, 291–309. New York: Oxford University Press.

Otto, Rudolph. 1958. *The Idea of the Holy: An Inquiry into the Non-Rational Factor in the Idea of the Divine and its Relation to the Rational*. Translated by John W. Harvey. New York: Oxford University Press.

Oz, Amos. 1994. *Israel, Palestine and Peace*. London: Vintage.

Putnam, Robert D. 1993. *Making Democracy Work: Civic Traditions on Modern Italy*. Princeton: Princeton University Press.

Ravven, Heidi M. 2013. *The Self beyond Itself: An Alternative History of Ethics in Brain Sciences and the Myth of Free Will*. New York: The New Press.

Rotberg Robert. 2006. *Israeli and Palestinian Narratives of Conflict: History's Double Helix*. Bloomington: Indiana University Press.

———, and Dennis Thompson. 2000. *Truth v. Justice: The Morality of Truth Commissions*. Princeton: Princeton University Press.

Sasson, Moshe. 1994. *Saba' Sanawat fi Bilad al-Massryeen* [*Seven Years in the Land of the Egyptians*]. Cairo and Damascus: Dar al-Kitab al-Arabi. (Originally published 1993 in Hebrew, translated into Arabic 1994).

Schaap, Andrew. 2005. *Political Reconciliation*. New York: Routledge.

Stevens, David. 2004. *The Land of Unlikeness: Explorations into Reconciliation*. Dublin: The Columba Press.

Tarusarira, Joram. 2013. "Civil Society and Generation of Trust in Zimbabwe." *A Journal of African Politics, Development and International Affairs* 40(2): 140–61.

Tiffanie, Wen. 2015. "Journey to the Other: Interview with Mohammed S. Dajani," https://www.guernicamag.com/interviews/journey-to-the-other/; accessed August 14, 2015.

Tutu, Desmond. 1999. *No Future without Forgiveness*. London: Rider.

———, and Mpho Tutu. 2010. *Made For Goodness*. London: Rider.

Wallach, John. 2000. *The Enemy Has a Face: The Seeds of Peace Experience*. Washington, DC: United States Institute of Peace.

Wüstenberg, Ralf. 2009. *The Political Dimension of Reconciliation: A Theological Analysis of Ways of Dealing with Guilt during the Transition to Democracy in South Africa and (East) Germany*. Grand Rapids: Eerdmans.

6

No Future without a Shared Ethos

Reconciling Palestinian and Israeli Identities

AVNER DINUR

> Forgiving and being reconciled are not about pretending that things
> are other than they are. It is not patting one another on the back
> and turning a blind eye to the wrong. True reconciliation exposes
> the awfulness, the abuse, the pain, the degradation, the truth. It could
> even sometimes make things worse. It is a risky undertaking but in
> the end it is worthwhile.
>
> —Archbishop Desmond Tutu, *No Future without Forgiveness*

In collective conflicts, not only armed forces are clashing but also identities.
Reconciliation studies are well aware of how identities cause conflicts
and suggest methods for dealing with identity as a major component in
conflicts. These studies, however, say little about the content of each collective identity. If identities need to be taken into account in reconciliation,
as these studies show, and if indeed any possible solution to a conflict
needs to be based on the specific identities that are clashing, then merely
pointing to the role of identities in conflict is insufficient with regard to
reconciliation. Only when the warring sides come to an understanding
of how their respective identities need to change, and also which parts
of their identities should not or cannot change, is it possible for them
to look at the wrongdoings of the past and examine the way they see
themselves in the present and future. The art of reconciling conflicts needs
to be nourished with insights from the field of identity research.

This chapter is about the need to change the stories we tell ourselves in order to reconcile conflicts in general, and the Palestinian-Israeli conflict in particular. In the first part, I argue that identities can be reconciled only through the shaping of a common ethos; a new story needs to emerge that both sides can agree on, a story that includes parts (and only parts) of the original identities involved in the conflict. I then argue that reconciliation is based on two contradictory moves that actually complement each other: Reconciliation as recognition of the other's ethos, and reconciliation as a demand presented to the other side to change their ethos. In the last part of this chapter, I offer a few preliminary cultural-political suggestions for the content of a future shared ethos for Israelis and Palestinians.

I want to begin with two preliminary notes, one on the main terms I am employing in this chapter and the other on what is at stake for me from a personal perspective.

Three terms are central to this chapter: *narrative, ethos,* and *identity.* In general, identities can be seen as perspectives people have in the present about the past and about the future. If we wish to reconcile conflicting identities, it is sometimes needed to be aware of the direction of our gaze: Is it directed at the past, the present, or the future? Being aware of this may lead us to use different terms that actually serve a similar need: to tell the world and to tell ourselves who we are. The term *narrative*—or metanarrative and master narrative[1]—usually refers to the past. Narratives are what Susan Dwyer calls "autobiographies of collectives" (1999, 87), stories about whatever has happened in the past and upon which we construct the way we see ourselves in the present. "Ethos" can be defined as the narrative of the present, "a complex of common social beliefs that creates an orientation about the present and the future for a specific society" (Bar-Tal 2007, 34). An ethos is a story that holds us together and that keeps us united. "Identity," finally, can be described as a "self-in-relation-to-the-world" (Northtrup 1989, 55). Identity has the dual function of identification (telling the world who we are) and differentiation (telling the world who we are not). An additional observation, close but different, shows that identity contributes both to uniqueness (my identity denotes who I, and only I, am) and to similarity (my identity is the way in which I am identical with others). Identification and differentiation, uniqueness and similarity, are all human needs which find fulfilment through stories people tell themselves and others. Although narrative, ethos, and identity can be differentiated, for the purpose of this chapter they will be used almost synonymously because the main question here is what kind of change these stories have to go through in order to reconcile conflicts.

As to the issue of what is at stake for me, I like to profess that I am not pursuing the ideas presented in this chapter from the perspective of a cold, objective analysis of conflict. Although I employ theoretical and analytical frameworks to understand reconciliation, I see this study as an existential journey serving a personal need—to explore my collective identity and see in what way it needs to change in order to make room for peace. This is a pressing question that is reflected in my daily life. Sderot, my hometown, has been under attack by missiles from Gaza for more than fifteen years. My house has been hit twice. My family and I live in a situation that can be described equally as post-traumatic and as an ongoing traumatization. Writing about reconciliation from a town under constant bomb threat leads to a certain degree of urgency: I may not have the time or patience to wait for a well-structured solution to solve the conflict. At any moment my writing can be interrupted by sirens that alert me to incoming missiles and force my family to run and seek shelter.

Writing from Sderot also means writing from within a surrounding in which ideas about peace and reconciliation may sound absurd. Residents of Sderot are very skeptical about the chances of any solution to the Palestinian-Israeli conflict. Since they have been threatened for so long, most people around me wish the Israeli government to use more drastic measures and solve the Gaza problem once and for all by force. I do not blame them, because just like most of them I feel this situation has to stop. However, the story they have in mind about how the constant threat from Gaza can be stopped or how the situation got started is quite different from the views I hold. Living in such an environment affects not only me but also my children. They have been variously called "traitors" and "Arab-lovers" (it is amazing to see how easily love can turn into a negative word) by their fellow Israeli schoolmates when they expressed their understanding (influenced by me) of current events, an understanding that challenges the narrative they hear from their teachers and other children. This is what this chapter is about: challenging a narrative and changing an ethos.

The Challenge of Changing an Ethos

Many peace-seekers and activists base their claims on universal ideas and on human rights concerns, and therefore believe that issues of identity are merely employed as tools of manipulation that would justify one group's imagined superiority over the other (Bartos and Wehr 2002,

43). Universalists believe that we should abandon our ethos and get rid of narratives, or at least reduce the impact of our narratives on rational decision making. They advise us to condemn passionate nationalists and to promote "civic nationalism" in lieu of "ethnic nationalism" (Ignatieff 1993, 249). In contrast to this universal tendency, my understanding of reconciliation goes hand in hand with Desmond Tutu's insight quoted in the epigraph above. It is based on the belief that only through a serious examination of our own ethos and the ethos of the other can there be a true and long-lasting reconciliation. Universalists might ask: Why do we need to be reconciled with the ethos of the other? Why can't we ignore the past and reconcile with the other simply on the basis of a common humanity? From Tutu I learned that the universalist approach is prob- lematic because it does not try to reconcile with real people, but with imagined entities that supposedly have no past. If people of one group say, "We are reconciled with you, but we totally reject your ethos; we think that the way you describe the past and the present is a total lie," what they are actually saying is that they are not yet brave enough to take the separate identities seriously. In such a case, reconciliation is reduced to an understanding that perceives the present disconnected from the past, as if the other group can be split into two collective identities: the one of the past, with whom we are not reconciled, and the other of the present, with whom we want to be reconciled. Such a split is, of course, absurd, as Jacques Derrida (2001, 39) and others have pointed out.[2]

Furthermore, in situations where there is great imbalance in terms of abuse and an asymmetry of power, we need to be aware that it is mostly the strong side or the perpetrators who wish to "leave the past behind," whereas the weak side and the victims perceive such a wish as immoral and impossible (Krondorfer 2008, 251). Usually, if one side advises to neglect the past, we can assume that this side is the perpetra- tor. Furthermore, an understanding of reconciliation that is based on the neglect to come to terms with a collective ethos ("We are reconciled with you, but not with your ethos") ignores the collective identity of the other and tries to reconcile with people merely on an individual level, thus leaving out a great part of who the other is. Archbishop Tutu insists that such a reduced understanding of the other does not open doors to reconciliation. Any attempt to reconcile without taking into account the need to reconcile the ethos of the other is doomed to fail.

Is it possible to change the ethos of collectives that are involved in identity conflicts? If so, when do collectives feel secure enough to make changes? In order to answer these questions, we can consult a few works in the field of reconciliation studies. Yehudith Auerbach and Hila Lowenstein, for example, define identity conflicts as conflicts in which "at least one side feels that the other has denied its legitimacy and thus negated its collective/national identity" (2011, 212). Following their definition, we can say that identity conflicts erupt not because of disagreement over material needs, and not even over ethos in general, but because denial takes place. Denial of legitimacy means that people in one group feel that they cannot be who they are as long as the others are who they are. In the case of Israelis and Palestinians, Donald G. Ellis writes:

> Israeli identity is formed in opposition to Palestinian identity, and the same is true for the Palestinians. . . . This has led to mutual denial of the identity of the other. Palestinians deny Jewish nationhood—"Judaism is a religion, not a people"—and the legitimacy of Jewish aspirations—"Zionism is racism." Israelis deny Palestinian distinctiveness—"Palestinians are just Arabs"— and territorial demands—"Jordan is Palestine." (2006, 158)

Such denials have a strong mirroring effect. Each side—whether Palestinian or Israeli—considers the identity of the other illegitimate in order to reaffirm their own side's identity. One reason for this reciprocal de-legitimation can be found in the similarity of both sides, as some scholars have pointed out. For example, Michael Ignatieff writes: "Everywhere I've been, nationalism is most violent where the group you are defining yourself against most closely resembles you" (1993, 244). On the other hand, we may locate the cause of conflict in the great differences between two geographically proximate societies. In such a view the conflict is seen as total—it is about every aspect of life: about religion, peoplehood, language, land, culture, and so forth. It is a conflict in which very few components of identity (or even no component at all) are shared by the two sides (in contrast, for example, to Ireland, South Africa, or Bosnia).

Auerbach observes that identity conflicts are harder to resolve since they are not solely inspired by material demands such as land, water, or oil (which can be divided), but rather by deeper beliefs rooted in history, which are perceived as nonnegotiable (2009, 295). Although Auerbach does not say so herself, we can take her insight to conclude that, contrary to what many assume, it is not negotiations that are needed in order to end identity conflicts but something altogether different.[3] Auerbach herself continues with a pessimistic tone: "Efforts at changing the metanarratives in identity conflicts are doomed to failure, at least when attempted too early, because they are perceived as a direct attack on the most cherished values and symbols of each protagonist" (2009, 298). As we shall see, Auerbach acknowledges that social identity needs to change. It is not so much that we should not try; rather, she warns us for not triggering this change too early and for not expecting too much. Other scholars approach conflicts in similar ways, using what they call "ripeness theory," according to which some conflicts are not yet "ripe" for reconciliation (Ellis 2006, 29). Tamar Herman notes that reconciliation processes can promote peace in cases that have a high potential to succeed, while in cases with high risk of failure (as in the Palestinian-Israeli case) more violence can erupt due to reconciliation efforts (Herman 2004, 41). Similarly, Trudy Govier and Wilhelm Verwoerd argue that reconciling narratives are "too far removed from the realities of relationships between individuals and groups to plausibly be constructed as the core of reconciliation. It is our conviction that fundamentally it is people—not their narratives or theories—who are alienated from each other and may need to reconcile" (2002, 183).

These cautious notes of researchers about the prospects of reconciling identity conflicts are echoed by the skepticism of public opinion about peace and reconciliation. At present, many Israelis submit to the view that the Israeli-Palestinian conflict is totally intractable and therefore one should not even try to find solutions. Instead, one should just learn to "live with the conflict"[4] or "manage the conflict"[5] to the best of one's self-interest. These ideas in the Israeli streets are mirrored by the "anti-normalization" campaign (*Tatbi'a* in Arabic) in the Palestinian streets. This campaign advocates for the rejection of any kind of dialogue between Palestinians and Israelis, because dialogue is seen by anti-normalizers as a sign that the Israeli occupation could be considered normal or acceptable by Palestinians. Anti-normalizers on the Palestinian side and conflict managers on the Israeli side are, of course, opponents, but they share a few basic beliefs: they both show contempt for peace activists and they believe that at the moment there is no partner for peace on the other side, that is to say, they believe the other side is unwilling to change. The perception that it is the other side that needs to change in order to make way for reconciliation can be judged as naively ethnocentric and egocentric; yet, it may also be based on a lack of understanding of the mirroring effect of conflicting identities. It is very hard to change one's own attitude when no trace of change is discernible on the other side. How, then, can the study of reconciliation help conflicting parties to realize in what ways each of them needs to change?

Terrel A. Northrup's differentiation of three levels of change may be helpful here.[6] On the first level of his account, each side acknowledges the need for change, but the change is only peripheral. This basic change can stop violence and may also lead to the next level of change. However, it does not yet require any change in the way the conflicting groups see themselves or in how they see the other side. Ceasefire agreements are a good example for this kind of first-level change. The second level involves changes in the relations between the parties. Here the image each side has about the other is modified, but this alteration does not yet involve a change in the identity of each side. On both the first and second levels, the conflict is approached in new and better ways, usually less violent ways, but the conflict itself stays intact. On the third level, however, the identity of each group is challenged.

Northrup uses a compelling example to show the difference between these levels. A married couple is fighting for years about different things. One day, they discover their son is a drug user. This new information may change the way they see their relationship (second level), but it can also change their self-esteem, the way the parents see themselves and judge their own actions (third level). Their shared responsibility leads them to reconsider the conflict and their identity. Something similar, according to Northrup, happens in collective conflicts when a new enemy comes into the picture and unites the two sides against it (Northrup 1989, 77). In the case of the parents of the drug user, it is the negative side, the drugs, that forces the couple to look at the conflict and at their identity in new ways, as well as the positive side that demands change (shared responsibility and love for their son, their shared "property"). Applied to the Israeli-Palestinian conflict, we might be able to see the land, the shared property, as a key for change. If both sides were to realize how much damage has been inflicted to their "shared child" by the conflict, it might lead to real transformation. I will return to this issue later.

Northrup suggests that changes in level one and level two are not enough for full reconciliation because "what has not changed is the general rigid construct that allows each party to perceive some other party as completely separate, as not-self." In contrast, a level three change happens when a sense of "'we' replaces the 'us/them' split" (Northrup 1989, 80).[7] Referring to the example of the new enemy in collective conflicts, Northrup suggests that a level three change is noticeable when the new enemy withdraws but the conflict no longer re-erupts. What has happened is that the shared threat enabled each side to stop seeing itself through the "us versus them" split. However, one important question is left open in Northrup's account: What will happen to the original identities of each side when the new "we" emerges? A few scholars believe that the influence of the original narratives should be reduced to a minimum. Ellis, for example, states:

> If group identities are going to play a significant role in the conflict resolution process, then they must change so that they no longer become the primary mechanism of interpreting meanings or assigning value. In other words, two groups such as Israelis and Palestinians will never progress towards acceptable coexistence if their own group-identities are rigid and hegemonic with respect to controlling meanings of political or cultural actions. Their identities must become more inclusive of the other. This poses significant questions about the possibility of real identity change. Are group-identities so strong and fundamental that they are not capable of significant change? Or can the creation of appropriate circumstances and conditions of interaction produce meaningful change? I feel confident change is possible. (Ellis 2006, 73)

Change in identity is needed and possible, but it is also very hard to achieve because it deals with the sense of "self" on both the individual and collective level. I agree with Ellis that in the Palestinian-Israeli conflict, there is a need for more inclusiveness in the structure of identities on each side, especially with regard to Jewish identity, where exclusiveness is a fundamental aspect of the nation's history.[8] Certainly, as Northrup puts it, the "us versus them" construct is blocking the way for peace. However, it does not follow from these observations that the needed change is linked only to lowering the impact of nationality or to finding room in the national ethos for more universal values, as Ellis implies (2006, 174). The issue of inclusiveness and of broadening the identities in the Israeli-Palestinian case might mean, alternatively, to make room in the national ethos for a third space, a broader identity that includes the national identities of both Palestinians and Israelis.

I contend that national identities can be strong, meaningful, and even "rigid," but ought not to be "hegemonic," to use Ellis's words. Identities are valuable assets and as such need not be excluded from the shared "we" that both Northrup and Ellis endorse. I believe the preservation of identities is in the fundamental interest of anyone who is committed to reconciliation; hence, it may be worthwhile to consider here differentiating between ethos and identity (contrary to the synonymous use of these terms elsewhere in this chapter). The new "we" is a shared ethos, but not a shared identity. It seeks to unite the sides, but only to a certain degree, for it remains respectful of the original identities of both sides. The goal of the new "we" is to enable the separate identities to hold a shared story that is needed for coexistence.

Whether the emergence of a shared ethos is possible remains open to debate. Herbert C. Kelman states that the forming of a new "transcendent identity" is very helpful for reconciliation but is not a necessary condition. The only thing he considers necessary is that "each party revise its own identity just enough to accommodate the identity of the other" (2004, 119). Susan Dwyer similarly does not expect a new "we" to emerge. She stipulates a more modest goal for a reconciliation process:

> In my account of reconciliation, the core notion is that of bringing apparently incompatible descriptions of events into narrative equilibrium. Hence the first thing that parties to reconciliation will require is a clear view of those events, where only the barest of facts—who did what to whom when—are relevant. The second stage will involve the articulation of a range of interpretations of those events. Finally, parties to the reconciliation attempt to choose from this range of interpretations some subset that allows them each to accommodate the disruptive event into their ongoing narratives. It is not required that all parties settle on a single interpretation, only that they are mutually tolerant of a limited set of interpretations. Sometimes this process will require the revision of aspects of the preexisting narrative. (Dwyer 1999, 89)

Similar to Northrup, Ellis, and Dwyer, Auerbach acknowledges the need for change in narratives but cautions us not to push for changes too early. She argues that a change in identity is possible only after a long process of other-side awareness—a process she analyzes using "the reconciliation pyramid." This theoretical construct mentions seven stages for reconciliation: (1) acquaintance of the other side's narrative; (2) acknowledging the

other narrative as authentic and legitimate without however accepting it
as true; (3) expressing empathy for the suffering of the other; (4) assuming
at least partial responsibility for the suffering of the other, caused through
the conflict; (5) expressing readiness for restitution or reparation for the
other side; (6) public apology and asking for forgiveness; (7) constructing
a common narrative (2009, 302–11).[9]

According to this model, the construction of a shared narrative should
be left to the top of the pyramid, to the very last stage of the process.
Auerbach's caveat needs to be considered. Yet, an additional barrier toward
peace, I suggest, might found at "stage zero," at the foundation of Auerbach's
pyramid, and it may cause even further delay in the process. In my view,
to engage in a reconciliation process that takes identity seriously, it is not
enough to be acquainted with the narrative of the other side or to accept
it. While getting to know the narrative of the other, it is important to
investigate one's own ethos. A collective ethos is far from being a linear
story or a static picture of reality agreed upon by all members of the
in-group.[10] Public examination of our own ethos is needed in order to
understand what we can let go of and what we deem necessary to retain.
This, undoubtedly, will affect the new shared ethos as it is constructed on
the highest level of the pyramid. For example, it is important for Israelis to
understand the complexity of state, nation, and religion in the construction of modern Jewish identity and how this impacts the struggle for a
"Jewish Democratic State." It is hard to imagine Israelis reconciling with
Palestinians without tackling these issues among themselves.

It is, indeed, risky to promote a shared ethos—the highest level of
Auerbach's pyramid—when the lower levels (including my proposed "zero
level") are not stable enough. Otherwise, expectations stirred by the talk
about peace might lead to much disappointment and, perhaps, to violent
acts from people on both sides who do not accept the premise of the
need for change. Should we wait for the basic levels of the pyramid to
be established before attempting to construct a shared ethos? I believe
the answer is no. A shared ethos needs to be considered while the flames
of the conflict are still burning. This suggestion might be perceived as
hasty recklessness. Let me, therefore, offer three reasons why we ought
to do so in the beginning of the process: First, we need to expand our
disciplinary base for understanding reconciliation. Most of the studies on
reconciliation derive from the work of social psychologists, sociologists,
and political scientists. I have cited several sources from these disciplines
when discussing the frameworks of identity conflicts (Auerbach's pyramid,

Northrup's three levels of change, etc.). Many of these studies interpret the role of identities in conflict without analyzing the content of a national ethos that might fit into their framework. I believe it is time for scholars with cultural, theological, historical, and philosophical backgrounds to take further steps within this theoretical framework and fill it with content. In other words, I think scholars have not paid enough attention to the content of a shared ethos in specific conflicts, not because they thought it was too early to do so, but because it was outside of their disciplined-bound purview.

Second, reconciliation should be done while the flames of conflict are still burning. In her contribution to this volume, Zeina Barakat calls this approach "The Hölderlin perspective." Because I am writing from Sderot, as I mentioned in my personal introductory notes, I share with Barakat a sense of urgency: we do not have the privilege to wait until a conflict ends. Moreover, in identity conflicts we cannot wait for the parties to be ready to alter their identity before reconciliation starts. Entrenched in their views, they may never be fully ready for change and yet change is needed and possible.

Third, and most importantly, if—by following a few of the studies I cited—we acknowledge that at some point in the process we will need to establish a common ethos, it is essential that we begin to examine its content already in the early stages. We will need to discuss ideas about structure and content of such ethos early on in order for the process to be open and clear to all sides. If we do not examine necessary identity changes from the very beginning, we actually throw sand in the eyes of the public, leaving both sides under the illusion that solving the conflict would be possible without major changes in identities. I believe the Oslo Accords are a good example of an attempt by both sides at staying who they have been (that is, to remain a Jewish nation-state versus insisting on the Palestinian right of return) while assuming the conflict can be solved. I believe, with others, that this oversight is one of the major reasons for the failure of the Oslo peace process.[11]

Reconciliation as Recognition and Demand

What is the change that each side's ethos needs to go through for real reconciliation to take place? Two competing directions can be suggested: First, reconciliation is recognition. It requires acceptance of the ethos of the other side as legitimate, reasonable, and needed. We recognize that "you are who you are" and we don't wish you to be anyone else for the sake of reconciliation. In other words, it is you whom we wish to reconcile with and not an imagined entity that will be convenient for us to reconcile with. Second, reconciliation is a demand. We demand that you change certain aspects of your ethos in order to make it possible for our two narratives to be reconciled.

The two directions are seemingly opposites. If we were to accept the identity of the other and affirm "you are who you are," how can we at the same time take the liberty to demand that the other will change? If we demand such of the other, do we not imply that we do not accept the ethos of the other? Or even worse—that we accept the other's ethos only partially, that is, only those parts that are convenient to our identity? For example, an Israeli can easily say that it is important to learn about Palestinian culture and support workshops in which Palestinians and Israelis are dancing *debka* and making hummus together,[12] but when it comes to the issue of land, the same Israeli might reject any Palestinian territorial claim. In this example, the Israeli only accepts those parts of the other's ethos that are convenient to him or her.

Arguing that both directions (recognition and demand) are needed, I am not overlooking the tension between them. Instead, I argue that both are needed because they balance each other out. In my account of reconciliation, "our" side will need to realize that the other side will keep on being who they are, but we can accept this only under the condition that the others will change enough to make room for us to keep on being who we are. And from the reverse perspective: We demand that the other will change but only under the condition that they do not lose their own sense of identity.

Two kinds of changes are needed in the ethos of conflicting parties: the first is becoming tolerant of the ethos of the other—each side will need to alter their ethos in a way that will leave enough room for the other side's ethos to be legitimate and reasonable. In other words, reconciling conflicting identities means moving from the situation described in Figure 1 into the configuration of Figure 2. The state of affairs in Figure 1, in which the meaning of ethos A is "not B" and vice versa, represents the feeling that "we are who we are because we are not them" and even: "we are who we are because they are not who they claim to be" (the "us versus them" split according to Northrup). In this logic, if we were to accept the other's ethos as reasonable, we cannot keep being ourselves. For

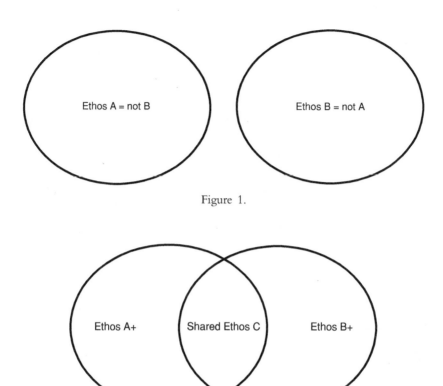

Figure 1.

Figure 2.

example, if we accept that they are the people of this land, we cannot see ourselves as the people of this land. The first move needed for reconciling identities is to change ethos A into A+, that is, into an ethos in which B+ (but not B) will make sense, and of course reciprocally to change B into B+, a new ethos in which A+ (but not A) will be legitimate. It is important to note that the change from A to A+ is based on respect of the ethos we held while in the conflict (A). Only the parts that make it impossible for our ethos to coexist with the new ethos established on the other side (B+) will need to change.

One example for such a change is the slow acceptance of the *Naqba* (Arabic for "catastrophe," the Palestinian description of the 1948 events) by the Israeli public.[13] In the past, there was hardly any discussion in Israel about the *Naqba*; the word itself was hardly known by most Israelis. This has changed in the last twenty years. One sign of this shift is an Israeli official law from 2011, according to which any institute that teaches lessons about the *Naqba* is at risk of losing all kinds of support from the Israeli government.[14] This law, although negative in itself, is paradoxically also a sign that some Israelis are slowly but surely moving from ethos A into ethos A+. They now accept the narrative of the *Naqba* as part of the way they see reality, which, in turn, caused the promulgation of the 2011 law, because it worried other Israelis who want to uphold ethos A.

For Palestinians, the *Naqba,* and Israel's responsibility for it, is central to their identity and probably will be part of any future Palestinian narrative (B+). Hence, I believe that if Israelis are not willing to take collective responsibility for the events of the *Naqba,* any real chance for reconciliation is questionable. When Israelis say that the *Naqba* never happened or that most Palestinians fled their homes voluntarily or upon pressure from foreign Arab armies,[15] they are actually saying that they are ready to reconcile with Palestinians only under the condition that they accept the Israeli ethos (A). Hassan Jabareen contends that Israelis open their culture only for "Zionist Arabs" (a paradoxical and ridiculous term), but not for real Palestinians (2002, 210). Following him, I suggest that reconciling with "real Palestinians" means to realize that the *Naqba* will be part of B+, but that this realization does not mean that the Israeli narrative about 1948 is completely false. On the other side, Palestinians who are Holocaust deniers or who claim the *Naqba* and the Holocaust are similar events, fall into the same trap, for it is very hard to imagine a Jewish identity in the near future that would neglect the Holocaust and its historical uniqueness.[16]

A second and more advanced move is that both sides leave room in their future ethos for a shared ethos (change A into A+ in a way that makes C possible). Contrary to some of the scholars mentioned above, I contend this move is inevitable. A closer look at Figure 1 will show why. The two circles in Figure 1 do not touch or overlap. There seems to be no contact between the conflicting sides. This, however, is actually misleading. If the Palestinian and Israeli identities were indeed as separated as Figure 1 suggests, it would not be hard to reconcile the two narratives without establishing a common sense of reality. In a case where there are no relations between two sides, narrative A would not imply in any way the negation of narrative B. For example, the Spanish national ethos does not imply in any way the dismissal of the Japanese national ethos, and therefore reconciliation is not needed. They are already in separate spheres.

The problem in all identity conflicts, however, is that neatly separating the national narratives is not really possible. The reason that A means "not B" is that identities are entangled. People from each side meet on a daily basis, and while doing so, identities interact, respond to each other, and are formed in opposition to one another. Furthermore, history is shared; the same events are described differently in both narratives. A shared ethos is needed because, in the first instance, each side's ethos included parts of the ethos of the other side, but these parts were described negatively in order to reaffirm one's own side view on the same events.

In other words, if a group changed its ethos from A to A+ and now is tolerant of the other side's narrative (B+), and yet there is no effort of trying to create a shared ethos (C), what we would end up with is that for the A+ group the ethos B+ will be perceived as legitimate and reasonable, though it will remains totally alien. We saw earlier that a few scholars (like Auerbach's pyramid level 2) find this state of affairs plausible. In my view, however, a stance that assumes the other side's ethos to be "legitimate" in itself, but "false for me," is problematic insofar as the events described in narrative B have something to say about the truth in the description of events in narrative A. "Legitimate, but false for me" actually implies that we do not accept B+ at all. For example, if Israelis say that the *Naqba* is nothing but a political manipulation that cannot be part of any future Israeli narrative (A+), in what ways could the same Israelis then claim that it is a legitimate Palestinian narrative of the 1948 events? Changing our ethos from A into A+ in order for their ethos (B+) to be legitimate is not sufficient until and unless we also create a shared ethos (C).

Having argued for the need for a shared ethos and the framework for its structure (recognition *and* demand), two warnings are in place. They have to do with what the shared ethos *should not* be: First, it should not be a melting pot. I use A+ to denote that the new ethos should be built on the basis of respect for the original ethos of each side. It should not dismiss A or B and melt the two identities into a totally new identity. In other words, it should not create an artificial, technocratic, civic identity in which cultural diversity and cultural depth are erased. Second, the shared ethos cannot be a surrender of one ethos to the other. In many cases, this is exactly what extreme nationalists on both sides demand: that the other side shall accept one's own ethos "as is," without any revision. For example, Salman Natour's *The Memory Talked with Me and Left* contains a collection of *Naqba* stories based on interviews. Reading the book from an Israeli perspective is a worthwhile but hard experience. The combined weight of all the stories of murder, rape, massacre, and brutal behavior of Israeli soldiers may make an Israeli reader feel that the 1948 war was not that far removed from the events of the Holocaust. From the Israeli point of view, one hesitates to confirm the truth of all these stories, for they miss a great deal of the other perspective on the 1948 events. They neglect, for example, the fact that Israel in 1948 was far from having a real army; hence, Natour's repeated descriptions of war crimes of a conquering army against civilians are not accurate. They also neglect to mention that Israel lost in that war 1 percent of its population at the time,[17] much more than the percentage of losses of Palestinians and of the Arab armies. Natour's book is an important reading material for the Israeli audience. It's a poetic work and not propaganda, but this does not mean that Israelis should accept the narrative drawn in it. A very different example from the other side is *Naqba-Charta,* booklets published by *Im Tirtzu,* an Israeli rightwing organization. The Arabic title of this Hebrew booklet is well understood by all Israelis because it uses a very common Hebrew slang, *Naqba*-Bullshit (=*charta*).[18] As is evident from the title, it does not leave any room for the narrative of the other side.

Contrary to such one-sided narratives, I believe that although the events of the 1948 war must become part of the shared ethos, they cannot be described either solely by Natour's book or by *Naqba-Charta,* because both would require a full surrender of one narrative to the other. This understanding might seem harder to accept for the ones who see themselves as the weaker side. I believe, however, that Palestinians must understand that in order to make way for peace their description of the events of the *Naqba* will be contested just as much as the Zionist narrative.

A Shared Ethos for Palestinians and Israelis: Preliminary Guidelines

What might a shared ethos look like? I now come to the most risky part of this chapter, in which I want to suggest a few basic ideas about the content of a future shared ethos for Israelis and Palestinians. I also want to explore the current practical consequences of these future components of a shared ethos. It is risky because the conflict at the present might not be "ripe" for a shared ethos to emerge. Hence, trying to construct it now could be perceived as "tying the cart in front of the horse," a danger that Auerbach and others have pointed out. Second, it is also risky because the following ideas are not based (and probably cannot be based) on objective sociological analysis of the conflict, but on a close, personal acquaintance with one side of the conflict and a somewhat adequate sense of the other side's needs. Third, it is also risky because the points I want to raise—and which I consider indispensable for a future shared ethos—are at the moment unacceptable by the majority of people on both sides. Still, I take the risk because, as I suggested earlier, one main reason for failures in previous rounds of peace talks between Palestinians and Israelis has been that both sides believed they can keep their ethos unchanged and still reconcile; they did not have a clear picture of the needed change in their ethos from the beginning of the process.

In my view, the following components are most important for a future shared ethos of Palestinians and Israelis:

- Land: both nations share attachment and responsibility to the whole of Palestine/land-of-Israel.

- Trauma: both nations are post-traumatic and can show empathy to the other side, based on this recognition.

- Violence: the history of violence between the warring sides needs to be rewritten for the sake of a shared ethos.

LAND

Since a great deal of the conflict is about land, it is clear why the land needs to be part of a shared ethos C (and also part of the separate ethos of A+, B+). Like a married couple fighting with each other while not acknowledging the damage they cause to their loved ones, I maintain that both nations need to acknowledge their connection to the whole land as a key element in a shared ethos. "The whole land" refers to the fact that Palestinians must acknowledge the Israeli connection to Hebron and Shchem (Nablus), and Israelis must acknowledge the Palestinian connection to Jaffa and Haifa. These connections cannot be divided or separated by fences. The connection of both nations to the land is deeper than valuing it as real estate. It is a homeland for both: *moledet* (Hebrew: the place of our birth) and *watan* (Arabic: geographical belonging). There can be different political solutions for the conflict—one state, two states, or other models[19]—but all of them must be based on mutual acknowledgment of the deep connection that each side has to the whole land.[20]

We can also reverse the suggested relationship of land and nations. A different way to understand the importance of land is not to say that the whole land belongs to the two nations inseparably but that the nations belong to the land. The Israeli poet Eliaz Cohen, a settler in Kfar Etzion and peace activist, pronounced this idea in remarkable words:

> We in Bnei Akiva, the yeshivas and Gush Emunim[21] were raised on the slogan, "The Land of Israel belongs to the people of Israel." But that is exactly what we have to release, let go of. We have to end the relations of "ownership." Rabbi Menachem (Fruman) always said that this is the land of peace, that the land is God's. Tremendous work is needed to liberate the consciousness, to recognize the fact that we are not the "lords of the land" or the owners of the land, but that we belong to the land. And then the slogan is reversed: "The people of Israel belong to the Land of Israel," and also "The Palestinians belong to the Land of Israel, to Palestine." (Quoted in Baram 2015)

On the Palestinian side, the attachment to the land does not need much elaboration. For Palestinians the land is probably the most central element of their identity (except, maybe, the fight against the occupation). Palestinian discourse might contribute to a shared ethos the concept of *tzumud,* which means in Arabic attachment, connection, and staying very close to the land, even in hard times. In the present Palestinian ethos, *tzumud* is used as a way of coping with the threat of forced evacuations from the land by the Israeli occupation. In future Israeli-Palestinian relations it might be used in a different way, a way that would express the interdependence of humans and land in a society that has become increasingly urban and less connected to the land.

The political consequences of seeing the land as part of a future shared ethos might help us to critically examine the peace talks of the last thirty years, which were based on separating Israelis and Palestinians and on uprooting Israeli settlers from what they perceive as their land. Peace initiatives in Israel and Palestine have so far assumed that painful concessions are needed for peace. Contrary to this paradigm of separation, I suggest to integrate into a future shared ethos both people's attachment to the land and hence look for a political arrangement in which people are not being separated from their land by fences. This means that a simple nation–state–based solution to the conflict, with two totally separated states, is not a real option and that a more sophisticated binational arrangement needs to be found.[22]

TRAUMA

Both nations need to acknowledge that the Jewish people and the Palestinian people are post-traumatic societies. They are "communities of trauma," which structure their self-understanding on painful events (Pdaia 2011, 45). This does not mean that the Holocaust and the *Naqba* are similar, or that comparing them is valid or helpful. It only means that the role of trauma in the national identity of both nations can be compared. It is hard to imagine Jewish identity in the present and near future without the Holocaust, as it is equally hard to imagine Palestinian identity without the *Naqba*. Both traumas are expected to be meaningful parts of the future identities (A+, B+), but they do not have to separate both peoples. Rather, they can build a shared space of empathy. A post-traumatic nation can find within itself empathy for the suffering of others if it does not see the suffering of the other as a threat. Attempts to compare the traumas are at the present a paralyzing element that makes compromise impossible (Sagiv 2015, 348–49).[23] The earlier trauma is employed by some Israelis as an excuse for the later trauma; the later trauma is magnified by Palestinians or, in reverse, demoted by Israelis on the basis of this comparison. This has led a few Israelis on the political Left to suggest that we should no longer remember the Holocaust at all (Elkana 1988). It has also motivated others to look for new ways of remembering, ways that might be part of a future shared ethos (Burg 2007). Borrowing a phrase from Vamic Volkan, one could say that the Holocaust and the *Naqba* are the "chosen traumas" of the two peoples (Cahanov 2015, 269; Chaitin 2011, 26–28). Palestinians and Israelis did not, of course, choose that traumatic events happened to them, but they have chosen to construct their identities on and around these events. The term *chosen trauma* might be useful because, if we acknowledge that traumas are "chosen" to construct narratives, this choice also opens the door for both nations to "choose" to employ their traumas in different ways: rather than competition, they could become entry points for mutual empathy and closeness.

The most obvious practical consequence of seeing trauma as part of a shared ethos is an educational one, namely, the need for both sides to become more acquainted with each other's trauma. Holocaust awareness projects for Palestinians and the work of the *Zochrot* organization have already taken place for the last two decades,[24] but very few Israelis and Palestinians heard of these efforts. These efforts are far from easy. My experience in Friendship Across Borders (FAB),[25] a German-Palestinian-Israeli organization that focuses on the traumatic past of the three nations, leads me to acknowledge that in many cases disrespect and frustration are the result of these encounters rather than respect for the trauma of the other side. Nevertheless, this work needs to be done.

Beyond these educational projects, there are also political consequences for seeing trauma as a central part of the shared ethos. I suggested earlier that Hebron is part of the Jewish ethos and Jaffa is part of the Palestinian ethos. Therefore, it is not a real option to divide the land into two nation-states and uproot people on either side. Considering the role of trauma in a future shared ethos, we might see the limits of this suggestion. The centrality of trauma in the future ethos leads to the conclusion that a democratic one-state ("a state of all its citizens") would be equally problematic as a two-states solution (Dinur 2008). Post-traumatic nations need security. They need to feel that their state belongs to them, not only as individual citizens but also as a strong collective. They need the state to take responsibility for their nation and make sure they will not be abused by the majority of citizens of their state. This means that the political solution Palestinians and Israelis need is a unique binational combination that has to be structured so that certain elements will unite the two nations (for example, one Supreme Court or one currency) while others will be kept separate (such as their educational systems).

VIOLENCE

Today, both sides present their violent actions in the conflict as if there was "no other choice." They say they want peace and reject the use of force and violence, but each blames the respective other side for causing violence. Both are caught in a circular pattern where it becomes impossible to know whether a specific act is cause or effect (Ellis 2006, 155). This must change. Both sides need to take responsibility for their violent acts and acknowledge that they did have other, less violent paths at their disposal. However, it does not follow from this pattern that the story of violence in the past century is a story of two sides with balanced forces. It is quite clear to any observer that Israel in the present and near past has possessed more military might than the Palestinians and, accordingly, the attitude toward violence and the need for a new story of violence are different for the two sides. It is much harder for the stronger side in conflict to change the way they see violence, accept responsibility for what happened, and admit that they had other choices apart from the use of force. It is important to note, though, that the weaker side also needs to find a way to differentiate between legitimate acts of objection to their oppression and illegitimate terror acts that should have been avoided (Rouhana 2001, 288).[26]

My experience with Palestinian-Israeli dialogue shows that for many Israelis it is important to hear Palestinians take responsibility for their part in the conflict. The Israelis I mention here are in most cases left-wingers who are ready to hear about Palestinian suffering; they did not come to the meetings to prove that Israel is right. Most of them would admit that the vast majority of the responsibility for the conflict is on the Israeli side, but still they want to hear the Palestinians condemn their own violent acts. Palestinians, however, find it hard in these encounters—at least in those I have witnessed—to condemn violent acts done by their "freedom fighters." I believe it is a hard work that both sides need to do: to admit that they had other choices.

Another important aspect of the new narrative of violence is its liberating effect for individuals who have participated in violent acts. We can learn from the experience of the South African Truth and Reconciliation Commissions that in reconciliation processes individuals can be partly excused from their personal wrongdoings that were done in the name of the old regime (Rouhana 2001, 292). This does not mean that any individual act of violence will be justified during reconciliation process, but it does show that a new story needs to be told and that this story must be shared by both sides. Such a narrative is told in order to enable people to live together by distancing themselves from the old regime. It allows them to say that they acted in the name of this regime but that they no longer see themselves as part of it.

As in the case of trauma, the question of violence has an immediate educational mandate. New history books need to be written and dialogue groups initiated so that the story of violence in Palestine/Israel can be rearticulated in such a way that it respects the narratives of all sides and illuminates nonviolent choices that leaders chose to ignore.[27] The immediate political consequences of such new approaches to violence are pressing: we need to put in front of the public and the leaders nonviolent alternatives to present actions of both sides and to stop the use of violence. This is a very complicated endeavor that I cannot even begin to articulate in this chapter. Among many things, it requires the breaking down of walls and checkpoints and the disarming of violent organizations.

Epilogue

If the acknowledgment of the need to establish a shared ethos were accepted, it would change the way Israelis and Palestinians see future peace talks. Instead of talking about material demands, such as borders, land, water, or economic arrangements, the identity of each side would be discussed. Indeed, this will not be the first time that ethos has been brought to the negotiation table. When Palestinian leaders demanded the right of return, while behind the scenes they acknowledged that this right could not be fully actualized, they negotiated ethos and not political arrangements. When Israeli prime minister Benjamin Netanyahu, in 2010, as a precondition for negotiation, insisted on Palestinians recognizing Israel as a Jewish nation-state, he was doing the same: his declaration meant that the peace process is not just about material issues, it is also about ethos. Although I did not agree with Netanyahu then, and though I do not think the demand of a Jewish nation-state is legitimate now, I see the prime minister's act as a sign of what is needed for reconciliation: debating the ethos of both sides.

I would like to end with a poem calling both sides to change their view of the respective other through a new approach to the land, the positive side of our future shared ethos. The connection of both nations to the land, I believe, holds the keys for reconciliation. It is a connection of strangers, not of owners, that stands at the center of Yitzhak Laor's (2004, 93) poem "New Occupation":[28]

> And then, another new spring night will come and occupy
>   the land
> will bend as a holy man over all the plants, thousands of insects
> will fly from a dry orchard to a deserted house, the dirt road
> will cover with caterpillars, the smell will rise like smoke,
>   the eyes of the flowers
> will open in the darkness, flower buds will open in the
>   trees, the direction of the wind
> will change, citrus smells will fill the noses. Aha, deserted
>   Chushchash[29] orchards,

our land is blossoming like an exited bride, and the grooms, women,
men, Jews, Arabs, barefoot, crowned with flowers, will stand
silent, remembering
the sanctity
of our lives
we are all
in it
guests
strangers.

Acknowledgments

I would like to thank the other contributors to this volume for a unique academic experience and an enriching dialogue that formed this book and contributed much to my thinking. I also thank Ellie Dinur and Julia Chaitin for their helpful comments.

Notes

1. Auerbach 2009, 294. Elsewhere, she writes, "Metanarratives, then, are stories about stories; that is, they place national narratives within a larger, all-embracing framework" (Auerbach and Lowenstein 2011, 213).

2. Derrida's debate concerns forgiveness and not reconciliation. I believe, however, that many of his insights are applicable for reconciliation. One example is his debate on "the split person." Other scholars use the same notion in interesting historical episodes such as the ability to reconcile with post-Nazi Germany. Marc Howard Ross claims that reconciling with Germany after the war was possible only through the understanding that the new German government was not a continuation of the Nazi regime. Paradoxically, according to him, the new government needed both to apologize for the crimes of the Nazis and to make clear that they were not their heirs (Ross 2004, 203). See more on the split person option in Benziman 2009, 86–88. Benziman differentiates between forgiveness and reconciliation. He sees reconciliation as leaving the past behind. For him forgiveness has a dialogical and never-ending nature. My understanding of reconciliation in this chapter is close to Benziman's understanding of the term *forgiveness* and far from his understanding of reconciliation. The difference between the two terms and the question whether forgiveness is needed for reconciliation is

discussed by many (including Verwoerd and Little in this volume) and is beyond
the scope of this chapter.

3. Many believe that conflicts in general and the Palestinian-Israeli conflict
in particular can be solved only through negotiations and only with strong and
determined leaders that sit together and sign peace agreements. See for example
Bar-Tal 2007, 307, 324. Bar-Tal sees the "official ending of the conflict," that is,
the signing of an agreement, as an inevitable stage in the process. See also Shimon
Peres in his "A New Middle East" (1993). My approach to reconciliation in this
chapter is very different.

4. See Daniel Bar-Tal's title *Living with the Conflict* (2007). The title should
not be seen as his consent to live with conflict, only as an analysis of how Israelis
in the present understand the conflict.

5. This approach is used by Avigdor Liberman, Moshe Ye'elon, and other
right-wing leaders in Israel. See http://www.iba.org.il/bet/?type=1&entity=984519
and http://www.93fm.co.il/radio/67836; retrieved July 25, 2016.

6. A similar account, using different terms, can be found in Rouhana
(2001, 279). Rouhana differentiates between "conflict resolution," "solving the
conflict," and "reconciliation," which are more or less parallel to each of the
three levels in Northrup.

7. See more on the "us versus them" perspective in Chaitin (2011, 44)
and in the many studies that she mentions there.

8. For an extended discussion on Jewish particularism and universalism,
see Werblowsky 1976.

9. Auerbach acknowledges that in some cases the order of these stages
might differ, but she does see them as a pyramid, in which the higher levels are
achievable only if they are laid on stable foundations at lower levels. She notes that
the first four levels are "people-to-people" levels, where dialogue is needed; until
this happens little can be achieved in the political sphere (Auerbach 2009, 302–11).

10. For an example of how to rethink "our" ethos, see Myers 2011.

11. For similar criticism on the Oslo Accords, see Peled and Rouhana
2004, 318–19.

12. *Debka* is a customary Arab dance widespread in many mid-Eastern
societies. Humus is a well-known dish. Both are usually associated with Palestinian culture.

13. According to Sammy Smooha, the number of Jewish Israelis who believe
"the Naqba didn't happen" decreased from 58 percent in 2010 to 52 percent
in 2012 (Smooha 2013, 66). The most active organization that deals with the
need for Israelis to remember the *Naqba* is Zochrot; see http://zochrot.org/en;
retrieved Feb 17, 2016.

14. The law is mostly declarative. Until the writing of this chapter, there
was not even a single incident of sanctions against institutions that teach lessons
about the *Naqba*. I can testify that regardless of this law teaching the narrative

of the *Naqba* to Israeli audiences leads to harsh reactions. See one incident (in Hebrew), at http://zochrot.org/he/article/54877; retrieved July 25, 2016.

15. See such a description of events in the booklet "*Naqba*-Charta," composed by an organization called *Im Tirtzu*; http://imti.org.il/publications/booklets/. For more on the debate about this organization, see: http://www.the7eye.org.il/66321. Both links retrieved Feb. 16, 2016.

16. According to a survey from 2012, 31 percent of Palestinians who are citizens of Israel did not think the Holocaust happened. It is quite likely that the percentage is even higher in the West Bank and Gaza, where Palestinians do not meet Israelis and their narrative on a daily basis. Sammy Smooha, who conducted the survey, believes this negation should not be seen as a denial of the Holocaust but as a protest against the use of the Holocaust as a justification for Israeli's actions (Smooha 2013, 64).

17. According to a few estimations, six thousand Israelis lost their lives in the 1948 war, more than any other war Israel conducted later. The total Jewish population in Palestine at that time was about six hundred thousand. Casualties on the Arab side (both Palestinians and Arab armies) were about eight thousand (Auron 2013, 42). For an extended discussion on the number of casualties on the Israeli side, see chapter 1 in Sivan 1991.

18. See note 16 above.

19. For a detailed analysis of the possible different solutions, see chapter 12 in Yiftachel 2006.

20. My use of the term "the whole land" is pointing at the actual borders of the state of Israel between the Mediterranean and the Jordan River, more or less parallel to the mandatory borders and to the de facto international borders of Israel after 1967. These borders can be contested and negotiated. At present they are seen by many as one geographical unit.

21. *Gush Emunim* is a movement of religious settlers in the West Bank. *Bney Akiba* is the main youth movement of religious Zionists.

22. For binationalism as a conceptual framework for dealing with the Palestinian-Israeli conflict, see Amnon Raz-Krakotzkin 2011. One political initiative that follows this direction is "Two States in One Home-land" (https://www.facebook.com/2states1homeland; retrieved Sept. 9, 2015). At the time of writing this chapter, this initiative is still "young" and preliminary. Other plans can follow similar patterns. It is too early to say how much political power these initiatives can gain. See more on public reactions to the binational ideas in Ghanem 2009.

23. For comparing the *Naqba* and the Holocaust, see Bashir and Goldberg 2015. Although almost every chapter in this book emphasizes that the Holocaust and the *Naqba* are incomparable, the title of the book, *The Holocaust and the Naqba: Memory, National Identity and Jewish-Arab Partnership*, inflamed a public debate; many called to ban the book based on the claim that it is comparing the two traumas.

24. For Palestinian Holocaust awareness, see http://www.haaretz.com/
nazareth-gets-first-holocaust-museum-for-arabs-1.159423; retrieved Feb. 17, 2016.
For *Naqba* awareness for Israelis, see Zochrot website (note 15 above).

25. See http://www.fab-friendshipacrossborders.net/index.php/en/; retrieved
Feb. 17, 2016.

26. My analysis of the need to change the ethos of conflicting sides
regarding the history of violence is close to Rouhana's analysis. He neither refers,
however, to the change in the ethos about land and trauma nor to the need for
a shared ethos.

27. For an example of new history books that take in account the narratives of both sides, see Bar-on, Adnan, Adwan, and Nawe 2003.

28. I would like to thank Laor for his permission to translate his poem
and for his helpful comments on my translation.

29. Arabic and Hebrew name for Bitter Orange. *Chushchash* is hardly proper
for eating. It was used in the past as a basis for grafting various citrus trees. Orchards
that are not properly cultivated sometimes turn back into *chushchash*. Laor used
this term to express the feeling of desertedness in nature before the new occupation comes (note based on personal email exchange with Laor, Nov. 13, 2015).

Works Cited

Auerbach, Yehudith. 2009. "The Reconciliation Pyramid: A Narrative-Based Framework for Analyzing Identity Conflicts." *Political Psychology* 30(2): 291–318.

———, and Hila Lowenstein. 2011. "The Role of National Narratives in Reconciliation: The Case of Mohammad al-Dura." *International Journal of Press/
Politics* 16(2): 210–33.

Auron, Yair. 2013. *The Holocaust, the Rebirth, and the Nakba.* Tel Aviv: Resling
(Hebrew).

Baram, Nir. 2015. "48 to 67." *Haaretz*, August 6. http://www.haaretz.com/st/c/
prod/eng/2015/greenLine/index.html; retrieved August 9, 2015.

Bar-On, Dan, Muslem Adnan, Sami Adwan, and Eyal Nawe, eds. 2003. *To Learn
the Historical Narrative of the Other: Palestinians and Israelis.* Translated by Yoav
Stern. Beit Jalla: Prime (Hebrew, Arabic, English).

Bar-Tal, Daniel. 2007. *Living with the Conflict: Socio-Psychological Analysis of the
Jewish Society in Israel.* Jerusalem: Carmel (Hebrew).

Bartos, Otomar J., and Paul Wehr. 2002. *Using Conflict Theory.* Cambridge and
New York: Cambridge University Press.

Bashir, Bashir, and Amos Goldberg, eds. 2015. *The Holocaust and the Naqba: Memory,
National Identity, and Jewish-Arab Partnership.* Tel Aviv: Van Leer, Hakibbutz
Hameuchad (Hebrew).

Benziman, Yotam. 2009. "Forgiveness and Remembrance of Things Past." *Azure*
35: 84–115.

Burg, Abraham. 2007. *Defeating Hitler.* Tel Aviv: Miskal (Hebrew).

Chaitin, Julia. 2011. *Peace Building in Israel and Palestine: Social Psychology and Grassroots Initiatives.* New York: Palgrave Macmillan.

Dajani-Daoudi, Mohammed S. 2008. "Big Dream/Small Hope: A Peace Vision." *Cross Currents* 58(2): 191–219.

Derrida, Jacques. 2001. *On Cosmopolitanism and Forgiveness.* Translated by Mark Dooley and Michael Hughes. London and New York: Routledge.

Dinur, Avner. 2008. "Arendt's 'Council System' and Israel as a 'State of all its citizens.'" In *Totalitarianism and Liberty: Hannah Arendt in the 21st Century*, edited by Gerhard Besier, Katarzyna Stoklosa, and Andrew Wisely, 289–302. Krakow: Ksiegarnia Akademica.

Dwyer, Susan. 1999. "Reconciliation for Realists." *Ethics & International Affairs* 13(1): 81–98.

Elkana, Yehudah. 1988. "In Praise of Forgetting." *Haaretz*, March 2) (Hebrew). Available online in English: http://ceuweekly.blogspot.co.il/2014/08/in-memoriam-need-to-forget-by-yehuda.html; retrieved January 17, 2017.

Ellis, Donald G. 2006. *Transforming Conflict: Communication and Ethnopolitical Conflict.* Lanham, MD: Rowman and Littlefield.

Ghanem, As'ad. 2009. "The Bi-National State Solution." *Israel Studies* 14(2): 120–33.

Govier, Trudi, and Wilhelm Verwoerd. 2002. "Trust and the Problem of National Reconciliation." *Philosophy of Social Sciences* 32(2): 178–205.

Herman, Tamar. 2004. "Reconciliation: Reflections on the Theoretical and Practical Utility of the Term." In *From Conflict Resolution to Reconciliation*, edited by Yaacov Bar-Siman-Tov, 39–60. New York: Oxford University Press.

Ignatieff, Michael. 1993. *Blood and Belonging: Journeys into the New Nationalism.* New York: Farrar, Straus and Giroux.

Jabareen, Hasan. 2002. "The Future of Arab Citizenship in Israel: Jewish-Zionist Time in a Place with no Palestinian Memory." In *Challenging Ethnic Citizenship: German and Israeli Perspectives on Immigration*, edited by Daniel Levy and Yfaat Weiss, 196–220. New York: Berghahn Books.

Kahanov, Maia. 2015. "The Unheard Cry for Recognition: The Challenges of Dialogue between Jews and Arabs in Israel about Collective Traumas." In *The Holocaust and the Naqba: Memory, National Identity, and Jewish-Arab Partnership*, edited by Bashir Bashir and Amos Goldberg, 268–97. Tel Aviv: Van Leer, Hakibbutz Hameuchad (Hebrew).

Kelman, Herbert C. 2004. "Reconciliation as Identity Change: A Social-Psychological Perspective." In *From Conflict Resolution to Reconciliation*, edited by Yaacov Bar-Siman-Tov, 111–24. New York: Oxford University Press.

Krondorfer, Björn. 2008. "Is Forgetting Reprehensible? Holocaust Remembrance and the Task of Oblivion." *Journal of Religious Ethics* 36(2): 233–67.

Laor, Yitzhak. 2004. *Leviathan City: Poems 2000–2004.* Tel Aviv: Hakibbutz Hameuchad (Hebrew).

Myers, David N. 2011. "Rethinking the Jewish Nation: An Exercise in Applied Jewish Studies." *Havruta* 6 (Shalom Hartman Institute): 26–33. Available online at http://hartman.org.il/Publications_View.asp?Article_Id=228&Cat_Id=310&Cat_Type=Magazine&Title_Cat_Name=Havruta; retrieved February 17, 2016.

Northrup, Terrel A. 1989. "The Dynamic of Identity in Personal and Social Conflict." In *Intractable Conflicts and their Transformation*, edited by Louis Kriesberg, Terrel A. Northrup, and Stuart Thorson, 55–82. Syracuse: Syracuse University Press.

Pdaia, Haviva. 2011. *Space and Place: An Essay on the Theological-Political Un-Conscious.* Bnei Brak: Hakibbutz Hameuchad (Hebrew).

Peled, Yoav, and Nadim N. Rouhana. 2004. "Transitional Justice and the Right of Return of the Palestinian Refugees." *Theoretical Inquiries in Law* 5(2): 317–32.

Peres, Shimon (with Arye Naor). 1993. *The New Middle East.* New York: Henry Holt.

Raz-Krakotzkin, Amnon. 2011. "Separation and Bi-Nationalism." *Jadal* 10: 1–4.

Ross, Marc H. 2004. "Ritual and the Politics of Reconciliation." In *From Conflict Resolution to Reconciliation*, edited by Yaacov Bar-Siman-Tov, 197–224. New York: Oxford University Press.

Rouhana, Nadim N. 2001. "Reconciliation in On-going National Conflict: Identity and Power in the Israeli-Palestinian Case." *Israeli Sociology* 3(2): 277–95 (Hebrew).

Sagiv, Asaf. 2015. "A Critique of Victim Consciousness." In *The Holocaust and the Naqba: Memory, National Identity, and Jewish-Arab Partnership*, edited by Bashir Bashir and Amos Goldberg, 328–49. Tel Aviv: Van Leer, Hakibbutz Hameuchad (Hebrew).

Sivan, Emanuel. 1991. *The 1948 Generation: Myth, Profile and Memory.* Tel Aviv: Maarachot (Hebrew).

Smooha, Sammy. 2013. *Still Playing by the Rules: Index of Arab-Jewish Relations in Israel.* Jerusalem: Israel Democracy Institute and Haifa University.

Tutu, Desmond. 1999. *No Future without Forgiveness.* London and Sydney: Rider.

Werblowsky, Zvi R. J. 1976. *Beyond Tradition and Modernity: Changing Religions in a Changing World.* London: Athlone.

Yiftachel, Oren. 2006. *Ethnocracy: Land and Identity Politics in Israel/Palestine.* Philadelphia: Pennsylvania University Press.

7

When Reconciliation Becomes the R-Word

Dealing with the Past in Former Yugoslavia

Heleen Touquet and Ana Milošević

In October 2015, both of us (Heleen and Ana) participated in the Memory Lab trip to Belgium. Memory Lab is an organization that brings together memory activists, scholars, and associations working on history, memory, and dealing with the past from the former Yugoslavia, France, Germany, Belgium, and Holland. Every year they organize a field trip during which the participants investigate how other countries handle their respective pasts, including museums and memorials. The main purpose is to learn from each other and to exchange views and experiences. Field trips in the past have included Germany, France, Bosnia, Croatia, and Serbia.

The aim of the October 2015 trip to Belgium was to "explore Belgian history and memorialization challenges, with a specific focus on World War One, colonial history and questions of European memory, and to connect the experiences from Belgium with the situations and remembrance-work in other European countries."[1] The lectures by Belgian academics and memory activists triggered vivid debates on responsibility, on dealing with the past, and on what constitutes European identity. In one of the exercises, we were asked to design a European museum of our own choosing. It led to a heated debate on whether European history is made only of wars, ashes, and human loss; it was ultimately a debate on what is Europe, if not the European Union.

At one point during that week, our conversations turned to the issue of reconciliation. It was a semantic discussion of sorts, whereby the participants reflected on why or why not they used the word *reconciliation* in their work. Not entirely a surprise, very few said that they use the concept. Some thought it was a tainted word and they would rather avoid it. In their mind, it is tainted because it implies forgiveness. Others objected to it because it has been used by both local politicians and the international community in disingenuous ways, diluting its meaning. Yet, despite the reluctance to use the term itself, the work they engaged in could still be described as reconciliation, at least in a broad sense. The participants all worked for museums, memorial centers, and NGOs, which, in their own ways, dealt with the difficult pasts of specific regions. One of us (Heleen) can recall a similar conversation with someone who had been working for the International Criminal Tribunal for the former Yugoslavia (ICTY) for several years. She called reconciliation the "R"-word. There is the G-word, she said, and the R-word. "G" stands for genocide, "R" for reconciliation. She added that there could not be any genuine reconciliation as long as victims didn't feel they received the justice they deserved and as long as entire nations could claim victimhood at the expense of others. Justice for victims, she argued, did not necessarily imply retributive justice but should also include restorative justice. Her thoughts sum up very well the inherent tensions in the reconciliation process in the Balkans: between justice and reconciliation, between the emphasis on retributive justice and the need of victims for restorative justice as well as rehabilitation and reparations.[2]

In this chapter we shall examine some of these tensions, focusing in particular on how the European Union (EU) accession process shapes definitions and interactions in reconciliation processes. First, we discuss the Franco-German model of reconciliation and how it is employed as part of the formal accession process of the European Union. We then discuss the case of the Serbian resolution on Srebrenica as an example of how the emphasis on normative reconciliation and symbolic politics of restorative justice leads to outcomes that have actually little impact on the lived experiences of war victims from either side of the conflict. In the last part, we reflect further on the findings we have presented and examine what is missing from conventional definitions of reconciliation both within the EU and local political discourse.

The European Union and the Franco-German Model

The model that dictates the way the European Union deals with the Western Balkans is that of Franco-German reconciliation after World

War II. This model signifies a particular way of "doing reconciliation" as a top-down process initiated by elites, where the rest of society is supposed to follow suit. In essence, it is conceived of as a political process that is measured through economic and regional cooperation and that should first and foremost lead to stability. More than just a model, the Franco-German reconciliation lies at the very core of European *mythe identitaire,* the myth that constitutes the identity of the EU: the EU itself is seen as the fruit of reconciling peoples who had previously been at war with each other (see Guisan 2011).

When the European Union received the Nobel Peace Prize in 2012, the statement of the Norwegian Nobel Committee read that it had rewarded the EU for its "successful struggle for peace, reconciliation and for democracy and human rights." The statement even alluded to the former Yugoslavia, noting that "the Nobel Committee also believes *that the question of EU membership is bolstering the reconciliation process after the wars in the Balkan States,* and that the desire for EU membership has also promoted democracy and human rights in Turkey" (emphasis added).[3] In other words, when European Union officials talk about reconciliation, they most often have the Franco-German model in mind. Eduard Kukan, the chair of the European Parliament's EU-Serbia delegation, believes that this model was a salient example for EU officials, who had applied it "not only between two countries (as in bilaterally), but also as an argument in some internal situations like . . . very tense situation between two political parties in Albania or Macedonia. . . . *The moral is look at France and Germany: if they could do it, you can do it*" (emphasis added).[4]

Even though the EU was from the beginning an economic endeavor, starting as the European Community of Coal and Steel, the fundamental rights myth (Smismans 2010) suggests that reconciliation is a core value of the European Union. It is precisely the connection between economic cooperation and stability that lies at the heart of the reconciliation model as it is being applied to the Western Balkans. The prospect of EU membership offered to the post-conflict Balkans was initially a step taken toward a long-term strategy of stability. As Doris Pack, a former member of the European Parliament with significant experience in the region, said in a 2014 interview: "Having them in, we are keeping them in peace."[5] The assumption is that regional and economic cooperation will *automatically* lead to reconciliation, creating a spillover effect from politics to citizens. If we were to take a look at the EU's annual reports on the progress of potential members of the EU, precisely regional cooperation and good neighborly relations are seen as tools to measure the overall success of regional reconciliation. Employing repetitive and technocratic language, when reconciliation is measured it often reads something like: "country X participated constructively in regional initiatives and worked to improve its bilateral relations in a spirit of reconciliation and good neighborly relations." Transitional justice or restorative justice are, however, rarely mentioned. Kukan explains: "Reconciliation is very difficult because it has to do also with this mindset and to change that it is very difficult and that is why any movement and any initiative that leads in that direction we support."[6] As David McAllister, the EP's liaison with Serbia, notes: "Reconciliation is a precondition for the future development in the region and in different countries in the Balkans."[7]

Reconciliation, in that sense, is seen as mainly an elite-driven political process. Implicit in this notion is that reconciliation happens top-down and is fostered through intensive regional cooperation and Europeanization through socialization. The expectation is that, over time, these processes shall lead toward a change in the mindset and help countries to find a common ground. In this model, focusing on the future is more important than dwelling on the past. In the words of former EU commissioner on Enlargement[8] Štefan Füle: "Reconciliation is not about finding where the guilt needs to be attributed, *but looking towards the future without limitations of the past*" (emphasis added).[9] The expectation is that ordinary citizens and grassroots efforts will follow changes at the top.

It is also, in essence, a very elite-led, top-down view of reconciliation—a political process between different ethnic groups. However, if we were to look at how the concept has been used historically in the region, we can see that it has an additional dimension. During the 1990s, regional political leaders narrated the Yugoslav war through the prism of ethnic hatreds and World War II, in which the past was not only revived but distorted in order to support nationalistic agendas. To this end, the narrative of "all-national reconciliation" (*nacionalno pomirenje*, used both in Croatia and Serbia) posited on reconciling, *within the nation*, the ideological differences stemming from World War II. As such, intra-ethnic reconciliation, paired with historical revisionism, built heavily upon pre-Yugoslav, ethno-national histories and memories (Milošević 2017). It was based on deepening the wounds of the past and a competition of victimhood, focusing on the number of victims killed by the "Other" (see Ramet 2011; Djokić 2009). In this sense, it can be argued that before reconciliation became a process *between* ethnic groups, it was a tool of state- and nation building. As such, it carries a certain political weight.

There are many instances of how the Franco-German model[10] is employed in the process of dealing with the past in the Balkans, in particular when it comes to the civil society initiatives that receive EU support. The Memory Lab initiative, for example, where our conversations on reconciliation took place, was sponsored by French and German organizations. It included the Franco German Youth Office (FGYO), which is one of the pillars of the Franco-German reconciliation process after World War II. FGYO has provided a platform for exchanges between French and German youth. Incidentally, FGYO has also taken the initiative to establish a similar office called Regional Youth Cooperation Office (RYCO) across the former Yugoslavia, modeled on its own experiences. In 2015, the Western Balkan states signed a joint declaration for the establishment of RYCO with the aim to "promote the spirit of reconciliation and cooperation between the youth in the region." Symbolically, the agreement was signed in the presence of French president François Hollande and German chancellor Angela Merkel, who both emphasized that Franco-German reconciliation and the know-how of the FGYO could help the region to "deal with the bitterness of the past."[11]

A second important example is the "Joint History Project" launched in 1999 by the Center for Democracy and Reconciliation in Southeast Europe (CDRSEE). Through the Instrument for Pre-Accession Assistance, the European Commission invested 1.5 million euros in the project to create joint history books in the Western Balkans. It aims to challenge the way history is taught in schools across the Balkans. So far, four books covering the period of World War II up to the 1990s have been published in eleven languages. Just as in the Franco-German case, the goal of these history books is not only to challenge and revise ethnocentric history lessons but also to encourage critical thinking and debate. Celebrating diversity and tolerance is also a curricular aim of these text books. However, the decision of whether to use these history text books, designed as complementary rather than standard works, is dependent on the willingness of teachers to embrace multiperspective history teachings (Fajfer 2013).

Reconciliation and Conditionality

Despite the emphasis on reconciliation as a crucial element of the *mythe identitaire*, the elements of dealing with the past and transitional justice have never been part of EU accession before the Enlargement ambitions regarding former Yugoslavia. In the 1980s, during the accession process of Spain, Portugal, and Greece, there was no mention of transitional justice, reconciliation, or dealing with the past. After the fall of communism in 1989, the driving narrative about the Eastern Enlargement process (when Poland, Hungary, Slovakia, the Czech Republic, and others became EU members in 2004) was the *Reunification of Europe*. The Enlargement toward the Balkans, however, was not framed in this way. The war in Yugoslavia (1991–95) was not only the first European war since 1945 but an important test for the EU in dealing with a major regional and European crisis. It became evident that the EU needed to assume its responsibilities in the field of conflict prevention and crisis management, but also to rethink its Enlargement strategy. For the post-conflict Balkans, Enlargement and Integration became intrinsically linked to transitional justice. Nevertheless, there is no tradition of encoding reconciliation or transitional justice in the conditions for EU membership that apply to acceding countries. The fact that reconciliation processes are seen as something that will happen rather automatically in response to regional integration and economic cooperation is also reflected in the conditions that the EU has set, both formally and informally. "Conditionality" refers to the rules that acceding countries should adhere to if they become members.

After the accession of Bulgaria and Romania, the EU adopted a "Fundamentals first" approach. This means that the so-called soft acquis (rule of law, fundamental freedoms, independence of the judiciary, democracy) are now discussed at the beginning of the negotiation process. It was only with the accession of Croatia that issues of dealing with the past became part of the EU Enlargement criteria. Full cooperation with the International Criminal Tribunal of former Yugoslavia (ICTY) was the EU's main demand. The expectation clearly was that retributive justice through cooperation with the ICTY would help the process of dealing with the past and would lead to reconciliation (Rangelov 2006). In addition to cooperation with the ICTY, domestic war crimes trials were also part of EU conditionality.[12] In this light, the domestic handling of war crimes cases and reconciliation "should include preparedness to face its recent past and to do all it can to establish an atmosphere conducive to deal with all war crimes" (EC 2016, 57).

No elements of restorative justice were actually included in EU Conditionality, despite the great need for restoration (Rangelov 2006). From 2009 onward, the EU also started to support the RECOM[13] initiative for a regional truth commission in the former Yugoslavia (Bonora 2014) that was established by local NGOs in 2008. It was a move to redress some of the gaps and to support an initiative for restorative justice. The idea was that this would increase the recognition of the role of civil society in the process of coming to terms with the past. The Human Rights Committee of the EU Parliament was the first to declare its support of RECOM in 2010, later to be followed by the support of several EU Commission officials. In 2008, the European Parliament's rapporteur for Serbia, Jelko Kacin, advocated for the creation of a regional truth and fact-finding commission, when RECOM was still in its infancy. RECOM was seen as a good complement to the focus on retributive justice that had previously dominated the EU approach. Seen as a bottom-up impulse for dealing with the past, RECOM, as a grassroots initiative in contrast to the ICTY, was recognized as a mediating factor between the EU and national governments; it played an important role in enhancing the process of awareness and reconciliation throughout the Western Balkan (EP 2011). However, the EU never included support for RECOM in its conditionality; as a result it could not demand local elites to support the initiative (Touquet and Vermeersch 2016). In addition, the RECOM project was dominated by the bigger donor-funded NGOs in the region; as a result, some victims' organizations in Kosovo and Bosnia opted to step out of RECOM.

Interestingly, while the RECOM initiative originally claimed to have set reconciliation as its goal, the concept was later abandoned in its Statute (Niesser n.d.). As Vesna Teršelič, the director of *Documenta*, a Croatian NGO, argued during the RECOM consultations: "I don't know if the word 'reconciliation' will find its way in the documents we plan to submit to our governments simply because people who have suffered a lot may feel they are being forced to accept it. And I think that a decision to reconcile is a deeply personal decision and that fact-finding will certainly help people make such a decision."[14] There are other famous examples of organizations that do not want to employ the term *reconciliation*. For instance, Munira Subašić, from the Movement of the Mothers of Srebrenica and Žepa Enclaves Association, Bosnia and Herzegovina, said: "I will say first of all, on behalf the Movement of the Mothers of Srebrenica and Žepa Enclaves Association that we salute all commissions, not only this one, but every commission in Bosnia and Herzegovina or elsewhere because it is always better to do something than to do nothing. We understand that dialogue is needed, but I must tell you that at this moment I am offended by the word 'reconciliation.' *I intimately know*

whether I can forgive somebody, whether I will be able to forget, but on behalf
of thousands of mothers I cannot decide . . . whether they will be able to forgive
or forget. So, I don't want this commission to mention the word reconciliation"
(emphasis added).[15]

One can only speculate whether the chance for dealing with the
past was missed by not making reconciliation a part of more strident
conditionality. Asked about the lack of transitional justice elements in
conditionality, Kukan explains:

> I think it's a mistake. Somehow, we take it, especially our
> colleagues from the Western European countries, as: let them
> reconcile and then we will see. Given the character of these
> relations, I think that it would have been better to include
> it. . . . It would be truly helpful for those who are truly
> interested in reconciliation, if they could find some legal kind
> of support for it from the documents of the EU. Instead it
> remained wishful thinking, interpreted through the "good
> neighborly relations."[16]

Srebrenica and Symbolic Politics

Apart from its support for RECOM, the EU also supports restorative
justice in the form of public apologies and other symbolic politics in
the region. Kukan acknowledges the importance of such symbolism: "I
think it is important, however symbolic it might be—but it reflects your
own attitude, your own position towards these issues *and these kinds of*
symbolic signals are very important in this whole process of reconciliation. That is
why we always support or encourage leaders to do gestures or acts like
this" (emphasis added).[17] One of the particular foci of the EU in terms
of symbolic politics is the recognition of the genocide in Srebrenica by
the Serbian Government.

The UNPROFOR-protected[18] enclave of Srebrenica in northeastern
Bosnia was attacked by Bosnian Serb Army of Republic of Srpska (VRS)
in July 1995, which murdered around eight thousand Muslim men and
boys. In 2004, during one of the most important cases handled by the
ICTY (the Krstić case[19]), the ICTY ruled that the atrocities of Srebrenica
constituted genocide. Radislav Krstić, the former officer of VRS, was the
first European on trial for genocide since the Nuremberg trials. Krstić was

found not guilty of genocide as a principal perpetrator, but guilty as an aider and abettor to genocide. Srebrenica has become one of the ultimate symbols of the suffering of the Bosniaks during the Yugoslav war. Yet, to this day the Serbian government has not officially acknowledged that a genocide took place there. In light of this situation, we will discuss in the remainder of this chapter how the EU has applied soft pressure on Serbia to deal with the acknowledgment of Srebrenica through a resolution by the European Parliament. Finally, we consider the relationship between symbolic politics and reconciliation, starting from the observation that the EU regularly lauds Serb politicians who visit the memorial site in Srebrenica for their efforts of reconciliation.

In 2009, the European Parliament adopted a resolution on the genocide in Srebrenica. Organizations such as the Mothers of Enclaves of Srebrenica, the Association of Concentration Camp Detainees of Bosnia and Herzegovina, and the Grand Mufti Mustafa Cerić presented a draft resolution to declare July 11 a day of mourning and remembrance in the European Parliament.[20] The resolution of the European Parliament was meant to set an example for the Serbian Parliament, which would adopt a similar declaration recognizing the genocide. The last paragraph of the Resolution (see EP 2009) explicitly instructs the president of the European Parliament to forward the resolution to the governments of the Western Balkan states as a way of encouraging them to follow suit.

After Serbia had formally submitted its request for EU membership in 2009, Serbian president Boris Tadić called on the Serbian Parliament in 2010 to adopt a declaration that would unequivocally condemn the crime in Srebrenica. Over the course of the next two months, a heated debate ensued over the wording of the text (Dragović-Soso 2012, 171). Serbian human rights NGOs protested in front of the Serbian Parliament, calling on the members of the parliament to pass a resolution modeled on the European Parliament's resolution.[21] In March 2010, a declaration condemning the crime against Bosnian Muslims in Srebrenica was finally adopted. Unlike the EU resolution, however, it calls for all countries of the former Yugoslavia to adopt similar resolutions condemning crimes committed against Serbs during the war. Jasna Dragović-Soso argues that in Serbia it was impossible "to adopt an official act focused solely on Srebrenica without simultaneously demanding a 'return apology' for crimes committed against Serbs" (2012, 172–73).

The Serbian Declaration also does not use the word *genocide* to describe the crimes committed in Srebrenica. In fact, the 2010 resolution was not so different from the one that had failed to be accepted by the Serbian Parliament in 2005 (*Deklaracija o osudi ratnih zločina na prostoru nekadašnje Jugoslavije* [Declaration on Condemnation of War Crimes Committed on the Territory of former Yugoslavia]). The text of the 2005 failed resolution illustrates the guiding principles behind the dominant attitudes of the Serbian political elites toward war crimes in the 1990s:

> Serbia has a special, vital and historical interest in the explanation and judgement of *all war crimes* committed in the recent history of Yugoslavia *in which the Serbian nation was the greatest victim*. First in the terms of victims, *Serbia must be the first in the judgement of all crimes*. The democratic party of Serbia in this declaration condemns all war crimes, without regard to who committed them, in the conviction that no crime is subject to statutes of limitation and no crime can be forgotten. . . . It is of fundamental importance in the condemnation of crime, we do not make distinction on the basis of the place where a crime was committed or the religion or nationality of the victim. Therefore, we unreservedly condemn the crime committed in Srebrenica. (DSS Deklaracija 2005; emphasis added)

The 2005 Declaration continues to list other "un-investigated and unpunished crimes against Serbian population" in Operation Flash, Operation Storm, Sarajevo, Tuzla, and elsewhere. A second element in this nationalist discourse is the expansion of the scope of war crimes going back to World War II. There were also references to Serb victimhood in World War II as well to the atrocities of the 1940s Ustaša movement in Jasenovac (MacDonald 2009).

Despite the absence of a true acknowledgment of the genocide in the 2010 Declaration, the high representative Catherine Ashton and Commissioner Štefan Füle issued the following statement: "The European Union welcomes the adoption by the Serbian Parliament of the declaration on Srebrenica. This is an important step for the country in facing its recent past, a process which is difficult but essential for Serbian society to go through. This is not only important for Serbia, *it is the key for the reconciliation for the whole region*. We appreciate the role of everyone who made such a step possible" (EU 2010; emphasis added). In its 2010 progress report on Serbia, the European Commission highlights the significance of "condemning the crime in Srebrenica" (EC 2010, 20).

We can ask, however, whether the EU support for such symbolic steps toward recognition of war crimes is counterproductive. Pablo De Greiff (2008) argues that an apology can only be considered as such if it includes an acceptance of responsibility and an expression of regret. The Serbian declaration on Srebrenica contained neither of those aspects. It is therefore unclear what the declaration means in terms of reconciliation, and why European Union officials chose to support it. When there is no admission of guilt, there is no recognition of what was done to the victims. The Serbian policy so far has pursued a course that does not recognize, or only partly recognizes, victims (there have been some small steps toward recognition through local war crimes court cases but not through compensation, memorialization, etc.). So far, EU criticism toward this stance by the Serbian government has been rather mild and formulated in a very polite way, despite the fact that genocide denial is clearly not acceptable to the EU. The 2012 EU progress report criticized newly elected Serbian president Tomislav Nikolić in the following words: "Some *unhelpful statements for reconciliation* in the region were made by the new Serbian President, Mr Nikolić, at the time of his election and taking office, *such as that denying the qualification of genocide for the crimes in Srebrenica.* Several regional leaders decided not to attend the inauguration of the new president. Serbia needs to continue to make a positive and constructive contribution to regional cooperation and reconciliation" (EC 2012, 21–22; emphasis added).

Serbian Prime Minister Aleksandar Vučić's visit to the Srebrenica memorial in 2015 is a good example of the way Serbia pleases the EU with certain gestures, while it shows a different face for domestic audiences. At his visit on July 11, 2015, Vučić refrained again from using the word *genocide,* since such a gesture would imply a statement of guilt. Vučić is, however, considered to be a controversial figure for the victims because of his former political allegiance with Vojislav Šešelj, an ICTY-acquitted Serbian politician. Vučić's visit to Srebrenica thus sparked a violent reaction by some of the mourners, who started to throw rocks which hit him in the face.[22] European officials did not hesitate to show their support for Vučić, calling his visit to Srebrenica a "historical choice." Federica Mogherini, the high representative for foreign affairs, tweeted: "My solidarity to @avucic who made the historical choice of being present in Srebrenica. Peace can be built only on reconciliation." The day before July 11, Serbian activists had gathered in front of the Serbian Parliament in Belgrade to commemorate the victims by lighting candles, thereby defying the Serbian authorities who had forbidden the event, citing security reasons. The authorities said that right-wing groups had threatened to interrupt the commemoration. The director of the Youth Initiative for Human Rights, Anita Mitić, was arrested that evening. In an interview with the news website Balkan Insight, she said: "It is proof that the Serbian PM can go to the Srebrenica genocide commemoration, but that Belgrade cannot have anything to do with it. It means that recognizing the Srebrenica genocide victims and holding people accountable is not permitted in Belgrade."[23] The strange double standard of visiting the Srebrenica memorial while at the same time punishing its own citizens wanting to hold a commemoration was not noted publicly by any EU officials.

Since the EU lauds public apologies and official visits, they are judged by many observers as well as victim groups as an easy way to please the EU rather than as sincere gestures of recognition and acknowledgment. The history of the debate on Srebrenica in the Serbian Parliament illustrates the point that a lot of these discussions have one goal: to please the EU rather than actively deal with the past, let alone to admit guilt. Declarative commitments on issues of the past are usually not followed by concrete measures or tangible policies that create a truly transformative effect for those who suffered injustices.

Reconciliation without Recognition

In spite of all the talk on reconciliation from above, as researchers working regularly in the field we cannot help but notice that very little has been achieved for people who have been victims of the war. Yet, the fate and role of victims are crucial for the process of reconciliation. While the EU has done its share to support retributive justice in particular, its competences do not reach far enough to have an impact on processes that benefit victims. According to renowned psychologist Judith Herman's research on what justice means for victims, neither retributive nor restorative justice can really help. The key for victims is recognition and acknowledgment by the community (Herman 2005). One kind of acknowledgment is acknowledgement by the state. State policies for the recognition of victims are often heavily politicized and follow their own norms with regard to who is considered a legitimate victim (Wilke 2007; Jacoby 2015). This is also the case in the Western Balkans, in particular when it comes to the recognition of victims of sexual violence. Given the knowledge we have about the impact of sexual assault and sexual violence on a human beings' capacity to connect and to enjoy life, it is clear that the consequences of sexual violence extend far beyond what happens to individual victims and stretch out over entire communities, as well as across different generations. There were numerous victims of sexual violence during the 1990s war in the Balkans. Though most victims were women, many men were also abused in the camps. Bosniaks suffered the highest number among victims of sexual violence, but there were also Croats and Serbs. The capacity of victims to connect is intimately linked to recognition. However, the recognition of victims and survivors of sexual violence is very uneven in the former Yugoslav states. Due to the ethnicized structure of the Bosnian state, survivors of sexual violence are not recognized at all in the Republika Srpska (Serbian part of Bosnia and Herzegovina). In the Federation (the Bosnian-Croat Federation), there is a very limited recognition for sexual violence survivors since 2006, as they can apply for a small compensation from the social welfare system.[24] However, in the Republika Srpska, people have to prove a physical disability of 60 percent in order to get any compensation, which is almost impossible to do for a victim of sexual violence. Similarly, in Croatia, sexual violence victims can apply for compensation only if they are Croat nationals. This policy neglects, for example, the Serb soldiers who were sexually tortured in the Lori prison camp. In Serbia, there is no recognition at all for sexual violence victims. In essence, transitional justice efforts (such as the recognition of victims and survivors of sexual violence) have fallen prey to the enduring competition between memory entrepreneurs who claim victimhood only for their own nation.

Victims are also not recognized because of the lack of memorials. Even though citizens demand the creation of more memorials, ethno-nationalist memory entrepreneurs dominate the official memorialization landscape relating to the war in Serbia, Bosnia, and Croatia. What is officially remembered has to fit into each respective ethno-national narrative (Pavlaković 2014). The political attention given to memorialization such as the annual commemorations in Srebrenica transforms these places of memory into a public stage. Instead of being a locus for mourning and remembrance for the victims, political elites become the central actors of these commemorations. Though it is conceivable that some gestures of political leaders, such as kneeling or asking forgiveness, are genuine acts of mourning and remorse, their actions should not be seen as an expression of collective attitudes.

In response to the politicization of memorials and commemora-tions, some victim and survivor associations create their own grassroots memorials and organize counter-commemorations. Private monuments have emerged in public spaces as alternative loci of grief and remem-brance for the victims for whom an official memorial has been denied. However, these bottom-up expressions of memory are not without their own controversies. In the municipality of Vareš in central Bosnia, for example, a multiethnic memorial was threatened with removal after local elections put a new mayor into office. In some instances, local economic development overshadows the need to commemorate, as in the case of city of Prijedor, where the former detainees of the Omarska camp are allowed a few days each year to commemorate. The former prison camp is now a factory owned by the Indian steel conglomerate ArcelorMittal. In an attempt to do something for the former detainees, ArcelorMittal organized meetings between the victims and the local Serb mayor, a man who had been part of the local Serb crisis staff during the war. The crisis staff (*Krizni štab*) took control over the town at the beginning of the war and established the three camps where Bosniak and Croat civilians were detained, abused, and killed (Omarska, Keraterm, and Trnopolje). The mayor and the victims could not reach an agreement, and to this day there is no monument (Sivac-Bryant 2014).

The problem with the lack of recognition of victims in favor of the recognition of collective victimhood of entire nations is that it further fuels exclusionist politics as it makes it easier for nationalist elites to mobilize the grievances of their own victims. Bizarrely enough, the argument that all victims should get recognition is also used by memory entrepreneurs. In 2015, Aleksandar Vučić proposed[25] to hold a Memorial Day for all victims, with the political purpose of establishing a narrative of the equalization of guilt, an idea that was welcomed by some EU officials, according to ICTY chief prosecutor Serge Brammertz.[26] He invited citizens to turn toward real problems and to the future, meaning economic reforms: "[F]rom hatred and digging up the wounds from the past we cannot and will not be able to live."[27] The narrative of the equalization of guilt is dangerous because it is linked to the idea of "ancient hatred" that marks some Western views on the wars in the former Yugoslavia: supposedly, people in the Balkans are really "other" and savages, who bear a deeply entrenched hatred for each other. In such a reading, everyone is equally guilty—and therefore no one is accountable.

The EU's adherence to the Franco-German model seems much more of a strategy of pacification and stabilization than an investment in a process that leads to reconciliation. While the European Commission acknowledges that the "lasting reconciliation requires efforts at all levels— government, civil society and the judicial system," reconciliation "is linked to the struggle against poverty and social exclusion" (EC 2010, 10). The idea seems to be that economic progress will automatically lead to the healing of people who have lived through the 1990s war. In 2016, one of us (Ana) was invited to the directorate general for Enlargement of the EU to share her experiences on reconciliation in the Western Balkans with human rights activists from African countries. At a certain point, a colleague from Zimbabwe asked: "What do the victims and their families actually want?" The answer of the Commission official was: "People in Bosnia are going in the streets saying 'we are hungry in three languages.'" The official was referring to the protests in Bosnia that were happen- ing at the time, when some people carried signs with the antinationalist slogan "We are hungry in three languages,"[28] stating they cared more about economic progress than nationalist issues. What the official seemed to suggest to our colleague from Zimbabwe was that bread and butter issues were more pressing concerns than victims' rights. While a poor economic performance, lack of employment opportunities, and alarming poverty levels are certainly pressing issues in the region, the improve- ment of economic conditions alone will not compensate for the lack of acknowledgment and recognition of victims and their families. Of course, this does not mean that there is not a lot of overlap between economic issues and recognition: victims' demands for material compensation and recognition have both been shortchanged (Dragović-Soso 2016).

Conclusion

The EU conceptualizes reconciliation as a top-down process, dominated by political elites and accelerated by regional economic cooperation. In the Western Balkans region, the EU pursues a concept of reconciliation founded on the idea of nation-states, with the effect that it reinforces local political elites and their nation-building projects, in which historical narratives are used for political mobilization. At the same time, due to the very nature of the EU Enlargement process, the EU does not have any impact on local transitional justice processes that have left large numbers of victims unrecognized. This lack of recognition for the victims and survivors of war leaves the door wide open for ethno-political memory entrepreneurs who mobilize these grievance-based, ethnicized identities. In other words, the EU Integration process invites a critical gaze toward the past but deals with the past only selectively; EU accession does not weaken the domestic monopoly over existing ethno-national narratives.

The current crisis of legitimacy in the European Union threatens the small steps that have so far been taken toward reconciliation. In the Balkans, the EU is (still) one of the most important drivers of change, but its influence has faded in the last years. Support for EU candidacy in the Balkan countries has diminished. Taken together with the impact of the economic crisis, the already fragile regional relations are eroding even further. In the past five years we have seen the worsening of Serbian-Croatian relations over the refugee crisis, the revival of old disputes, and a renewed historical revisionism that tends to invert the efforts toward reconciliation. Ironically, the EU accession of Croatia only augmented these tensions. Today, the battle for one's own view of the past is not only fought regionally but also in the European Parliament.

Our analysis begs the question of what can be a way forward for the EU, the local elites, and grassroots associations. We believe that reconciliation requires a willingness to go beyond one's (political) comfort zone. It requires a willingness to critically address the past and to depoliticize issues concerning victims. The process of Europeanization in the Western Balkans must therefore fully develop its transformative potential and go beyond symbolic reconciliation. It cannot be limited to interactions between politicians and power holders but, instead, must be built upon a partnership with all citizens and upon the recognition of victims, independent of their ethnic belonging. No matter how small grassroots initiatives might be, when they support victims across boundaries, they deserve support. The challenge for the EU is to question its own exceptionalism and its preconceived notions of what reconciliation is and should be. As such, the current crisis of legitimacy might also be an opportunity for self-reflection.

Notes

1. "Memory Lab: Trans-European Exchange Platform on History and Remembrance." http://www.memorylab-europe.eu/workshop/2015-belgium; retrieved January 30, 2017.

2. Interview with anonymous official of the ICTY (Heleen Touquet, May 13, 2014).

3. Nobel Media AB 2014. "European Union (EU)—Facts." Nobelprize. org. http://www.nobelprize.org/nobel_prizes/peace/laureates/2012/eu-facts.html.

4. Interview with Eduard Kukan (Ana Milošević, May 24, 2016).

5. Interview with Doris Pack (Ana Milošević, April 10, 2014).

6. Interview with Eduard Kukan (Ana Milošević, May 24, 2016).

7. Interview with David McAllister (Ana Milošević, June 17, 2015).

8. The term *European Enlargement* refers to the process of expanding the European Union through the accession of new member states.

9. Interview with Štefan Füle (Ana Milošević, December 21, 2016).

10. For a discussion on whether it can be seen as a model, see Moll 2008.

11. "Joint declaration on the establishment of the regional youth cooperation office in the Western Balkans. Annex 2." *Vienna Western Balkans Summit.* 2015. https://rycoblog.files.wordpress.com/2015/12/annex_1_jointdeclaration_establishment-youth-cooperation-office-western-balkans-1.pdf; retrieved January 30, 2017.

12. See in chapter 23 the EU negotiations. Balkan Insight 2015. Interview with Pierre Mirel. War Crimes Justice Remains Key to EU Accession. http://www.balkaninsight.com/en/article/war-crimes-justice-remains-key-to-enlargement; retrieved January 30, 2017.

13. RECOM (Regional Commission for the Establishment of facts about the war crimes and other serious violations of human rights committed in the former Yugoslavia between 1991 and 2001) is a regional network of civil society associations and individuals established in 2008.

14. RECOM, Local consultation with civil society, Prijedor, Bosnia-Herzegovina, May 13, 2009, CP, 93.

15. Ibid., 267.

16. Interview with Eduard Kukan (Ana Milošević, May 24, 2016).

17. Ibid.

18. UNPROFOR—The United Nations Protection Force—was the first United Nations peacekeeping force in Croatia and in Bosnia and Herzegovina during the Yugoslav Wars.

19. Radislav Krstić, a former officer of the VRS, was the third person ever convicted by an International Tribunal under the 1948 Convention on the Prevention and Punishment of the Crime of Genocide. See more, ICTY Court records. Case reference: *The Prosecutors vs. Krstić* (T-98-33). http://www.icty.org/case/krstic/4; retrieved January 30, 2017.

20. "Diana Wallis meets Mothers of Srebrenica in Brussels." Wallis, Diana. October 16, 2008. https://dianawallis.org.uk/cy/article/2008/0064074/diana-wallis-meets-mothers-of-srebrenica-in-brussels; retrieved January 30, 2017.

21. "Žene u crnom za mir i pravdu." *B92,* January 10, 2010. http://www.b92.net/info/vesti/index.php?yyyy=2010&mm=01&dd=11&nav_id=403259; retrieved January 31, 2017.

22. "Serbia's president condemns 'savage' attack on PM at Srebrenica." *The Guardian*, July 21, 2015.

23. "Serbian Activist Faces Court for Commemorating Srebrenica." *Balkan Insight*, January, 26, 2016. http://www.balkaninsight.com/en/article/serbian-activist-faces-trial-for-commemorating-srebrenica-01-28-2016#sthash.jNfKIE5K.e96fLMzZ.dpuf; retrieved January 31, 2017.

24. Essentially, this is a law on social benefits for war victims that was adapted to include an exception for sexual violence survivors in 2006. Since then, sexual violence survivors no longer have to prove a 60 percent disability. Also, there is no longer a statute of limitations for this particular category. It is thus not a recognition through compensation.

25. "Vučić: Bilo bi dobro da imamo zajednički Dan sećanja na sve žrtve na prostoru bivše Jugoslavije." *Buka*, August 7, 2015.

26. Interview with Serge Brammertz (Heleen Touquet, August 26, 2015).

27. "Vučić: Bilo bi dobro da imamo zajednički Dan sećanja na sve žrtve na prostoru bivše Jugoslavije." *Buka*, August 7, 2015.

28. The slogan, *Gladni smo na tri jezika*, was spray-painted onto a wall in the industrial town of Tuzla, where the protests started. It went on to become a popular slogan in protests and grafitti.

Works Cited

Bonora, Catarina. 2006. "Opening Up or Closing the Historical Dialogue: The Role of Civil Society in Promoting a Debate About the Past." *Dialogues on Historical Justice and Memory Network Working Paper Series* No. 4.

Defrance, Corine. 2016. "La 'reconciliation' après les conflits: un 'savoir-faire' européen? Éléments d'introduction." *Les Cahiers Sirice* 2016/1(15): 5–14.

De Greiff, Pablo. 2008. "The Role of Apologies in National Reconciliation Processes: On Making Trustworthy Institutions Trusted." In *The Age of Apology: Facing Up to the Past*, edited by Mark Gibney et al., 120–36. Philadelphia: University of Pennsylvania Press.

Dragović-Soso, Jasna. 2012. "Apologising for Srebrenica: The Declaration of the Serbian Parliament, the European Union and the Politics of Compromise." *East European Politics* 28(2): 163–79.

———. 2016. "History of a Failure: Attempts to Create a National Truth and Reconciliation Commission in Bosnia and Herzegovina, 1997–2006." *International Journal of Transitional Justice* 10: 292–310.

Djokić, Dejan. 2002. "The Second World War II: Discourses of Reconciliation in Serbia and Croatia in the late 1980s and early 1990s." *Journal of Southern Europe and the Balkans Online* 4(2): 127–40.

DSS—Democratic Party of Serbia [*Demokratska partija Srbije*]. 2005. *Deklaracija o osudi ratnih zločina na prostoru nekadašnje Jugoslavije*. Belgrade: DSS.

EC. 2010. *Strategia di allargamento e sfide principali per il periodo 2010–2011 [The Enlargement Strategy and Main Challenges for the Period 2010–2011]* COM(2010) 660 definitivo [final]. November 9.

EC. 2012. *Progress Report on Serbia. Enlargement Strategy and Main Challenges 2012–2013*. COM (2012) 600 final. October 10.

EC. 2016. *EU Progress Report on Serbia 2016*. SWD (2016) 361 final. November 9.

EP. 2011. Stabilisation and Association Agreement between the EC and Serbia: Resolution on the European integration process of Serbia. P7_TA (2011) 0014. January 19.

EU. 2010. Joint Statement by High Representative Catherine Ashton and Commissioner Štefan Füle on the Serbian Declaration on Srebrenica. A 45/10. Brussels. March 31. Retrieved at: https://www.consilium.europa.eu/uedocs/cms_data/docs/pressdata/EN/foraff/113647.pdf.

Fajfer, Lubo. 2013. "Reconnecting History—The Joint History Project in the Balkans." In *History Education and Post-Conflict Reconciliation: Reconsidering Joint Textbook Projects*, edited by Karina Valentinovna Korostelina and Simone Lässig, 140–54. Abingdon: Routledge.

Guisan, Catherine. 2011. "From the European Coal and Steel Community to Kosovo: Reconciliation and Its Discontents." *JCMS* 49(3): 541–62.

Herman, Judith Lewis. 2005. "Justice from the Victim's Perspective." *Violence against Women* 11(5): 571–602.

Jacoby, Tami Amanda. 2015. "A Theory of Victimhood: Politics, Conflict and the Construction of Victim-Based Identity." *Millennium-Journal of International Studies* 43(2): 511–30.

MacDonald, David. 2009. "From Jasenovac to Srebrenica: Subaltern Genocide and the Serbs." In *Genocides by the Oppressed: Subaltern Movements and Retributive Genocide*, edited by Nicholas Robins and Adam Jones, 103–21. Bloomington: University of Indiana Press.

Milošević, Ana. 2017. "Back to the Future, Forward to the Past: Croatian Politics of Memory in the European Parliament." *Nationalities Papers* 45(5): 893–909.

Moll, Nicolas. 2008. "La réconciliation franco-allemande et les Balkans: une motivation, pas un modèle." *L'Europe en Formation* 3: 33–54.

Niesser, Jacqueline. "'Nemoj mi samo o miru i ljubavi!' Versöhnung als Tabu auf dem Gebiet des ehemaligen Jugoslawien?" Kakanien Revisited, n.d., http://www.kakanien.ac.at/beitr/re_visions/JNiesser1/; accessed March 20, 2015.

Pavlaković, Vjeran. 2014. "Fulfilling the Thousand-Year Old Dream: Strategies of Symbolic Nation-building in Croatia." In *Strategies of Symbolic Nation-Building in South Eastern Europe*, edited by Pål Kolstø, 19–50. Ashgate: Farnham.

Ramet, Sabina P. 2002. *Balkan Babel: The Disintegration of Yugoslavia from the Death of Tito to the Fall of Milošević*. Oxford: Westview Press.

Rangelov, Iavor. 2005. "Civil Society and Transitional Justice in the Balkans: Three Models of Interaction." *SiT Working Paper* WP/01/15.

————. 2006. "EU Conditionality and Transitional Justice in the Former Yugoslavia." *Croatian Yearbook of European Law and Policy* 2(2): 365–75.

Schaap, Andrew. 2008. "Reconciliation as Ideology and Politics." *Constellations* 15(2): 249–64.

Sivac-Bryant, Sebina. 2015. "The Omarska Memorial Project as an Example of How Transitional Justice Interventions Can Produce Hidden Harms." *International Journal of Transitional Justice* 9(1): 170–80.

Smismans, Stijn. 2010. "The European Union's Fundamental Rights Myth." *JCMS: Journal of Common Market Studies* 48(1): 45–66.

Touquet, Heleen, and Peter Vermeersch. 2016. "Changing Frames of Reconciliation: The Politics of Peace-Building in the Former Yugoslavia." *East European Politics and Societies and Cultures* 30(1): 55–73.

Wilke, Christiane. 2007. "Recognizing Victimhood: Politics and Narratives of Rehabilitation in Germany." *Journal of Human Rights* 6(4): 479–96.

Epilogue

Memory versus Reconciliation

VALERIE ROSOUX

The future does not belong to the dead, but to those who speak for them, who explain why they are dead.

—Georges Bernanos, *Les enfants humiliés: Journal 1939–1940*

In the aftermath of wars, an infinite series of actions must be treated as urgent: disarming, demobilizing, reintegrating, rebuilding, governing, judging, etc. In addition to these priorities, policymakers and peacebuilders face a plurality of narratives that reflect divergent and often contradictory memories of the conflict. Calls for inclusive narratives do not preclude the transmission of incompatible—and highly emotional—representations of the past, and therefore of the Other. In such circumstances, how can former enemies gradually negotiate a common language, in order to draw a line between the past and the present?

The contributions gathered together in this book suggest new ways to tame a conflictual past in order to move forward. They particularly emphasize the importance of interpersonal relationships. For, even if rapprochement seems necessary to the representatives of each party, it cannot be imposed by decree. Violent conflicts provoke an infinite series of individual fires that need to be extinguished one by one. From this perspective, it is worth highlighting specific dynamics and dilemmas. Rather than giving black and white explanations, this book dares to investigate grey areas and does not ignore the pitfalls of transformative processes. It invites us to adopt a research posture that favors both a reflective and a creative analysis.

Reflective Analysis

Throughout this volume, the authors reflect on their own commitment and beliefs. Rather than identifying themselves as strictly external analysts, they explain why they work on postwar reconstruction, to what extent this issue emotionally resonates with their own personal life, and how they manage to deal with their own expectations. This sensitive stance differs from two attitudes that often characterize research on post-conflict settings. First, scholars can adopt an attitude that is fundamentally normative. The objective is to tell people affected by war how they should cope with the past. This approach is maximalist: it tends to favor the shift from enmity to amity, from darkness to optimism. To allow such radical transformation, reconciliation is systematically associated with forgiveness (Bercovitch and Jackson 2009, 153). The language refers to either a theological framework (in terms of purification) or a psychological framework (in terms of healing). One of the advantages of this prescriptive attitude is its clarity. However, little attention is paid to local needs and resistance—and yet, these are legitimate.

Second, scholars can adopt a realist attitude that does not describe reconciliation as a panacea, but as an illusion. Emphasis is placed on the balance of power between parties, the main idea being that former enemies are driven fundamentally by their interests and not by an altruistic willingness to (re)build anything *with* the former enemy. The added value of this approach is that it stresses the importance of power asymmetries. However, in reducing the protagonists to rational actors, such an approach can miss their emotional side. This dimension certainly varies from one individual to another, but it can hardly be denied in the aftermath of a war. Another limitation of this attitude is the quasi exclusive attention paid to the macro level (state level) and the subsequent neglect of the mezzo and micro levels, which are key to understanding postwar changes.

The attitude suggested in this book is different. Far from providing an idealistic to-do checklist, or systematically skeptical counterarguments denying the impact of any emotional process, the authors propose a pragmatic attitude based on practical engagement. Their observation of, and often participation in, various post-conflict settings includes all levels of society (individuals, associations, leaders). Their studies consider small gestures and modest changes that might seem insignificant at first glance, but signal fundamental shifts in symbolic terms. By taking seriously the relational aspect of transformative processes, they show that reconciliation is definitely "hard work" and a "costly process" (see the chapter by Krondorfer), but that it is nevertheless a path that must be taken in order to turn the page.

As "scholars and practitioners," most authors question the role of third parties in the aftermath of a war. The role they play may be questionable. What is the legitimacy of outsiders in the eyes of local communities? How much credibility do they have? To put it in a more personal way, what can we say about dealing with mass atrocities if we are not survivors? A brief anecdote allows us to put these questions into perspective. During my first stay in Rwanda, I visited a rather poor area of Kigali with a Rwandan PhD student. Far from the crowded streets of the center, we were walking down a deserted alleyway when we saw an old lady who looked at me bitterly and pronounced a couple of words in Kinyarwanda. Confused by the coldness of her glance, I asked my PhD student to tell me what she had just said. Hesitantly, he translated: "Go back home, it's too late." The lady had already disappeared into the surrounding neighborhood, and there was anyway nothing to add. Nonetheless, her voice and her message remained with me during the whole trip. They forced me to reflect on my intentions, my hopes, and even my own personal story. They provoked a kind of "low-profile" reaction that was perhaps useful to avoid the syndrome of *Tintin in the Congo*. From then on, I started thinking about what Susan Sontag calls the dilemma of the third party facing the pain of others: being either "a spectator" or "a coward, unable to look" (Sontag 2003, 34).

The question is not only an ethical one. It also has a political dimension. Scholars working in the field of conflict resolution can easily position themselves as combatants on a battlefield. They choose sides and become part of the fight that they are supposed to observe from outside. The need not to become politically involved in favor of one party over the other may seem obvious. It is, however, not always so clear-cut, practically speaking. In a very tense political context (such as those emphasized in this book), scholars and practitioners can be bombarded with militant claims, which are mostly incompatible. Thus, a talk I gave in Geneva about "dealing with the past in Rwanda" provoked the anger of some Rwandans offended that I could call into question certain specific decisions made by the Rwandan authorities, while others bitterly regretted the lack of strong denunciations of the same authorities.[1]

Something similar happened when, ten years later, a Rwandan student explained to me that he was puzzled that I had not chosen sides, at least not publicly. He therefore asked me to tell him, in secret, which side I supported, since I needed to support one of them. In such circumstances, the objective of neutrality comes under fire. It is, however, the only practical means to explore the perceptions and positions of all parties, and, therefore, the only way to understand the interactions and dynamics observed in the aftermath of mass atrocities.

In the literature on social science methodologies, scholars are sometimes compared to spokespersons. They try to understand a specific context—in this particular case post-conflict settings—by listening to all parties. Their preliminary question is simple: How does it work? To answer this question, scholars need to understand who talks to whom, when, for what reasons, with what impact. Nevertheless, they cannot properly depict the interactions between parties by reporting only the voices of these parties. They also need to comprehend their silences—in the plural. In the aftermath of wars, a wide range of silences signals emotions as diverse as shame, guilt, fear, mistrust, suspicion, sadness, or merely respect. As shown in all the chapters of this book, these emotions remain very strong, even many years later. From Zimbabwe to Bosnia, these emotions are key to understanding postwar dynamics and deadlocks.

The role of peacebuilders and facilitators goes beyond this purpose. By becoming personally involved in the transformation of relationships between former enemies, they are faced with the political and moral dimensions of one of the most crucial post-conflict challenges: To what extent can they really help to "redress," "compensate for," "repair," or "rectify" past injustices? The irreversible character of the violence that is committed during a war (be it a civil war or an international conflict) reminds us that the aim is not only to make peace with the adversaries. It is also—and above all—to make peace with the past, or, in other words, with the world as it is.

This ambitious objective emphasizes a fundamental tension that characterizes all war-torn societies, namely, the tension between memory and reconciliation. On the one hand, people need to commemorate and honor the dead. Survivors need to know that the violence they suffered will be punished, or at least that it will never be forgotten. Policymakers and practitioners, however, often call for rapprochement in order to ensure a better future for the next generations. Both objectives are important. However, they are not easily compatible.

This tension particularly affects the families of survivors and victims, who may, quite legitimately, be reluctant and skeptical about any rapprochement with those who committed violence. It underlines the ambivalence of a process that can increase social capital, while decreasing individual well-being, at least for some victims (Ciliers, Dube, and Siddiqi 2016). This ambivalence brings us back to the initial question emphasized by Björn Krondorfer in the introduction to this book: Is reconciliation always possible, and even desirable? How can this notion resonate with all the components of the populations of devastated societies, since individual experiences, emotions, and expectations are dissimilar and fundamentally dissonant? Does reconciliation actually make sense in intractable conflicts?

Most of the authors gathered together in this book seem to see the need for a bottom-up process of reconciliation, even in the midst of the conflict. The chapters written by Zeina Barakat and Avner Dinur are very interesting in this regard. As scholars *and* peace activists, they both took the risk of becoming personally involved in a rapprochement with the "enemy," and therefore know the price that must be paid. This personal wish to bridge emotional and cognitive gaps is, as such, thought-provoking. Why are some individuals determined to give a chance to the other camp, while the vast majority of their fellow countrymen see the objective of reconciliation as indecent? Which variables can explain their resolve to (re)build a society *with* the adversary? Is there a specific feature in their personal trajectories that can explain their urge to imagine a scenario which is not divisive?

Applauded as visionary and audacious pioneers in New York, Brussels, or Berlin, these "reconciliatory" figures are often stigmatized and denounced as insensitive traitors by their own group (as is established in several chapters of this book). So where do they find the energy to resist group pressure? Is the ability to speak the language of the Other—and therefore to listen to alternative narratives—critical to distancing oneself from the traditional stories transmitted from one generation to the next? Is this personal experience behind the belief that "a continuous human contact will prepare [the parties] for better times," as Krondorfer put it?

The experience of interpersonal reconciliation leading to the gradual humanization of the enemy is certainly key to understanding the motivation behind each commitment to engage with the Other. The criticisms leveled at the intergroup contact theory in the field of social psychology do not negate our conviction that interpersonal encounters do make a difference. Further questions can still be put as to the impact of these encounters: How can we make sure that they do not only affect particular niches in society? How can participants deal with the psychological dissonance that inevitably marks their return back home? How can they maintain their vivid experience of the so-called enemies and resist the usual representations shared in their large-group community? To sum up, how can we ensure that the (re)humanization process is contagious?

Creative Analysis

All these questions are addressed in this book. They encourage us to explore the issue in at least three ways. The first relates to timing: When do protagonists start thinking in terms of reconciliation (if they do so), and until when does it make sense? The second question regards the process as such: What is "memory work"? The third one is more provocative: What if reconciliation is not on the agenda?

RECONCILIATION: HOW TO START AND HOW TO END?

The notion of *post-conflict* is well established. In 1995, the United Nations secretary general, Boutros Boutros-Ghali, created a task force to draw up an inventory of "post-conflict peacebuilding activities." More generally speaking, the notion of post-conflict is defined in handbooks, dictionaries, and encyclopedias. Practitioners and analysts regularly refer to it (Junne and Verkoren 2004; Chesterman 2005; Chetail 2009). However, the duration of these "post-conflict" environments can still be uncertain. What are the basic criteria that determine when a conflict is over? Traditional categories, such as conflict prevention/resolution/transformation, become less helpful in the case of intractable conflicts. New forms of violence also call into question any clear-cut distinctions between the stages that are supposed to occur "before," "during," and "after" an armed conflict. These conceptual difficulties do not invalidate categories that remain, to a large extent, useful to any analysis. However, they encourage us to engage in innovative thinking and to take a more flexible approach to issues such as timing, sequencing, and duration.

The chapter by Zeina Barakat illustrates the suitability of a flexible perspective with respect to sequencing. According to her, the reconciliatory process "paves the way for negotiations in good faith." Her own experience as an insider challenges the more traditional view on the subject (see Galtung 2000). The usual chronological sequence is: negotiation followed by reconciliation as a long-term goal that may or may not occur—and, when it does, mostly long after the negotiation processes. Rather than seeing reconciliation as an aspirational horizon, Barakat considers it as a necessary precondition to moving forward. In her view, reconciliation is a *process* rather than an ultimate goal, that is important not only *after,* but also *leading up to and during* the conflict resolution phase.

This viewpoint gives reconciliation a more immediate and ongoing significance for negotiations. However, is it realistic to expect negotiators to adopt a reconciliatory posture if security is not ensured? The answer probably depends on the level of reconciliation expected. From a minimalist perspective (according to which reconciliation is almost synonymous with conflict management), parties can be described as reconciliatory as soon as they agree to sit down at a common table. Mistrust, if not hatred, probably remains. But parties' representatives signal that they could begin to work toward common interests in the name of future generations. From a maximalist perspective (which identifies reconciliation with the notion of forgiveness), few negotiations could be seen as reconciliatory. Most who take this view consider that, in order to move ahead, it is crucial to put the past aside.

The peace process in the Middle East exemplifies this position very well. In the course of the Oslo process, for instance, parties initially repeated accounts of their past and demands for reparations and punishment as the basis of their position. But as the Palestinian negotiator Abu Ala'a said after the initial exchanges of grievances between the two sides, "Let us not compete on who was right and who was wrong in the past. Let us see what we can do in the future." In response, his Israeli counterpart, Uri Savir, recalls telling him, "I'm sure we can debate the past for years and never agree. Let's see if we can agree about the future" (quoted in Zartman 2005, 291). The decision not to argue about the past allowed the parties to move beyond an endless wrangling over right and wrong. Robert Malley, who participated in the Camp David talks, shares this future-oriented perspective. To him, "discussing the future would mean reconciling two rights, not re-addressing ancient wrongs." In his view, the objective of any political agreement is not to assess historical realities. As

Malley explains: "In the Middle East, each side develops a narrative of its own history. But negotiators cannot deal with representations that have been shaping the identities of the parties for decades." His conclusion is clear: "Firstly the political conditions for peace. Afterwards the work of memory."[2]

Various case studies show that the parties involved in a negotiation process leading toward a peace settlement need to feel sufficiently secure before they can agree to recall episodes and positions that shame them as well as those which show them in a good light. And the achievement of such security may require a decade, a generation, or even more, of silence. Even though seeking accuracy about the past and allowing victims to tell their stories are vital steps in the reconciliation process, truth in itself rarely favors effective negotiation, at least not immediately upon the cessation of hostilities.

This remark stresses the duration of the process. Several chapters of the book emphasize this dimension. The introduction and the first chapter highlight the long-lasting effects of war. The notion of "a two-hundred-year present" is telling in this regard. During workshops specifically devoted to the intergenerational transmission of "traumatic memories," Krondorfer realized that family memories are often passed on to new generations "below the surface of conscious cognition and reflection." In this regard, clinicians sometimes distinguish between intergenerational and transgen-erational processes of transmission. The former concerns the transmission of narratives from one generation to the next, while the latter regards the transmission of emotions without text, that is to say, unconsciously. Accordingly, as chapter 1 illustrates, facilitators try to help individuals not to pass on this "poison" to their children and grandchildren.

The attempt to balance loyalty toward ancestors with responsibil-ity toward future generations is extremely important to attempt to move forward. Nonetheless, the duration of such a process raises several meth-odological questions. How can we assess the long-term impact of a war, knowing that this impact lasts not only for years, but indeed for decades? How can we detect emotional and unconscious processes? How can we measure the transformation of representations from one generation to the next? These questions do not invalidate this approach. On the contrary, they point to a need to improve the currently available tools and methods in order to build bridges between the fields of conflict resolution and memory studies. Interdisciplinary teams of scholars would seem indispensable to tackle this task. Political scientists already work with historians, sociologists, and anthropologists, but they all could learn a lot by cooperating further with clinicians and social psychologists (see Luminet et al. 2012).

Beside methodological considerations, the duration of the process also implies a need for management of expectations by third parties trying to facilitate the transformation of the conflict. As a former veteran explained to Alistair Little and Wilhelm Verwoerd, "A lot of people want us to move forward very quickly. They say why do you always talk about the past? Let's move on" (see chapter 2). "Time to move on"—this formula was often chosen by Western diplomats (French, Belgian, and American) interviewed in the course of research on Rwanda (Rosoux 2014). This insistence on the need to turn the page as soon as possible is not new (see Alvarez 1998). However, it became particularly striking around the time of the commemoration of the twentieth anniversary of the genocide in Rwanda: the feeling seemed to be that a period of twenty years was as such a guarantee that the country had recovered (Montgomery 2014). This wishful thinking completely contradicts the actual duration of the "effects" and "after-effects" (to use the terms emphasized by Krondorfer) of the war.

This reflection on timing suggests that we could differentiate between protagonists not only on the basis of their interests but also according to their respective time frames. The time frames of survivors, perpetrators, and bystanders vary. Similarly, the time frames of peacebuilders, policymakers, and descendants have little in common. In this respect, the notion of "generation" seems to be central to expressing the plurality of post-conflict tempos. This concept has been studied by several sociologists (Mannheim 1952; Pichler 1994). Yet, it is far less studied in the field of international relations. Further research on this matter could help to address the following questions: How long do the notions of victim and perpetrator make sense? When does the victors/vanquished dichotomy lose its meaning? Until when are the labels "occupiers/occupied" relevant? What is the appropriate unit of measurement in peace studies: years, decades, or generations?

Memoria Post-Bellum

Each of these questions shows how delicate it is to manage what we could call *memoria post-bellum*. This phrase refers to the set of conflicting memories that accumulate at the close of armed conflicts. These memories are made up of individual memories and official representations (transmitted by group representatives). The way in which a society deals with its past through official discussions, commemorations, and monuments is a constant negotiation process in which identities are reinforced. The socially constructed nature of memory offers possibilities for change—even if change is neither easy nor systematic—and, therefore, opportunities for conflict transformation.

In the short term, attempts to work on memory may appear to be inappropriate and counterproductive. However, while dealing with the past can be postponed, it cannot be eternally avoided. Ignoring burning memories does not really act as a barrier to the recollection of past somber episodes. All case studies demonstrate that unspoken silences reemerge in the public sphere and cannot be beaten back forever. As a result, the real question is probably not whether or not the past should be confronted, but rather when, how, and by whom such an exercise should be carried out.

Memory work does not really concern the reality of the events that occurred (these cannot be denied by anybody), but rather the meaning and the emotional connotations that are attached to them. While working on this meaning, those involved in memory work attempt to establish a narrative that may favor a rapprochement with the Other. As stated in the introduction of this book, the aim of this process is not to discover *the* Truth. It is rather to examine the past in the light of the cooperation which is being sought.

In many cases, the memories that constitute the deepest layers of the *memoria post-bellum* were already included in the *memoria ad bellum* (that justi-fied the recourse to force) and *memoria in bello* (that governed the conduct of hostilities). References to additional episodes that took place during the most recent conflict constitute a new layer of this "multilayered memory," but they rarely contradict the perceptions of historical wrongs (see Volkan's "chosen trauma," mentioned by Krondorfer) and/or glorious victories, which constitute the core of each party's identity. The ultimate purpose of the memory work is to ensure a progressive differentiation between the meaning given to the *memoria post-bellum* on the one hand, and the meaning given to the *memoria ad bellum* and *memoria in bello* on the other.

The Franco-German case illustrates this process particularly well. It demonstrates that "yesterday's hereditary enemies" may become "determined friends" (de Gaulle 1970, 428–29). In particular, it shows that, despite their undeniable rigidity, national memories are potentially negotiable. Thus, the change in the meaning given to the battle of Verdun during World War I is revealing. The number of victims—a quarter of a million young soldiers—in addition to the ruthless nature of the combats created fearful memories seared into people's minds on both sides. As early as 1916, separate patriotic representations of the combats were developing in France and in Germany. Twenty years later, the Franco-German rapprochement paved the way for a new interpretation to be given to this event. Verdun gradually became a symbol enabling tribute to be paid to all combatants, French *and* German, killed or mutilated, finally sharing in a common martyrdom.

This reinterpretation was expressed symbolically when Mitterrand and Kohl stood hand in hand in front of the ossuary at Douaumont (France). The wars fought against each other in the past were then presented as a common past of collective suffering. The groups ceased to be presented in the official memory as combatants on opposite sides. They somehow lost their character of groups living separately from each other, and were now considered as brothers all of whom suffered as a result of a tragedy they all had to endure. As underlined in the chapter by Verwoerd and Little, taking on a new perspective of the past as "tragic" for all sides may pave the way to a common approach that is acceptable to all parties.

Even in the Franco-German case, often presented as a model/ example, the memory work that allowed the rapprochement did not develop directly and spontaneously; rather, it emerged only gradually and painstakingly. It was an open-ended process that did not do away with divergences and misunderstandings, but that made it possible to identify and soften these (Gardner-Feldman 2002). Moreover, despite reconciliation, Franco-German relations have suffered a series of crises and tensions, which can easily reopen deep scars. This example confirms that searching for "a shared ethos" (see the chapter by Dinur) does not imply the elaboration of *one* common narrative, but rather expresses the will of all protagonists to consider the conflictual past with all its complexity and its tensions.

Various chapters of the book refer to this process (see for instance the *Training for Transformation* initiative described by Joram Tarusarira). In the *Beyond Dehumanisation* research project, the changing narrative of the veterans who have become bridgebuilders is also particularly telling (see the chapter by Verwoerd and Little). The shift from a representation of the past based on the idea that they "were right" to a representation of the same past based on the idea that they had "good reasons" but that "those things were wrong" shows that the meaning given to the past is never fixed once and for all.

This process attempts to provide. the same opportunity to recount and recognize different narratives, so that divergence forms the focus of

interaction. To French philosopher Paul Ricoeur, such an ambition requires
the creation of new narratives of the same historic events ("*histoires au
second degré*") in order to find points of intersection between the initial
narratives (Ricoeur 1992, 110). Consideration of several points of view
does not imply that all perceptions are to be taken as equivalent. A sort
of plurality appears to be inherent to the representations parties have of
the past. Recognizing this plurality does not imply a questioning of the
existence of a reality beyond representations. The idea of a shared language
about the past is not based on a theory where everything is presented as
relative to a peculiar perspective (relativism). It entails, rather, the hope
that alternative futures exist (Olick 1999). To sum up, the aim is to live
with the memories rather than without them or against them (Rousso
1998, 47; Chaumont 1997, 314).

Analytically speaking, the only option is probably to go beyond
nationalistic visions of the past, and therefore revenge. It would, however,
be naive to consider the recognition of others' interpretations of the past
in a normative way. Memory work can only emerge from the parties
themselves. That implies several conditions. The first concerns the leaders on
each side. Knowing that the process is costly in terms of self-examination
and collective narcissism, they will only become involved in this process
if they are convinced that there is no other way to proceed. The second
regards the attitude of the population. Memory work cannot be reduced
to a top-down process that automatically impacts private spheres. A change
in the official narrative does not guarantee that the majority of the population will agree to call into question their own perceptions of the past.
In this regard, it is worth asking whether a change in the official account
and/or textbooks does actually have an impact on individual memories.
Do official statements, monuments, museums, or commemorations have
any effect on the individual transmission of memories? Nongovernmental
organizations, faith-based peacebuilders (see the chapter by Zilka Spahic
Siljak and Julianne Funk), and citizens' associations can play the role of a
bridge between the official and the public levels. However, all case studies
presented in this book illustrate the inescapable tensions that exist between
public and private practices, official and underground memories.

Beside these difficulties, it is worth recalling the limitations of memory
work based on reciprocal empathy (see chapter 1). Such an exercise is
only possible if wrongs are shared. In the case of atypical conflicts which
are not characterized by belligerents on each side, but by clearly identified
victims and perpetrators, it would be morally unfair to require a reciprocal

effort of empathy to promote rapprochement. Victims and perpetrators are not interchangeable. Innocent people who have been tortured, teenagers who have been raped, and devastated individuals cannot be put on the same level as the criminals, be they repentant or not. In the aftermath of irreversible crimes, the moral responsibility of offenders cannot be taken lightly. This point is crucial if we are not to disregard the victims. The same can be said of their descendants. We must be aware of the irrevocable dimension of past violence and realize that, for some, the mourning process remains and will remain unfinished.

What If Reconciliation Is Not on the Agenda?

Heleen Touquet and Ana Milošević have shown how loaded the word *reconciliation* can be. As representatives of the Movement of the Mothers of Srebrenica and Zepa Enclaves Association, many survivors, from Chile to Rwanda, explain that they are "offended" by this word. This reaction reminds us that the notion of reconciliation is fundamentally ambivalent. On the one hand, most official representatives, scholars, and NGO workers consider reconciliation as the ultimate achievement. On the other hand, victims or their relatives largely distrust this notion. Many of them feel bitterness toward what they perceive as an unbearable injunction that does not do proper justice to their sufferings.

The gap between these attitudes underlines a tension that cannot be avoided when speaking about reconciliation: the legitimate need to look forward at a collective level risks ostracizing people who are permanently traumatized by the conflict. This tension does not detract from the significance of efforts made to bring about a rapprochement between former adversaries. Nonetheless, it reminds us that the question for practitioners, especially peacebuilders and facilitators, is not only, "How can we favor a reconciliation process?" but also, "What do we do if reconciliation is not on the agenda?"

A brief comparative analysis allows us to shed light on this question. Thus, it is interesting to compare the failed Treaty of Friendship between France and Algeria with the successful Elysée Treaty between France and Germany. Why was closure impossible in one case and not in the other? An analysis of the negotiation processes involving experts and policymakers in both cases indicates the variables that explain why Franco-Algerian relationships can apparently not be "normalized," namely, leadership, international context, domestic resistance, and the long-term relationship between the parties. This last variable is intimately linked with the nature of the past violence.

Many observers use the same label of "reconciliation" in both the Franco-German and the Franco-Algerian cases. They explain that both contexts involved massive human rights abuses (be it during World War I, World War II, or the Algerian war) and thus that there was a common need for a Friendship Treaty. However, these contexts differ fundamentally as regards the figure of the Other. In the framework of the Franco-German wars, the other was the *enemy* to fight. In the colonial system, the other—as depicted by the colonial authorities—was a backward *child* to be educated and/or a *barbarian* to be exploited. These representations are not incompatible. However, they do not have the same long-term effects on the population affected.

The Franco-German case was characterized by a paradoxical mixture of hatred and esteem. In fact, respect for French culture was commonplace among the German elite. Likewise, a long tradition of French intellectuals and artists expressed their admiration for German writers and composers. This reciprocal admiration, as ambivalent as it was, guaranteed a form of symmetry between the enemies despite the battlefields and even the defeats. The Franco-Algerian situation was totally different. First, colonialization can hardly be characterized as a period of reciprocal admiration. Scorn and humiliation were felt on a day-to-day basis. Second, the nature of the war was very different. Far from being a war between similar combatants on both sides (as in the case of Verdun during World War I, for instance), the fighting between the French army and the *fellagha* (Arabic, designates the Algerian guerrilla soldiers) cannot be described as symmetrical. Third, the war ended in a particular way. In Algeria, the hostilities ceased after a negotiated agreement (the Evian Accords in 1962), and not after a crushing defeat by one of the parties. From that perspective, the notion of winners/losers is obviously less relevant than in other circumstances. Last, the Franco-Algerian case did not lead to any common language about the past. Between France and Germany, a common language developed gradually, based on (1) the distinction between Germans and Nazis, and (2) the notion of European construction. In the Franco-Algerian case, there is absolutely no consensus on the meaning of the Algerian war. The gap is not only between the French and Algerian sides. It is also—and above all—between various groups in France ("pro-*Algérie française*" and some of their descendants, who did not take part in a mourning process; *harkis*, Muslims who fought alongside the French against their fellow Algerians, who cannot see the war as a war of Liberation; members of the military who felt betrayed by the French politicians who negotiated the Evian Agreements, etc.). All these groups are still struggling with the meaning of the past and cannot, therefore, see the end, and therefore a new beginning.

This example shows that it is futile, if not counterproductive, to require reconciliation and friendship whatever the circumstances. I would personally call for a less ambitious view. Rather than expecting a process that entails friendship or forgiveness, I would insist on the importance of being realistic in terms of timing (changes in this area do not take years but generations) and setting achievable aims (coexistence is already a remarkable goal after mass atrocities).

Conclusion

The irreversible character of certain wounds cannot be underestimated. The layers of violence that accumulate during a war provoke festering wounds—physical as well as mental. These wounds are at the origin of an intense hatred that must be taken seriously. In most conflict resolution textbooks, hatred is considered as a strictly "negative" emotion. Might it not be more appropriate to see it as neither positive nor negative? The purpose is neither to call for it, nor to attempt to crush it by all means.

Another meeting in Rwanda shows the importance of this point. A Rwandan survivor who was particularly involved in local reconciliation projects geared toward perpetrators who had killed all her relatives was asked to explain where she could find the energy to go to jail, visit the criminals, and bring them food. After a sigh, she just said: "I took the time for hatred. It took me ten years. I hated the entire world. Now, I can think about reconciliation." This reaction is edifying. It is not, however, systematic. I will always remember the eyes of a Colombian woman who tragically told me: "Don't touch my hatred. That is the only thing that's left. They took all I had—except for my hatred." These reactions confirm that the response to past atrocities is ultimately an individual one.

The diversity of individual reactions forces us to question our own assumptions and brings us back to the reflective perspective underlying the whole book. Is the aim to distinguish between "good" (forgiving) victims and "bad" (resentful) victims? Probably not. A maximalist conception of reconciliation addresses *our* need for hope and closure. But anyone involved in reconciliation processes also ought to ask: Does it help *them*?

Notes

1. Conference, "L'histoire comme arme de guerre. L'instrumentalisation du passé en situations de crises," organized by the University of Geneva and the International Museum of the Red Cross and Red Crescent (September 3–4, 2004).

2. Robert Malley, "Au Proche-Orient, on en reviendra toujours à l'équation posée par Bill Clinton," *Le Monde* (January 23, 2001).

Works Cited

Alvarez, José. 1998. "Rush to Closure: Lessons of the Tadić Judgment." *Michigan Law Review* 96(7): 2031–2112.

Bercovitch, Jacob, and Richard Jackson, eds. 2009. *Conflict Resolution in the XXIst Century.* Ann Arbor: University of Michigan Press.

Bernanos, Georges. 1949. *Les enfants humiliés: Journal 1939–1940,* Paris: Gallimard.

Brudholm, Thomas, and Valerie Rosoux. 2009. "The Unforgiving: Reflections on the Resistance to Forgiveness after Atrocity." *Law and Contemporary Problems* 72: 101–17.

Chaumont, Jean-Michel. 1997. *La concurrence des victimes, génocide, identité, reconnaissance.* Paris: La Découverte.

Chersterman, Simon 2005. "Rough Justice: Establishing the Rule of Law in Post-Conflict Territories." *Ohio State Journal on Dispute Resolution* 20(1): 69–98.

Chetail, Vincent, ed. 2009. *Post-Conflict Peacebuilding: A Lexicon.* Oxford: Oxford University Press.

Ciliers, Jacobus, Oeindrila Dube, and Bilal Siddiqi. 2016. "Reconciling after Civil Conflict Increases Social Capital but Decreases Individual Well-Being." *Science* 352 (6287): 787–94.

de Gaulle, Charles. 1970. *Discours et messages.* Paris: Plon.

Eisikovits, Nir. 2010. *Sympathizing with the Enemy: Reconciliation, Transitional Justice, Negotiation.* Dordrecht: Martinus Nijhoff.

Gardner-Feldman, Lily. 2002. "The Principle and Practice of 'Reconciliation' in German Foreign Policy/Relations with France, Israel, Poland and the Czech Republic." *International Affairs* 75(2): 333–56.

Galtung, Johan. 2000. *Conflict Transformation by Peaceful Means: The Transcend Method.* Geneva: United Nations.

Junne, Gerd, and Willemijn Verkoren, eds. 2004. *Post-Conflict Development: Meeting New Challenges.* Boulder: Lynne Rienner.

Luminet, Olivier, et al. 2012. "The Interplay between Collective Memory and the Erosion of Nation States." *Memory Studies* 5(1): 1–15.

Malley, Robert. 2001. "Au Proche-Orient, on en reviendra toujours à l'équation posée par Bill Clinton." *Le Monde,* January 23.

Mannheim, Karl. 1952. "The Sociological Problem of Generations." In *Karl Mannheim: Essays*, edited by Paul Kecskemeti, 276–322. London: Routledge.

Montgomery, Sue. 2014. "Rwanda: 20 Years Later: The Burden of Survival." *The Gazette*, April 1.

Olick, Jeffrey. 1999. "Genre Memories and Memory Genres: A Dialogical Analysis of May 8, 1945 Commemorations in the Federal Republic of Germany." *American Sociological Review* 64(3): 381–402.

Pichler, Jane. 1994. "Mannheim's Sociology of Generations: An Undervalued Legacy." *British Journal of Sociology* 45(3): 481–95.

Ricoeur, Paul. 1992. "Quel ethos nouveau pour l'Europe?" In *Imaginer l'Europe: Le marché intérieur européen, tâche culturelle et économique*, edited by Peter Koslowkli, 107–16. Paris: Cerf.

Rosoux, Valerie. 2014. "Réconciliation : les limites d'un conte de fée." In *Quelle justice pour les peuples en transition?*, edited by Kora Andrieu and Geoffroy Lauvau, 113–26. Paris: Presses universitaires de Paris Sorbonne.

Rousso, Henry. 1998. *La hantise du passé*. Paris: Textuel.

Sontag, Susan. 2003. *Regarding the Pain of Others*. New York: Picador.

Zartman, I. William. 2000. "Ripeness: The Hurting Stalemate and Beyond," In *International Conflict Resolution after the Cold War*, edited by Paul Stern and Daniel Druckman, 225–50. Washington, DC: National Academy Press.

———, and Victor Kremenyuk. 2005. *Peace versus Justice: Negotiating Forward and Backward-looking Outcomes*. Lanham, MD: Rowman and Littlefield.

Contributors

Zena Barakat is a Jerusalem-born Palestinian who confronts taboos and challenges outdated traditions. She got her MA in American studies at Al-Quds University in 2006, and attained her PhD from Friedrich-Schiller University in Jena, Germany, where she is currently a postdoctoral fellow. She is the Palestinian coordinator for the trilateral project "Heart of Flesh not Stone." She is author of *Sexual Harassment*, one of the few books in Arabic that deal with this sensitive topic from social and legal perspectives. She also co-authored the Arabic textbook *Holocaust: Human Agony: Is There a Way out of Violence*, with Mohammed Dajani and Martin Rau (2012). She has taught at Al-Quds University in Jerusalem, Al-Istiqlal University in Jericho, and Friedrich-Schiller University in Jena. Her research interests include gender and feminism, American politics and society, conflict resolution, reconciliation and moderation, as well as democracy and pluralism.

Avner Dinur is a lecturer at Sapir College and Seminar Hakibbutzim College, Israel. He teaches medieval and modern Jewish philosophy with a focus on secular Jewish identity. His doctoral thesis dealt with aspects of Judaism and universalism in the philosophy of Hannah Arendt and Hans Jonas. He published a few papers on themes such as secular theology and Jewish feminism. He works as facilitator of different dynamic groups that deal with questions of identity and politics. He is vice chairperson of *FAB: Friendship Across Borders*, an NGO working to create trialogue between Germans, Palestinians, and Israelis. He is also a member of *Migvan*, an urban kibbutz in Sderot. He is married to Nitza and father of Omri, Rotem, and Shaked.

Julianne Funk is a peace scholar-practitioner focusing on the Western Balkans, especially Bosnia and Herzegovina. She divides her time between teaching peace and conflict studies at the University of Zurich, Switzerland,

and working for local NGOs in the former Yugoslavia. Currently she is coordinating the project "Trauma, Memory and Healing in the Balkans and Beyond" for the TPO Foundation in Sarajevo and co-editing the forthcoming book *Unhealed Trauma: Engaging Healing and Peacebuilding in Bosnia & Herzegovina*. She received her PhD in social sciences and MA in peace and conflict studies at the Katholieke Universiteit Leuven, Belgium. Her recent research and publications include the themes of peacebuilding/conflict transformation, lived religion, Bosnian Islam, *suživot* (mutual life), trauma and healing.

Björn Krondorfer is director of the Martin-Springer Institute at Northern Arizona University and endowed professor of religious studies in the Department of Comparative Cultural Studies there. His field of expertise is religion, gender and culture, (post-) Holocaust studies, and reconciliation studies. Among his publications are *Male Confessions: Intimate Revelations and the Religious Imagination* (Stanford University Press), *Men and Masculinities in Christianity and Judaism* (London, SCM), and *Remembrance and Reconciliation* (Yale University Press). He also published three volumes in German on the cultural and theological legacy of the Holocaust. His scholarship helped to define the field of Critical Men's Studies in Religion. Nationally and internationally, Krondorfer facilitates intercultural encounters on issues of conflict, memory, and reconciliation. He has been invited to speak, present his research, and facilitate workshops and seminars in South Africa, Australia, South Korea, The Netherlands, Finland, Poland, United Kingdom, Bosnia and Herzegovina, Italy, Israel/Palestine, Belgium, Germany, Switzerland, Austria, and Canada.

Alistair Little is a former loyalist political prisoner from an Ulster Volunteer Force. With a Protestant background, he became involved in the conflict in and about Northern Ireland at the age of fourteen, was imprisoned at the age of seventeen, and served almost thirteen years in prison. Upon his release, he qualified as a counsellor, and for more than twenty years has worked on peace, reconciliation, and conflict transformation in Northern Ireland, Ireland, the Balkans, the Middle East, and South Africa. Exploring the human cost of violent conflict, he works with former combatants, survivors, and members of wider society through a process entitled *Journey through Conflict*. Presenting at numerous international conferences on conflict and reconciliation, he has also participated in local and international TV programs, most recently "Moving Beyond Hatred" for NHK, Japan.

His journey from political violence to becoming a conflict transformation practitioner is the subject of the award-winning BBC film, "Five
Minutes of Heaven" (2009), starring Liam Neeson and Jimmy Nesbitt.
He is director of Beyond Walls CIC. His publications include *Give a Boy
a Gun: From Killing to Peacemaking* (2009).

Ana Milošević is a PhD candidate at the University of Leuven in Belgium and the University of Maastricht in the Netherlands. Her research
interests cover collective memories, identities, and European integration in
post-conflict societies, with a special focus on coming to terms with the
past. For several years she worked on the post-conflict transformation both
in the Balkans and in sub-Saharan Africa. In northern Uganda, she worked
with UN volunteers and local NGOs on projects directed to war orphans
and child soldiers. Between 2008 and 2014, she was closely involved in
the process of EU accession of the Western Balkans, collaborating with
the EU institutions and both state and nonstate actors. Currently, she is
collaborating with the European Observatory at the University of Bar-
celona on topics related to transnational memory, activism, and European
politics of memory.

Valerie Rosoux is a senior research fellow at the Belgian National
Fund for Scientific Research (FNRS). She teaches international negotiation and conflict transformation at the University of Louvain (UCL). In
2010–11, she was a senior fellow at the United States Institute of Peace
(Washington, D.C.). She has a License in philosophy and a PhD in international relations. Her research interests focus on the uses of memory in
international relations. Her publications include "Post-Conflict Reconciliation: A Humanitarian Myth?" (in *The Humanitarian Challenge* 2015),
"Is Reconciliation Negotiable?" (*International Negotiation* 2013), and "The
Unforgiving: Reflections on the Resistance to Forgiveness after Atrocity,"
(in *Theorizing Post-Conflict Reconciliation* 2013).

Zilka Spahić Šiljak holds a PhD in gender studies. Her scope of work
addresses cutting-edge issues involving human rights, politics, religion,
education, and peacebuilding. With more than fifteen years experiences
in academic teaching and working also in governmental and nongovernmental sectors, she heads the TPO Foundation Sarajevo and teaches at
several universities, including in the United States and Bosnia and Herzegovina. As post-doctoral research fellow at Harvard University, she has

published *Shining Humanity: Life Stories of Women Peacebuilders in Bosnia and Herzegovina* (Cambridge Scholars, 2014). She also published *Contesting Female, Feminist and Muslim Identities: Post-Socialist Contexts of Bosnia and Herzegovina and Kosovo* (2012), and *Women Religion and Politics* (2010). Her current research at Stanford University focuses on intersections of leadership, gender, and politics.

Joram Tarusarira is assistant professor of religion, conflict, and peace-building at the University of Groningen in the Netherlands. He is also the deputy director of the Centre for Religion, Conflict and Public Domain at the same university. He attained his PhD from the University of Leipzig (Germany), where he was a German Research Foundation (DFG) doctoral candidate of the Research Training Group "Religious Non-Conformism and Cultural Dynamics." His research interests include religion in conflict and its transformation, religious nonconformism and cultural dynamics, religion and civil society, social movements, peace and reconciliation. He is the author of the book *Reconciliation and Religio-Political Non-Conformism* (2016, Routledge).

Heleen Touquet is a researcher and lecturer in international relations at the KU Leuven, Belgium. She has specialized in issues related to post-confict peacebuilding in the Balkans, studying postethnic political mobilization in Bosnia-Herzegovina, the framing of the reconciliation process by local and international actors, and the Europeanization of LGBT rights in the region. She co-edited a book on the last topic in 2016 (Palgrave-MacMillan). Her articles have appeared in, among others, *Europe-Asia Studies, Nationalism and Ethnic Politics, Reproductive Health Matters*, and *East-European Politics and Societies*. Her current research interest is gender and post-conflict, with a focus on male victims of sexual violence and the use of sexual violence as a tool for political demobilization. She teaches courses on international intervention and ethnic conflict as well as nationalism and political mobilization in Leuven.

Wilhelm Verwoerd is currently a research fellow at the Beyers Naudé Centre for Public Theology, within the Faculty of Theology, University of Stellenbosch, South Africa. Previously he has worked as a researcher within the South African Truth and Reconciliation Commission (SATRC) from 1996–98, during a decade when he taught as lecturer in political philosophy and applied ethics at the University of Stellenbosch. A number of academic articles, co-edited books, and his PhD thesis focused on conceptual and moral questions raised by the SATRC, such as national reconciliation, apologies, forgiveness, shared responsibility, and the complex dynamics between victims and perpetrators. He gained extensive reconciliation practitioner experience in Ireland (2002–11) as coordinator and facilitator with the Glencree Survivors and Former Combatants program (www.glencree.ie). He worked closely with Alistair Little to develop the *Journey through Conflict*—a process of Life Histories ("storytelling"), Deep Dialogue, and Wild Nature to deepen and humanize relationships between people divided by intense conflict. A reflective introduction to this process has been published as a *Journey through Conflict Trail Guide* (www.trafford. com). In 2012, Dr. Verwoerd moved back to South Africa to continue his reconciliation work and to explore creative ways to help transform the complex legacy of apartheid and cultivate sustainable communities.

Index